D1065372

ART AND
ARCHITECTURE
IN THE POETRY
OF ROBERT BROWNING

ART AND ARCHITECTURE IN THE POETRY OF ROBERT BROWNING

An Illustrated Compendium of Sources

Charles Flint Thomas

The Whitston Publishing Company
Troy, New York
1991

Library of Congress Catalog Card Number 87-50834

ISBN 0-87875-349-4

Printed in Singapore

In memory of my dear mother,
Mrs. John Harold Thomas,
formerly Grace Helen Lewis
and Mrs. Crawford Burbank Waterman

Henry Charles Fehr
Robert Browning
South London Art Gallery
(see the Introduction and THOMA under the Key to Bibliography)

CONTENTS

Map of Florence

Map of Rome

NOTICE

The first edition of a reference work that is meant to be comprehensive and detailed cannot help exemplifying one of Browning's favorite themes, the Doctrine of the Imperfect. The second edition of this work, then, in an effort to be definitive, is projected for the near future and is in current preparation. Readers who wish to make corrections and/or contributions for journal publications to precede and be included in the second edition are sincerely invited to send them to the following address:

> Notes & Queries
> *Studies in Browning and His Circle*
> Baylor University
> P. O. Box 97152
> Waco, TX 76798-7152

PREFACE AND ACKNOWLEDGMENTS

Personal observation during my first trip to Europe in 1968 convinced me that (1) a comprehensive source study on the numerous references and allusions to art and architecture in the poetry of Robert Browning needed to be done, and (2) that such a study not only necessitated the usual historical and biographical library work but also continued firsthand observation of the art and architecture itself. The empirical nature of this study, then, is what distinguishes it from other source studies on the same subject, none of which has involved such intensive field work. In addition to the trip mentioned above, twelve others have been made spanning over sixty months of travel throughout Italy, England, France, Germany, Belgium, Austria, Switzerland, and the United States. As a result, most of the edifices and art objects that Browning *refers* to in his poetry have been observed and noted, and a large number of the buildings, paintings, and sculptures that Browning *alludes* to have been presumably uncovered and nominated as possible sources. By replicating Browning's movements, probing museums and libraries near the various residences where he lived, and sometimes just stumbling across sources by chance, I have come up with the bulk of my discoveries. In many cases my findings have depended on personal interviews with art curators, museum directors, church historians, and reference librarians living in the above-mentioned countries. To them and my various readers, all of whom have given so generously of their time and energy, I would now like to express gratitude and make acknowledgment.

Specifically, I would like to thank the following scholars for reading my manuscript: Robert G. Collmer, Professor of English and Dean of Research and Graduate Studies at Baylor University; David DeLaura, Professor of English and Chairman of the English Department at the University of Pennsylvania; John Ecker, former Professor of Education at Howard Payne University; Marvin Eisenberg, Professor of the History of Art at the University of Michigan; Jack W. Herring, Professor of

English and former Director of the Armstrong Browning Library at Baylor University; William M. Jensen, Associate Professor of Art at Baylor University; and Leonée Ormond, Professor of English at King's College, London. The range of specialization embraced by these scholars in the areas of literature, art, and education is extensive, and I am particularly indebted to them for their individual expertise as it applies to the various aspects of this study: to Professor Collmer for his assistance with the emblematic tradition in literature; to Professor DeLaura for his understanding of the life and works of Robert Browning as applied to the painter poems; to Professor Ecker for his analysis of the format of this study from a pedagogical point of view; to Professor Eisenberg for his help with Medieval and Renaissance Italian art; to Professor Herring for his insight into the life and works of Robert Browning as applied to biographical sources; to Professor Jensen for his assistance with Greco-Roman art; and to Professor Ormand for her understanding of the life and works of Robert Browning as applied to nineteenth-century English art. Finally, I would like to thank Mrs. Rita S. Humphrey, Administrative and Editorial Assistant to the Director of the Armstrong Browning Library, for proofreading the textual aspects of this study; Dr. Philip Kelley, Director of the Wedgestone Press, for verifying and locating various artifacts owned by the Brownings; to Mrs. Betty A. Coley, Librarian of the Armstrong Browning Library, for providing many important source materials; and to Fukuoka Jo Gakuin College, Department of English Cultures, for making a grant available to help reproduce the many color illustrations in this study.

For the numerous art curators, church historians, museum directors, and reference librarians that have assisted me, I refer the reader to the Key to Bibliography for specific names and to the following list of institutions that they represent. Included in the list are numerical references to photographs that have been authorized by the institutions for reproduction in this work. Almost all of the other photographs not listed on the following pages are provided either by myself or by my photographers Mr. Kalle Valdma, of Santa Monica, California, and Dr. James W. Cady, former Vice President of Academic Affairs at Howard Payne University.

Alte Pinakothek, Munich (Fig. 4)

Armstrong Browning Library, Baylor University, Waco (Figs. 71, 81, 197.5)

Biblioteca di Foligno (Figs. 242, 243)

Biblioteca Marucelliana, Florence (Figs. 42, 167)

Bibliothèque Municipale, Nantes (Figs. 40, 60)

Bibliothèque Nationale, Paris (Fig. 6)

Birmingham Museum and Art Gallery (Fig. 250)

British Museum, permission granted by the Trustees of the British Museum (Figs. 95, 97, 99, 107, 122)

Browning Institute, New York (Fig. 252, 259)

Comune di Spello (Figs. 242, 243)

Detroit Institute of Arts (Fig. 91)

Dulwich Picture Gallery, by permission of the Governors of Dulwich Picture Gallery (Figs. 16, 63, 89, 117, 157, 237, 245, 247, 248, 249)

Fitzwilliam Museum, Cambridge (Fig. 38)

Gabinetto Fotografico Nazionale, Rome (Figs. 13, 14, 15, 17, 65, 68, 69, 70, 88, 119, 120, 121, 133, 134, 135, 136, 160, 176, 177, 178, 181, 182, 185, 186, 190, 191, 192, 193, 194, 195, 196, 233, 251)

Gabinetto Fotografico, Soprintendenza alle Gallerie, Florence (Figs. 1, 5, 8, 47, 48, 49, 50, 51, 54, 55, 56, 58, 72, 73, 86, 87, 98, 100, 102, 103, 105, 106, 108, 111, 113, 114, 119, 124, 140, 141, 143, 144, 145, 156, 209, 210, 213, 214, 219, 222, 223, 225, 238, 246)

Galleria Corsini, Rome (Fig. 19)

Gemäldegalerie, Staatliche Museen Preussischer Kulturbesitz, Berlin-Dahlem (Figs. 78, 104)

Gipsoteca di Possagno (Fig. 130)

Glyptothek, Munich (Fig. 96)

Harewood House, Yorkshire (Fig. 101)

Keble College, Oxford (Fig. 77)

Kensington Palace, London, reproduction by permission of the Lord Chamberlain's Office, St. James's Palace, London (Fig. 10)

Kunsthalle, Bremen (Fig. 129)

Leighton House, London (Fig. 36)

Louvre, Paris (Figs. 112, 142, 260)

Mills College Library, Oakland, courtesy of the Goewey Collection (Fig. 149)

Musée National du Château de Fontainebleau (Figs. 25, 26, 27, 28)

Museo dell' Opera del Duomo di Siena (Fig. 23)

Museo di Roma (Fig. 121)

National Gallery, London (Fig. 45)

National Gallery, Parma (Fig. 12)

National Museum of Villa Giulia, Rome (Fig. 258)

Offentliche Bibliothek, Aachen (Fig. 67)

Palazzo Barberini, Rome (Fig. 231)

Palazzo Ducale, Venice (Fig. 241)

Residenz, Munich (Fig. 240)

Services d'Archives de Loire-Atlantique, France (Figs. 40, 60)

Soprintendenza per i Beni Artistici e Storici delle Province di Pisa, Livorno, Lucca, e Massa-Carrara (Figs. 235, 236, 244, 255, 256)

South London Art Gallery (Frontispiece)

Staatliche Kunstsammlungen, Dresden (Fig. 109)

Tanenbaum, Joseph M., of Toronto (Fig. 7)

Tate Gallery, London (Figs. 74, 75)

Vatican Museums (Figs. 110, 135, 162, 211)

Windsor Castle, Royal Library, reproduction by gracious permission of Her Majesty Queen Elizabeth II (Fig. 82)

INTRODUCTION

This reference tool identifies sources for art and architecture mentioned or implied in the poetry of Robert Browning. Spanning over 70 poems, it comprises the greatest number of such sources ever brought together in a single study. Of the approximately 500 source notes entered (not counting obvious repetitions of sources) the author advances over 100—or more than one out of five—that purport to be original discoveries. For a detailed account of this claim, see the Index of Sources with Locations and the Index of Miscellaneous Sources. Another original feature of this study is the Summary of Composite Sources. The some 140 sources listed in this section, which is more than one out of four of the total number entered in the study, indicate that a theory of composite sources is a viable part of Browning's creative method. Also included in this study are numerous seldom-seen illustrations, identifications of a number of little-known locations, and much new evidence supporting sources nominated by other authors. All in all, the single most important new finding in this study is, as the author assesses it, the Castellani *fleur-de-lis* ring, in *The Ring and the Book*; the most important groups of original discoveries are the conflations of sources for imaginary art and architecture, which are listed in the Summary of Composite Sources.

The source entries in this work are based on references to real, imaginary, and unspecified pictures, sculpture, and architecture. Pictures include paintings, drawings, etchings, emblems, illustrations in books, stained-glass windows, and tapestries. Sculpture embraces statuary, bas-reliefs, castings, and jewelry. Architecture includes single structures, such as palaces, homes, portals, colonnades, bridges, etc.; and structural complexes, such as streets, squares, and—in some cases—cities as a whole. Other types of sources included in this study are books on art and art history, and literature, when related to art and architecture.

The references to the art and architecture are, for the most part, identified by illustrations (about 70% in color), locations, and names of artists. The more than 260 illustrations, the two maps, and the three indexes are provided in order to facilitate the identification of the sources, the locations, and the artists. In the cases where the references in the text are allusions to imaginary or unspecified pictures, sculpture, or architecture, evidence is introduced in order to establish sources for the allusions. Allusions to unspecified and imaginary art and architecture that entail a conflation of possible sources are listed in the Summary of Composite Sources. In the cases where possible sources are introduced with a modicum of evidence, their inclusion may be justified by their value as subjects for future research.

This study is designed to codify old and new information through alphabetizing, numbering, and indexing; as such, it is basically descriptive, yet it contains two or three dozen, mostly original, analytical comments. If more critical commentary is desired, however, the reader is directed to books and dissertations entered in the Key to Bibliography under AL, BERM, CON, CRO, EISS, GRIF, KO, and THOMAS. For analysis on a smaller scale, the reader should see the articles by ALB, CROW, DAH, DEL, DELA, DO, LEI, and ORM, although this is by no means a comprehensive list of articles. Citations from Browning's poetry are taken from the 1895 Cambridge edition of Browning's works by Porter and Clarke. The line numbering for *The Ring and the Book* is based on Cook's *Commentary*. Indexing is maintained through the alphabetical arrangement of poems by titular head letters, the ordering of the line numbers of citations taken from each poem, the cross-references within the notes on each poem, the Index of Artists, the Index of Sources with Locations, and the Index of Miscellaneous Sources. References to the two maps may be found in the notes to the text and in the Index of Sources with Locations. The Supplement to Citations and Notes was added at publication time and coordinates with the main body of citations and notes. Of particular interest in the Supplement, among many new findings, are the additional notes under *The Ring and the Book* that enrich the discovery of the Castellani *fleur-de-lis* ring.

For information about the Frontispiece, see THOMA under the Key to Bibliography. The marble bust of Robert Browning illustrated by the Frontispiece was, along with a marble bust of Elizabeth Barrett Browning, uncovered by the author in the South London Art Gallery and is reproduced here with the permission of the curator of the gallery.

TABLE OF CHRONOLOGY

This chronology lists major events in Browning's life and important readings, travels, and associations with personages contributing to Browning's education and writing about art and architecture. For a general yet detailed chronology, see Philip Kelley and Ronald Hudson's *The Brownings' Correspondence: a Checklist* (The Browning Institute and Wedgestone Press, 1978), pp. 491-98.

1812	Robert Browning is born in Camberwell, London.
1814	Dulwich Picture Gallery opens and in subsequent years is visited by RB with his father and Alfred Domett. RB's early education is under the tutelage of his father. He reads the following books about art: Francis Quarles's *Emblems, Divine and Moral*; Gerard de Lairesse's *The Art of Painting*; Daniel Bartoli's *Simboli*; Nathaniel Wanley's *Wonders of the Little World*; and the *Biographie Universelle*.
1834	RB visits Aix-la-Chapelle, St. Petersburg.
1836	RB meets D. Maclise.
1838	RB visits Trieste, Venice, Castelfranco, Treviso, Asolo, Bassano, Solagna, Oliero, Possagno, Verona, Trent, Innsbruck, Munich.
1844	RB visits Naples, the Amalfian Coast, Rome; reads extensively in Giorgio Vasari's *Lives*.
1845	RB reads *De la poésie chrétienne*, by Alexis F. Rio.
1846-47	RB marries Elizabeth Barrett Barrett in London; travels with her continually until her death in 1861; goes to Paris and meets Mrs. Jameson there; travels to Pisa; resides in Casa Guidi, Florence; visits

Massa-Carrara, Vallombrosa; meets Hiram Powers and William Wetmore Story in Florence.

1848-49   RB visits Arezzo, Fano, Loreto, Rimini, Bagni di Lucca; reads Ruskin's *Modern Painters*; Robert Wiedemann Barrett Browning (Pen) is born; RB meets Seymour Kirkup and George Mignaty in Florence.

1850   RB resides briefly near Siena.

1851-52   RB visits Parma, Padua, Venice, Paris, London; meets D. G. Rossetti in London and also meets there, possibly this early, Millais and Woolner; returns to Florence; reads in Baldinucci's *Notizie* and familiarizes himself (probably at an earlier date) with guidebooks published by John Murray.

1853   RB visits Assisi; resides in Rome; meets Lord Leighton and Harriet Hosmer in Rome; lives in Florence; makes excursions to Prato and Bagni di Lucca.

1855-56   RB visits Paris, London.

1858   RB resides at 43 Bocca di Leone, Rome.

1859   RB visits Viterbo.

1860   RB buys *The Old Yellow Book* in Piazza San Lorenzo, Florence.

1861   EBB dies and is buried in the Protestant Cemetery, Piazza Donatello, Florence; RB returns to London.

1862   RB vacations in Pornic, France.

1872   RB visits Paris and Fontainebleau.

1877   RB visits the Villa la Saisiaz, near Geneva.

1889   RB visits Asolo; dies in Venice; is buried in Westminster Abbey.

LIST OF ILLUSTRATIONS

CITATIONS, NOTES, AND ILLUSTRATIONS

ABT VOGLER

2-4, 13-24

Bidding my organ obey, calling its keys to
their work,
Claiming each slave of the sound, at a touch, as
when Solomon willed
Armies of angels that soar, legions of demons
that lurk....

And one would bury his brow with a blind
plunge down to hell,
Burrow awhile and build, broad on the roots
of things,
Then up again swim into sight, having based
me my palace well,
Founded it, fearless of flame, flat on the
nether springs.

And another would mount and march, like the
excellent minion he was,
Ay, another and yet another, one crowd but
with many a crest,
Raising my rampired walls of gold as transparent
as glass,
Eager to do and die, yield each his place to
the rest:
For higher still and higher (as a runner tips
with fire,
When a great illumination surprises a festal
night—
Outlined round and round Rome's dome from
space to spire)
Up, the pinnacled glory reached, and the
pride of my soul was in sight.

Compare the physical likeness between Milton's Pandemonium
in *Paradise Lost* and Abt Vogler's palace of music here.   The

foundation of Pandemonium, built of "Gold" on the "liquid fire" of "Hell," rises like columns of air "as in an organ . . . with the sound / of Dulcet Symphonies and voices sweet" (*P. L.* I.690-712); the foundation of Vogler's palace of music, built "flat on the nether springs" of "hell . . . fearless of flame," rises as Vogler, the organist, improvises his "walls of gold."

The "great illumination . . . round Rome's dome"—the dome of St. Peter's Church in the Vatican—occurred during festivals, especially Easter (BER, 7; POR, V, 308; Figs. 133 and 134). For other references to the Church of St. Peter, see below under "The Boy and the Angel," 47-52; *Christmas-Eve,* 10:526-76; *Easter-Day,* 26:798-802; "The Pope and the Net," 13-15; *Prince Hohenstiel-Schwangau, Saviour of Society,* 861-65; and *The Ring and the Book,* III.566-72.

For a study showing the relationship between Pandemonium in *Paradise Lost* and the Church of St. Peter in the Vatican, see Rebecca W. Smith, "The Source of Milton's Pandemonium," *Modern Philology,* 29 (1931), 187-98. For other images implying a criticism of the Catholic Church, see below under *Prince Hohenstiel-Schwangau, Saviour of Society,* 861-65, and *The Ring and the Book,* III.103-04.

ANDREA DEL SARTO

1-3

> But do not let us quarrel any more,
> No, my Lucrezia; bear with me for once:
> Sit down and all shall happen as you wish.

DeVane thinks that the poem "Andrea del Sarto" is a reading of a presumed painting by Andrea del Sarto that Browning saw in Palazzo Pitti (DEVA, 245; Map F:9G). The painting was originally described in nineteenth-century catalogues of Palazzo Pitti (cat. no. 118) as a portrait of Andrea with his wife. Freedberg, however, in line with earlier critics, no longer identifies the painting with Andrea, attributes it tentatively to Toschi, and gives it the title *Portrait of a Man and a Woman* (FRE, 223; Fig. 1). The painting is thought to be a composite of two separate portraits because the left arm of the man is too long as it extends over the woman's shoulder (DEVA, 248; CHI; DOM).

For a correction of DeVane's report on Browning's correspondence, which presumably verifies the association of the poem with the painting, see Julia Markus's "Browning's 'Andrea' Letter at Wellesley College."   Markus's point is that because of inaccuracies in the letter at Wellesley referred to by DeVane, the best evidence that we have confirming Browning's intention of writing the poem as a reading of the painting is a report of a conversation between Browning and Frederick J. Furnivall on Sunday morning, November 20, 1881, twenty-six years after the poem was published (MARK, 52-55).

Looking at the painting from Browning's point of view —that is, presumably as a portrait of Andrea del Sarto and his wife Lucrezia—we see that Lucrezia is holding a letter in her

Fig. 1
Andrea del Sarto (formerly attributed to)
Portrait of a Man and a Woman
Palazzo Pitti
Florence

hand. Andrea, with his right arm over her shoulder, is pointing to the letter with his left hand. Turner believes that the letter is the cause of a quarrel between Andrea and Lucrezia, but he does not say why and does not connect the letter with the passage here (TUR, 348). I think that not only a quarrel is connected with the letter but that the specific nature of the quarrel is probably explained by an annotation in the second edition of the Palazzo Pitti catalogue, which describes the painting (CHIA, 59):

> It seems that the look [of Andrea] alludes to the dolorous past in the life of Andrea when, invited by letter from Francis I to return to France, she [Lucrezia] impeded him from it.

This annotation, which is based on an 1837 source in the library of the Uffizi Gallery (DOM), was current when Browning was in Florence and might have been familiar to him when he was writing the poem in 1853. If Browning had this annotation in mind, then line 229, "How I could paint, were I but back in France," connects with line 1, "do not let us quarrel any more," and the letter in the painting signifies that Andrea lets "all happen as you wish"—as Lucrezia wishes—and does not heed the letter of Francis I requesting that Andrea return to France.

41-43

> There's the bell clinking from the chapel-top;
> That length of convent-wall across the way
> Holds the trees safer, huddled more inside . . . .

Andrea del Sarto lived on 22 Via Gino Capponi at the corner of Via Giuseppe Giusti, just off the Piazza Santissima Annunziata, in Florence. For evidence supporting the idea that Andrea is speaking from this residence, see below under 211-13. The "convent-wall across the way" from Andrea's residence is probably that of the Servites, which adjoins the Church of the Santissima Annunziata in the piazza of the same name (Fig. 2; Map F: 6I,7I). Andrea is buried in the church, in the chancel on the left hand side under the pavement. In Piazza Santissima Annunziata stands Palazzo Budini-Gattai and the equestrian statue of Ferdinand I, both of which are discussed below under "The Statue and the Bust," 1-6, 202-05. For another reference to the Church of the Santissima Annunziata and/or the Servites, see below under 259-63 and under "Up at a Villa—Down in the City," 51-52.

Fig. 2
Background: Church of the Santissima Annunziata
Foreground: Giovanni da Bologna, statue of Duke Ferdinand I
Right: Foundlings Hospital
                   Florence

57-59

> . . . that cartoon, the second from the door
> —It is the thing, Love! so such thing should be—
> Behold Madonna!—I am bold to say.

The source for this unspecified "cartoon" could be any number of Madonnas that were modelled by Andrea after his "Love," his wife Lucrezia (VAS, III, 262-63). Compare below under 177-79 and 230-31.

97-98

> Ah, but a man's reach should exceed his grasp,
> Or what's a heaven for?

Compare this famous statement of Ruskin's Doctrine of the Imperfect with the diction ("grasp"), meter (iambic pentameter), and content of the epigram from Emblem II, Book II, from *Emblems, Divine and Moral*, by Francis Quarles (Fig. 3):

> Nor cease his Cares, till this low World's vast round,
> Within his vain, the eager Grasp he found.

Fig. 3
Francis Quarles
Emblem II, Book II
Emblems

For a discussion of another emblem from the same book by Quarles, see below under "The Glove," 189-90.

103-12

> Yonder's a work now, of that famous youth
> The Urbinate who died five years ago.
> (T is copied, George Vasari sent it me.)
> Well, I can fancy how he did it all,
> Pouring his soul, with kings and popes to see,
> Reaching, that heaven might so replenish him,
> Above and through his art—for it gives way;
> That arm is wrongly put—and there again—
> A fault to pardon in the drawing's lines,
> Its body, so to speak: its soul is right. . . .

The "copied" "work" of the "Urbinate" Raphael, with its "fault to pardon in the drawing's lines, / Its body, so to speak," is possibly an allusion to the *Madonna of the Palazzo Tempi*, in the Alte Pinakothek, in Munich (Fig. 4). This idea is suggested by David DeLaura in reference to a passage from Alexis François Rio's *De la poésie chrétienne. . . .*" (DEL, 383; RIO, 217):

> The Virgin of the Palazzo Tempi, formerly at Florence and now in the gallery of the King of Bavaria, is remarkable for the greater boldness of its design: we see that the artist now begins to give a freer development to his genius. The position of the infant Christ, when his mother poses tenderly to her bosom, offers certain technical difficulties to be overcome; and in the incorrect foreshortening of the hand on which he rests we discover the uncertainty of a first attempt. In grace and power this picture is, however, perfect.

DeLaura shows that Browning was familiar with Rio's work (DEL, 370), and this leads to the connection between Browning's description of the "arm [that] is wrongly put" and Rio's account of the "incorrect foreshortening of the hand" in the painting. To further advance Raphael's Madonna as a source in this context, I would point out five facts: first, Browning passed through Munich in 1838 on his return to London from Italy (KELL, 492); second, the *Madonna of the Palazzo Tempi* had been housed in the Alte Pinakothek of Munich since 1835 (DUS, 21), three years before Browning's visit there; third, in *Pippa Passes*, I.375-94 (see below under this citation), the First Student speaks of Jules as having seen Canova's *Psiche-fanciulla* in Munich; fourth, in "Old Pictures in Florence," 13:97-104 (see below under this citation), the statue of Paris in the Glyptothek, in Munich, is described; and five, the Glyptothek is in close proximity to the Alte Pinakothek, where the Raphael is housed. From these facts

Fig. 4
Raphael
Madonna of the Palazzo Tempi
Alte Pinakothek
Munich

we can conclude that Browning not only passed through Munich but unquestionably observed art objects in the city and most likely acquainted himself with the holdings in the Alte Pinakothek before publishing "Andrea del Sarto" in 1855.

Jacob Korg, on the other hand, nominates for this passage Raphael's painting *Leo X with Two Cardinals*. As Korg points out, Vasari's name is mentioned in connection with a picture by Raphael that has been copied ("'T is copied, George Vasari sent it me"), and Browning presumably predicts that Andrea will improve the copy by re-copying it himself but that he will not improve it to the point where it will be as good as the original by Raphael. Vasari relates in his *Vite* that Andrea did indeed copy the *Leo X with Two Cardinals*, and this suggests that Browning, who relies heavily on the *Vite* throughout the poem, is also drawing on Vasari here. Korg goes on to quote John Shearman, who describes Andrea's copy of the Raphael as imperfect because of its emotionally static "prismatic clarity" (KO, 120-21; SH, I, 125, 126). That Browning—at a much earlier date, of course—shared Shearman's view of the copy as distinguished from the original is conceivable, in that Browning could have compared the paintings. The original by Raphael has been in the Uffizi since 1797 (DUS, 46), where Browning undoubtedly saw it sometime from 1846 on. And the copy by Andrea has been in the Palazzo Capodimonte since 1735 (SH, I, 265), where Browning could have seen it when he passed through Naples in 1844 (KELL, 492).

But there are two points that weaken Korg's nomination of this source. First, there is nothing in Vasari about any imperfections in Andrea's copy (VAS, III, 179-81), and, second, Korg does not account for the particular reference in the text to "the arm [that] is wrongly put." My own view is that a composite theory might apply here, and I have accordingly entered in the Summary of Composite Sources both the *Leo X with Two Cardinals* and the *Madonna of the Palazzo Tempi* as possible sources. The *Madonna of the Palazzo Tempi*, as discussed above, explains the improperly drawn arm—or hand, to be exact—and the *Leo X with Two Cardinals*, in conjunction with Browning's reading in Vasari, allows for the copying process.

148-49

> That Francis, that first time,
> And that long festal year at Fontainebleau!

For a discussion relating this passage to the painting *Portrait of a Man and a Woman*, see above under 1-3. For another reference to Francis I and the Palace of Fontainebleau, see below under "Cristina and Monaldeschi," 5-14ff, 81-88, and 105-12. (Continued under this reference in the Supplement to Citations and Notes.)

177-79

> "Rafael did this, Andrea painted that;
> The Roman's [Raphael's] is the better when you pray,
> But still the other's [Andrea's] Virgin was his wife"....

See above under 57-59 and below under 230-31 for other references to Andrea's wife Lucrezia as a model for the Holy "Virgin." For other references to Raphael, see above under 103-12 and below under 185-87, 259-63.

185-87

> ...Rafael...
> ...the young man was flaming out his thoughts
> Upon a palace-wall for Rome to see....

The frescoes of Raphael in the Vatican are no doubt referred to here. Also, see above under 103-12, and below under *Prince Hohenstiel-Schwangau, Saviour of Society*, 850-55, and *A Soul's Tragedy*.

211-13

> Come from the window, love—, come in, at last,
> Inside the melancholy little house
> We built to be so gay with.

The particular setting for this poem is the "little house" that Andrea had "built" in Florence at 22 Via Gino Capponi, on the corner of Via Giuseppe Giusti (KO, 122-23, Map F:6I). Vasari tells us that Andrea bought the ground and had the house built in 1520 after returning from his trip to France (VAS, III, 266n). On the façade of the residence today is a tablet which reads in part, *"In questa casa abitò il pittore senza errori*—"In this house lived the painter without errors." The general Florentine setting for the poem is established by a direct mention of "our Florence" (190), and the indication of the outlying geographical landmarks

"Fiesole" and "Mount Morello" (15, 40, 92, 208). Compare 41-43
above.

230-31

> One picture, just one more—the Virgin's face
> Not yours this time! I want you at my side....

For other references concerning Andrea's use of his wife as a
model for the Holy "Virgin's face," see above under 57-59 and
177-79. (Continued under this reference in the Supplement to
Citations and Notes.)

259-63

> In heaven, perhaps, new chances, one more chance—
> Four great walls in the new Jerusalem,
> Meted on each side by the angel's reed,
> For Leonard, Rafael, Agnolo and me
> To cover....

In the Church of the Santissima Annunziata, in the Cloister of
the Madonna, Michelozzo designed an enclosed portico covering
"four great walls" on which are painted frescoes by Andrea del
Sarto, Pontormo, Rosso Fiorentino, and Baldovinetti, to name a
few. What brings these particular four walls to mind is the close
proximity of the Church of the Santissima Annunziata to the
setting of the poem, Andrea's home a couple of blocks away
from the church (see above under 41-43), and the fact that the
church is where Andrea is buried, where Andrea, in spirit,
might paint while "In heaven." (Continued under this reference in the Supplement to Citations and Notes.)

ANY WIFE TO ANY HUSBAND

77-78

> Yet, while the Titian's Venus lies at rest,
> A man looks.

"Titian's Venus," who "lies at rest," could be any one of a number of paintings by Titian showing Venus reclining. In particular, because of its sensuality, Turner nominates the *Venus of
Urbino*, in the Uffizi Gallery (TUR, 324; Fig. 5; Map F:8H). Other
possibilities are the *Venus and Cupid*, also in the Uffizi; the

Venus with the Organ-player, in the Gemäldagalerie of the Staatliche Museen, in Berlin-Dahlem; a painting of the same name in the Prado, in Madrid; the *Venus with the Lute-player,* in the New York Metropolitan Museum; and the *Venus, Pardo,* in the Louvre. Browning no doubt saw the two paintings in the Uffizi and the one in the Louvre some time prior to publishing his poem in 1855.

Fig. 5
Titian
Venus of Urbino
Uffizi
Florence

APPARENT FAILURE

Epigraph, 1-3, 10-11

"We shall soon lose a celebrated building."
                    Paris Newspaper.

No, for I'll save it! Seven years since,
          I passed through Paris, stopped a day
To see . . .

. . . the Doric little Morgue!
          The dead-house where you show your drowned. . . .

The "celebrated building" that Browning hopes to "save" is the
"Doric little Morgue," which, at the time the poem was published in 1864, was located on the east point of the Ile de la Cité,
behind the apse of Notre-Dame. DeVane states in his 1955
Handbook that the Morgue still stands (DEVA, 312-13), but in
1914 the Morgue was demolished, over forty years before the
Handbook was published.   Fig. 6, which is an illustration of
Meryon's famous 1854 drawing of the Morgue, shows one of the
corner pilasters, in accord with the text, surmounted with a
"Doric" capital. Browning obviously saw the Morgue when he
"passed through Paris" in 1855-1856, a little more than "Seven
years" before the 1864 publishing date.

BALAUSTION'S ADVENTURE

2672-97

I know, too, a great Kaunian painting, strong
As Herakles, though rosy with a robe
Of grace that softens down the sinewy strength:
And he has made a picture of it all.
There lies Alkestis dead, beneath the sun,
She longed to look her last upon, beside
The sea, which somehow tempts the life in us
To come trip over its white waste of waves,
And try escape from earth, and fleet as free.
Behind the body, I suppose there bends
Old Pheres in his hoary impotence;
And women-wailers in a corner crouch
—Four, beautiful as you four—yes, indeed!—
Close, each to other, agonizing all,
As fastened, in fear's rhythmic sympathy,
To two contending opposite. There strains

Fig. 6
Meryon
The Morgue
Bibliothèque Nationale
Paris

The might o' the hero 'gainst his more than match,
—Death, dreadful not in the thew and bone, but like
The envenomed substance that exudes some dew
Whereby the merely honest flesh and blood
Will fester up and run to ruin straight,
Ere they can close with, clasp and overcome
The poisonous impalpability
That simulates a form beneath the flow
Of those gray garments; I pronounce that piece
Worthy to set up in our Poikilé!

The "great Kaunian painter" DeVane identifies as Frederic Leighton, whose painting *Hercules Wrestling with Death for the Body of Alcestis* depicts "a picture of it all," that is, a scene from Euripides's *Alcestis*, the play which *Balaustion's Adventure* describes. The painting was exhibited by the Royal Academy in 1871, at the same time Browning was publishing his poem (DEVA, 352-53). Ormond records that Browning visited Leighton's studio while the painting was in progress (ORMO, 78). Today, the picture is owned by Mr. and Mrs. Joseph M. Tanenbaum, of Toronto (Fig. 7).

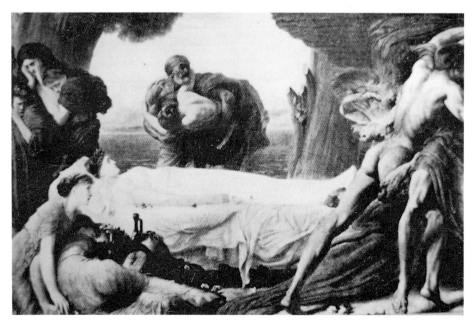

Fig. 7
Frederic Leighton
Hercules Wrestling with Death for the Body of Alcestis
Owned by Mr. and Mrs. Joseph M. Tanenbaum
Toronto, Canada

BEATRICE SIGNORINI

17-24

> ... "Desire"
> With starry front for guide, where sits the fire
> She left to brighten Buonarrotti's house.
> If you see Florence, pay that piece your vows,
> Though blockhead Baldinucci's mind, imbued
> With monkish morals, bade folk "Drape the nude
> And stop the scandal!" quoth the record prim
> I borrow this of: hang his book and him!

The painting entitled *Desire* (*L'Inclinazione*), by Artemisia Gentileschi, can still be seen in "Casa Buonarroti," in Florence. It is a ceiling piece in the room designated La Notte (PRO, 177-78; Fig. 8). As Browning correctly describes it, in the upper right-hand corner of the painting there is a "starry front for guide," and on a cloud "sits the fire," that is, a beautiful woman personifying desire. According to Baldinucci's *Notizie dei professori del disegno*—"the record prim"—the figure in the painting was originally nude but was later draped by Baldassarre Volterrano (DEVA, 543). Other poems which rely on Baldinucci's *Notizie* as a historical source are discussed below under "Filippo Baldinucci on the Privilege of Burial," 31:241-244ff; "Of Pacchiarotto, and How He Worked in Distemper," 5:64-75; and "Parleying with Francis Furini," 1:3-7.

245-61

> They parted. Soon instead
> Of Rome was home,—of Artemisia—well,
> The placid-perfect wife. And it befell
> That after the first incontestably
> Blessedest of all blisses (—wherefore try
> Your patience with embracings and the rest
> Due from Calypso's all-unwilling quest
> To his Penelope?)—there somehow came
> The coolness which as duly follows flame.
> So, one day, "What if we inspect the gifts
> My Art has gained us?"
>   Now the wife uplifts
> A casket-lid, now tries a medal's chain
> Round her own lithe neck, fits a ring in vain
> —Too loose on the fine finger,—vows and swears
> The jewel with two pendent pearls like pears
> Betters a lady's bosom—witness else!
> And so forth, while Ulysses smiles.

Fig. 8
Artemisia Gentileschi
Desire
Casa Buonarroti
Florence

DeVane (DEVA, 543) associates this passage describing Ulysses, Calypso, and Penelope with a presumably real painting of Ulysses by Romanelli, but, as far as I can determine, there is no record of such a picture (FAL).

306-15

> Whereat forth-flashing from her coils
> On coils of hair, the *spilla* in its toils
> Of yellow wealth, the dagger-plaything kept
> To pin its plaits together, life-like leapt
> And—woe to all inside the coronal!
> Stab followed stab,—cut, slash, she ruined all
> The masterpiece. Alack for eyes and mouth
> And dimples and endearment—North and South,
> East, West, the tatters in a fury flew:
> There yawned the circlet.

As DeVane reports it, the incident described here derives from an account in Baldinucci's *Notizie de' professori del disegno* (DEVA, 543-44). The account traces the lives of the artists Artemisia Gentileschi (1597-1652) and Francesco Romanelli (1617-1662), and the wife of Romanelli, Beatrice Signorini. Baldinucci relates that a portrait of Gentileschi was rendered by Romanelli inside a circlet surrounded by a decorative fruit design fashioned by Gentileschi. Beatrice Signorini, upon seeing the painting brought into her home in Viterbo, Italy, surrounded the face and part of the face itself with closely spaced holes made with a bodkin or, as Browning calls it, a "*spilla.*" Browning, however, exaggerates Baldinucci's account by having Beatrice stab out the face "in a fury" until "There yawned the circlet." Baldinucci further records that the painting was handed down to the Romanelli heirs in Viterbo, but whether or not the portrait still exists is, according to officials in the Civic Museum in Viterbo, not known (also see FAL). The home of the Romanelli family in Viterbo, however, does exist; it functions today as an apartment house and stands in good repair on Via Romanelli (Fig. 9).

 Berdoe observes that Artemisia Gentileschi was a beautiful woman and that she rendered a *Self-portrait* (BER, 67; Fig. 10), but he does not relate the painting to the present text. Perhaps Browning saw this handsome—if not beautiful—*Self-portrait* and found in it a justification for his exaggerated interpretation of Beatrice Signorini's violent act of jealousy in response to her husband's—to Romanelli's—portrait of Gen-

Fig. 9
Former home of the Romanelli family (center)
Viterbo
Italy

Fig. 10
Artemisia Gentileschi
Self-portrait
Kensington Palace
London

tileschi. Today, Gentileschi's *Self-portrait* is in Kensington Palace, London, where it was originally housed before 1835 and after 1973. Between 1835 and 1973 it was kept in Hampton Court Palace (CRI). Therefore Browning could have conveniently seen the painting at almost any time while in London.

BISHOP BLOUGRAM'S APOLOGY

3-9

> We ought to have our Abbey back, you see.
> It's different, preaching in basilicas,
> And doing duty in some masterpiece
> Like this of brother Pugin's, bless his heart!
> I doubt if they're half baked, those chalk rosettes,
> Ciphers and stucco-twiddlings everywhere;
> It's just like breathing in a lime-kiln: eh?

The phrase "We ought to have our Abbey back" refers to Bishop Blougram's hope for the reversion of Westminster Abbey (Fig. 85) from an Anglican to a Catholic church, it having been in the hands of the Anglicans since the time of Henry VIII (TUR, 339). Turner believes that the word "basilicas" refers to the basilicas of Italy (TUR, 339), while Ormond thinks that it more likely refers to the architecture of English Catholic churches, which tend to be in the Greco-Roman Baroque style rather than the Gothic style of Westminster Abbey (ORMON). The "masterpiece" of "Pugin," that is, Augustus Welby Pugin, is quite probably St. George's Cathedral, in Southwark, London (Fig. 11). I advance this idea in an article by showing the relationship between Pugin and one of the probable historical models for Blougram, Cardinal Nicholas Wiseman. My argument is that the only church by Pugin that can be connected with Wiseman is St. George's Cathedral, which Wiseman, while a Bishop, opened in 1848, seven years before Browning published his poem (THOM, 27-33).

For another reference to Westminster Abbey, see below under "The Last Ride Together," 6:65-66.

Fig. 11
Augustus Welby Pugin (architect)
St. George's Cathedral (1939, before the blitz)
Southwark, London

113-17

> And Parma's pride, the Jerome, let us add!
> 'T were pleasant could Correggio's fleeting glow
> Hang full in face of one where'er one roams,
> Since he more than the others brings with him
> Italy's self,—the marvellous Modenese!

The "Jerome" is clearly a reference to the famous painting the
Virgin with St. Jerome and Mary Magdalen, by the "Modenese,"
Correggio—Antonio Allegri—who was born in Correggio, near

Modena (BER, 79; POR, V, 294; Fig. 12). The painting— "Parma's pride"—can be seen in the National Gallery of Parma. A copy of the work by Federico Baroccio is in the Palazzo Pitti, in Florence (KO, 130; Map F:9G).

Fig. 12
Correggio
Virgin with St. Jerome and Mary Magdalen
National Gallery
Parma

513-16

> He [Shakespeare] leaves his towers and gorgeous palaces
> To build the trimmest house in Stratford town;
> Saves money, spends it, owns the worth of things,
> Giulio Romano's pictures. . . .

Shakespeare's "trimmest house" in "Stratford Town," that is, Stratford-on-Avon, probably refers to the New Place, which Shakespeare rebuilt in 1597. It does not exist today, although Shakespeare's birthplace still stands in the same city.

The reference to "Giulio Romano's pictures" calls to Korg's mind Shakespeare's famous encomium about Romano in the statue scene of *The Winter's Tale*, V. ii. 97-100 (KO, 130-31):

> . . . that rare Italian master, Julio Romano,
> who had he himself eternity and could put breath
> into his work, would beguile Nature of her custom,
> so perfectly he is her ape. . . .

Lionel Stevenson considers Leontes and the statue scene from *The Winter's Tale* a source for the Duke and the portrait of his Duchess in Browning's earlier poem "My Last Duchess" (STEV, 26-27; see below under My, 1-4).

704-07

> Up with the Immaculate Conception, then—
> On to the rack with faith!—is my advice.
> Will not that hurry us upon our knees,
> Knocking our breasts. . . .

Compare the reference to Correggio's painting the *Virgin with St. Jerome and Mary Magdalen* above under 113-17 and the paintings of St. Jerome by Filippo Lippi listed below under "Fra Lippo Lippi," 70-75. DeVane places the composition of "Bishop Blougram's Apology" to 1850 and "Fra Lippo Lippi" to February, 1853 (DEVA, 216, 240). Consequently, the present passage is a possible literary source for the text in "Fra Lippo Lippi" which describes "Jerome knocking at his poor old breast / With his great round stone to subdue the flesh" (73-74). For a later dating of the composition of "Fra Lippo Lippi," see that poem below under 145-63 and under "By the Fireside," 14:66-68, 18:86-90.

THE BISHOP ORDERS HIS TOMB AT SAINT PRAXED'S CHURCH: ROME, 15—

20-28

> Yet still my niche is not so cramped but thence
> One sees the pulpit o' the epistle-side,
> And somewhat of the choir, those silent seats,
> And up into the aery dome where live
> The angels, and a sunbeam's sure to lurk:
> And I shall fill my slab of basalt there,
> And 'neath my tabernacle take my rest,
> With those nine columns round me, two and two,
> The odd one at my feet where Anselm stands....

With some modifications, several features in this passage correspond with details that can be found in the interior of the Church of St. Praxed, that is, the Church of Santa Prassede, in Rome. There is an "aery dome" in the Cappella San Carlo Borromeo (Fig. 233), where a "sunbeam's sure to lurk" in the lantern surmounting the dome of the chapel; there is a "choir" behind a balustrade on each side of the main altar; there are "angels" in the form of mosaics on the wall behind each choir; there is a portable wood "pulpit," which was once in the nave— not on the "epistle-side" of the main altar—and is now in storage (Fig. 13); and there is a "tabernacle" that forms part of the sculptured tomb of Cardinal Cetti (Fig. 14). For other references to the tomb of Cardinal Cetti, see below under 56-61 and 106-12. For the "nine columns round" the Bishop's tomb, see Fig. 17 and below under 85-90.

42-49

> Some lump, ah God, of *lapis lazuli*,
> Big as a Jew's head cut off at the nape,
> Blue as a vein o'er the Madonna's breast...
> Sons, all have I bequeathed you, villas, all,
> That brave Frascati villa with its bath,
> So, let the blue lump poise between my knees,
> Like God the Father's globe on both his hands
> Ye worship in the Jesu Church so gay....

Rolfe and Hersey correctly identify the "lump . . . of *lapis lazuli*" as the globe that surmounts the altar-tomb of Ignatius Loyola, in the chapel on the left side-aisle of the "Jesu"—Gesù—Church, in Rome; Rolfe and Hersey incorrectly agree with the text that "God the Father's globe" rests "on both his [God's] hands" (ROL, 167;

Fig. 13
Church of Santa Prassede (Saint Praxed)
Interior (pulpit on left side)
Rome

cf. COOKE, 59-60). Actually, the globe is poised on the hands of
an angel below the sculptured figures of Christ and God. Furthermore, the reference to the altar-tomb is an anachronism in light
of the dating of the poem. The sub-title specifies "Rome, 15—,"
but Loyola's altar-tomb was constructed by the Jesuit Andrea
Pozzo between 1695 and 1704, and the statue of God was done by
Bernardino Ludovisi, who died in 1749, and Lorenzo Ottoni,
who lived between 1645-1736. For another reference to the Gesù
Church, see below under *The Ring and the Book*, III.103-04.

56-61

> The bas-relief in bronze ye promised me,
> Those Pans and Nymphs ye wot of, and perchance
> Some tripod, thyrsus, with a vase or so,
> The Saviour at his sermon on the mount,
> Saint Praxed in a glory, and one Pan
> Ready to twitch the Nymph's last garment off....

Commentators have suggested that Browning, while visiting the
Church of St. Praxed in October, 1844, was inspired by the marble
tomb of Cardinal Cetti or, as Rolfe and Hersey and DeVane refer
to him, Cardinal Cetive (ROL, 166; DEVA, 166-67). But the commentators say nothing about the tomb of Cardinal Cetti that relates it in *detail* to the description of the Bishop's bas-relief on
the tomb that he orders in the poem. The *Handbook for
Travellers in Central Italy*, which was published by John Murray
and was known to Browning (LIN, 577; OG, 38; KEL, 144, item
A1692), describes the tomb of Cardinal Cetti as follows (MUR,
382):

> The tomb of Cardinal Cetti (1474), in the 4th chapel on the rt.,
> with portraits of himself, St. Peter, St. Paul, and statues of S.
> Prassede and S. Pudenziana is interesting as a work of art of
> the 15th century.

As Figures 14 and 15 show, the statue on the far left is that of
Santa "Prassede"—St. Praxed—and is in "bas-relief" as the text
indicates. Behind the head of the statue is a minuscule halo
surrounded by a shelled vault giving the effect of a nimbus
radiating from the halo, especially when seen from below, as in
Fig. 15. The halo and the effect of the radiating nimbus, then,
support the text in that they show "St. Praxed in a glory" (EISE).
Moreover, no other statue or bas-relief of St. Praxed that I know
of exists in Rome as part of a tomb. There is a bas-relief stone

portrait of St. Praxed on the façade of St. Pudens—Santa Pudenziana—the sister church on Via Urbana, near the Church of Santa Prassede, and the sister churches both have portraits of St. Praxed either in the form of mosaics or frescoes, but none of these portraits is connected with a tomb. Furthermore, Mrs. Jameson, in *Sacred and Legendary Art*, records no churches

Fig. 14
Tomb of Cardinal Cetti
Church of Santa Prassede
Rome

Fig. 15
St. Praxed
Tomb of Cardinal Cetti (detail)
Church of Santa Prassede
Rome

other than Santa Prassede and Santa Pudenziana as having any
art object depicting St. Praxed (JAME, II, 622-24). Finally, the case
for the bas-relief statue of St. Praxed on the tomb of Cardinal
Cetti should not be materially weakened by the fact that the
statue is not "in bronze" as the text indicates. As is pointed out
above under 42-49, there are historical discrepancies in the

Bishop's reference to Loyola's altar-tomb in the Gesù Church, and the discrepancy here is not inconsistent with Browning's free historical treatment of the poem as a whole. For other details in the poem that correspond with the tomb of Cardinal Cetti, see above under 20-28 and below under 106-112.

Another feature of the bas-relief on the tomb as ordered here by the Bishop is the scene of "Pan / Ready to twitch the Nymph's last garment off." A possible source for this scene was brought to my attention by Professor Jack W. Herring, of Baylor University. It is a painting entitled *Pan and Syrinx* and is in the Dulwich Picture Gallery, in London (Fig. 16). Griffin and Minchin point out that the painting was one of many at the Dulwich Gallery that shaped Browning's taste in art (GRI, 14), but they do not identify the painting as a source for the present poem. In Browning's time the painting was attributed to Gerard de Lairesse (Flemish-Dutch, 1641-1711), the same Lairesse whom Browning writes about in "Parleying with Gerard de Lairesse"; and as late as 1914 the catalogue of the Dulwich Gallery attributed the painting to Lairesse (DUL, 108, cat. no. 179). The 1953 catalogue, however, attributes the painting to Gerard Hoet (Dutch, 1648-1733; DULW, 23, cat. no. 179).

On the other hand, there is a possibility that the source here is a painting in the National Gallery of London by Hendrick van Balen (c. 1575-1632), a follower of Jan Brueghel I. The painting is named *Pan Pursuing Syrinx,* and it indeed shows "Pan / Ready to twitch the Nymph's last garment off." The painting was probably influenced by Hendrick Goltzius's print *Pan and Syrinx,* which also inspired a painting of the same name by Rubens in collaboration with Jan Brueghel I. But the museum catalogue enters 1860 as the acquisition date of Balen's painting and it notes that before this date the painting was in the Edmond Beaucousin collection (MART, 9-10). Consequently, whether or not Browning saw the painting by Balen prior to publishing the present poem in 1845 is not known. As for the print by Goltzius and the painting by Rubens-Brueghel, evidence that Browning saw them is yet to be uncovered. (Continued under this reference in the Supplement to Citations and Notes.)

68-69

> . . . all of jasper, then!
> 'T is jasper ye stand pledged to. . . .

DeVane attributes the reference to "jasper" and the other rich

Fig. 16
Gerard Hoet
Pan and Syrinx
Dulwich Picture Gallery
London

marbles in the poem to Daniel Bartoli's *De' simboli trasportati al morale* (DEVAN, 57).   Melchiori specifies the passage from Bartoli which supports DeVane's claim and draws on Gerard de Lairesse's *The Art of Painting in All Its Branches* as a collateral source for the rich marbles (MEL, 29ff).   For other references to Lairesse's book, see below under 106-12 and 116-17. The copy of Lairesse's book that was owned by Browning is in the Yale University Library, in New Haven, Connecticut.

85-90

> For as I lie here, hours of the dead night,
> Dying in state and by such slow degrees,
> I fold my arms as if they clasped a crook,
> And stretch my feet forth straight as stone can point,
> And let the bedclothes, for a mortcloth, drop
> Into great laps and folds of sculptor's-work. . . .

In the Chapel of the Crucifixion in the Church of St. Praxed, in Rome, there is the tomb of Cardinal Anchero (d. 1286), which is in the style of the Cosmati (BAE, 241; EISE; HARE, II, 51; CROWE, I, 85). As Fig. 17 shows, the tomb is surmounted by an effigy of the Cardinal, who is covered with "bed-clothes" that "drop / Into great laps and folds of sculptor's-work," and whose protruding feet "stretch . . . forth straight as stone can point." Also, as described in line 27 and illustrated in Fig. 17, there are, as viewed from the entrance of the chapel, "nine columns round" the tomb of the Cardinal.

Actually, there is a total of eleven columns if the columns on all three sides of the tomb are counted (the fourth side is adjacent to the wall of the chapel and shows no columns). But, if we assume that this tomb is a model for Browning's poem, we may be sure that Browning is recalling the view of the nine columns on the two sides visible from the entrance to the chapel because he places "Anselm" by the "odd" column at the "feet" of the Cardinal (line 28), that is, Browning gives the reader a view of the nine columns in Fig. 17 by positioning Anselm by the third or odd column, which is at the corner of the tomb nearest the chapel entrance, the only place where Anselm could comfortably stand next to an odd column at the feet of the Cardinal.

106-12

> . . . heighten my impoverished frieze,
> Piece out its starved design, and fill my vase
> With grapes, and add a visor and a Term,
> And to the tripod ye would tie a lynx
> That in his struggle throws the thyrsus down,
> To comfort me on my entablature
> Whereon I am to lie . . . .

Fig. 17
Tomb of Cardinal Anchero
Chapel of the Crucifixion
(view from the chapel entrance)
Church of Santa Prassede
Rome

On Cardinal Cetti's tomb, discussed above under 20-28 and 56-61, the Cardinal's effigy lies on an "entablature." As may be seen in Fig. 14, the bas-relief "frieze" of the entablature features a "vase"—actually two vases—and the bas-relief square pilasters on either side of the entablature frame two stands, each of which would have a "tripod" as a base if the tripods could be shown in full relief.

Melchiori notes that the words "frieze," "vase," "grapes," "visor," "Term," and "thyrsus" may be found as ornamental motifs in *The Art of Painting in All Its Branches*, by Gerard de Lairesse (MEL, 28ff). For other references to this book, see above under 68-69 and below under 116-17.

Greenberg puts forth Pugin's *Contrasts* as a source for Browning's concern here with the inconsistent mixture of Christian and pagan elements (GRE, 1589). For example, the entablature with its frieze, as described above, is an element in the Classical or Greco-Roman style of architecture, and Pugin holds that the Classical style is more suggestive of a pagan temple than a Christian edifice. For another reference to Pugin, see above under "Bishop Blougram's Apology," 3-9.

116-17

> Gritstone, a-crumble! Clammy squares which sweat
> As if the corpse they keep were oozing through....

Barbara Melchiori compares this passage with the following from Gerard de Lairesse's *The Art of Painting in All Its Branches* (MEL, 38):

> Some stones, being more weak and brittle than others, and cor-
> roded by the air, dampness and drought, are broke[n] in pieces
> by the pressure of those over them and thus leave gaps and
> breaks....

For other references to Lairesse's treatise, see above under 68-69 and 106-12.

THE BOY AND THE ANGEL

47-52

> 'T was Easter Day: he flew to Rome,
> And paused above Saint Peter's dome.
>
> In the tiring-room close by
> The great outer gallery,
>
> With his holy vestments dight,
> Stood the new Pope, Theocrite....

The "great outer gallery" of St. Peter, in Rome, is no doubt Bernini's colonnade (Fig. 133), which is mentioned below under *Christmas-Eve*, 10:526-76. Also, compare references to the Church of St. Peter above under "Abt Vogler," 2-4, 13-24; and below under *Easter-Day*, 26:798-802; "The Pope and the Net," 13-15; *Prince Hohenstiel-Schwangau, Saviour of Society*, 861-65; and *The Ring and the Book*, III.566-72.

BY THE FIRESIDE

2:6-8

> I shall be found by the fire, suppose,
>   O'er a great wise book as beseemeth age,
> While the shutters flap as the cross-wind blows. . . .

The setting here is undoubtedly Casa Guidi (DEVA, 222). For a description of the fireplace in the drawing-room of Casa Guidi, see below under *The Ring and the Book*, I.472-83, 497-501; for an illustration of the fireplace in the drawing-room and the one in the dining room of Casa Guidi, see Figs. 149 and 150, respectively.

14:66-68, 18:86-90

> And yonder, at foot of the fronting ridge
>   That takes the turn to a range beyond,
> Is the chapel reached by the one-arched bridge. . . .
>
> It has some pretension too, this front,
>   With its bit of fresco half-moon-wise
> Set over the porch, Art's early wont:
>   'T is John in the Desert, I surmise,
> But has borne the weather's brunt. . . .

Various attempts have been made to explain this setting for the "chapel" by the "one-arched bridge" and the fresco of "John in the Desert." J. S. Lindsay claims that the scene is based on a description of the area around Lake Orta in Piedmont as found in the *Handbook for Travellers in Switzerland, the Alps of Savoy and Piedmont*, one of the guidebooks published by John Murray and one known to have been owned by Browning (KEL, 144, item A1692). The words in the poem that could have been derived from the guidebook are "Alp," "Pella," and "little lake," which is presumably Lake Orta near the village of Pella (LIN, 577). The guidebook mentions that there are many chapels in the Lake Orta area, but none of them is identified with a fresco of "John in the Desert" (MURRA, 234). Furthermore, Browning is not known to have visited the Lake Orta area, and so the incomplete description in the guidebook is all that we have to go on in trying to identify the chapel and painting according to Lindsay's claim. DeVane, on the other hand, recounting the notes of William Wetmore Story, places the scene near Bagni di Lucca. In 1853 the Brownings made an eleven-mile climb to Mount Prato Fiorito, and Mrs. Browning specifically mentions in a letter a little chapel seen during the climb (DEVA, 222; JAM, I, 273-74). Italian state officials, however, inform me that there are numerous chapels in the Prato Fiorito region and that none of them has a painting of "John in the Desert" (LUC). Jacob Korg puts aside both Lindsay and DeVane and maintains that there are contradictions in trying to identify the scene of the poem with any one locale and that the setting is "essentially imaginary, not a transcription from life" (KOR, 147). More recently, M. B. M. Calcraft has corroborated DeVane's view and convincingly identified the chapel near Bagni di Lucca as the Refubbri Chapel, or Oratorio di Rifubbri (CAL, with ilustrations; also, in this study see Figs. 235 and 236). My proposal, instead, is that Browning's description of the setting is imaginary as a whole, as Korg maintains, but that in particular it is a composite of several Italian features: the Lake Orta region, near Pella; the Oratorio di Rifubbri, near Bagni di Lucca; and a fresco designated *St. John in the Desert*, which is a detail from the *Life of John the Baptist*, by Filippo Lippi, in the Cappella Maggiore of the Duomo of Prato (Fig. 18).

In the summer of 1853, just prior to the Mount Prato Fiorito excursion, the Brownings visited the city of Prato (TAP, 272) and saw paintings in the Duomo of Prato, which Browning later incorporated in the poem "Fra Lippo Lippi" (see below under "Fra Lippo Lippi," 31-36, 194-98, and 323-32). In the probable recalling of the excursion to Prato Fiorito and Lippi's fresco of *St. John in the Desert* in the Duomo of Prato, Browning could have confused Prato proper and Prato Fiorito in point of time and could have associated them in name. Furthermore, just above the fresco of *St. John in the Desert* in the Cappella Maggiore of the Duomo of Prato is Lippi's lunette-shaped *Birth of St. John* (VAS, II, 72-73; MAR, 210, item 46, plate 92). Perhaps Browning, through his own observations in the Duomo and his reading in Vasari, derived his image in the poem of the "fresco half-moon wise" from his recollection of Lippi's lunette at Prato. (Continued under this reference in the Supplement to Citations and Notes.)

CENCIAJA

15-29

Shelley, may I condense verbosity
That lies before me, into some few words
Of English, and illustrate your superb

Fig. 18
Filippo Lippi
St. John in the Desert (detail)
from the *Life of John the Baptist*
Duomo
Prato

> Achievement by a rescued anecdote,
> No great things, only new and true beside?
> As if some mere familiar of a house
> Should venture to accost the group at gaze
> Before its Titian, famed the wide world through,
> And supplement such pictured masterpiece
> By whisper, "Searching in the archives here,
> I found the reason of the Lady's fate,
> And how by accident it came to pass
> She wears the halo and displays the palm:
> Who, haply, else had never suffered—no,
> Nor graced our gallery, by consequence."

There is no painting by Titian of Beatrice Cenci, nor is there any portrait of her that I know of showing that "she wears the halo and displays the palm." Nevertheless, I think that Browning, in this passage, could have had in mind the presumed portrait of Beatrice Cenci attributed to Guido Reni. Shelley gives a detailed account of Reni's portrait in his Preface to his play *The Cenci*, and since Browning uses the play—Shelley's "superb / Achievement"—as a basis for his poem, he certainly was familiar with Shelley's Preface to the play. Reni's portrait, "famed the wide world through," is housed in the Palazzo Corsini, in Rome (Fig. 19; Map R: 8F). Compare Hawthorne's use of the same portrait in his *The Marble Faun*, especially Chapter VII, which is entitled "Beatrice." Browning, we know, owned a copy of Hawthorne's book (KEL, 99), and the Hawthornes visited the Brownings in Casa Guidi in 1858 (Hawthorne, *The Italian Notebooks*, entry for June 9, 1858).

175-77

> He left home, in July when day is flame,
> Posted to Tordinona-prison, plunged
> Into a vault where daylong night is ice....

For another reference to the now defunct "Tordinona-prison," see below under *The Ring and the Book*, V. 324-25.

228-30

> So, the Marchese had his head cut off,
> With Rome to see, a concourse infinite,
> In Place Saint Angelo beside the Bridge....

See Fig. 146 and compare other references to the Castle or "Place Saint Angelo" below under *The Ring and the Book*, X.1010-12, 2106-11; and *Sordello*, IV.1014-22.

266-69

By death of her, the Marquisate returned

Fig. 19
Guido Reni (attributed to)
Beatrice Cenci (identified with)
Palazzo Corsini
Rome

To that Orsini House from whence it came:
Oriolo having passed as donative
To Santa Croce from their ancestors.

The sixteenth-century "Orsini" Palace, in Rome, was built inside
the Theater of Marcellus. Fig. 20 shows the Theater of Marcellus,
the third story of which is part of the Orsini Palace (Map R: 8H).

Fig. 20
Theater of Marcellus (left)
Palazzo Orsini (third floor of theater)
Rome

Near the Orsini Palace is the Cenci Palace (Fig. 21; Map R:
8H), which, though not specifically mentioned in Browning's
poem, provides an important setting for Shelley's play *The
Cenci* (see above under 15-29 for the reference to Shelley's
"superb / Achievement").

Fig. 21
Middle and right: Palazzo de' Cenci
Rome

"CHILDE ROLAND TO THE DARK TOWER CAME"

Mrs. Orr mentions an unspecified painting that Browning supposedly saw in Paris that served as an inspiration for this poem (OR, 274), but who painted it and what it depicts in the poem she does not say.

A more clearly demonstrated source is Gerard de Lairesse's *The Art of Painting in All Its Branches*, which provides depictions of the landscape for the poem (DE, 426-32).

13:76-78

> One still blind horse, his every bone a-stare,
> Stood stupefied, however he came there:
> Thrust out past service from the devil's stud!

The Rev. John W. Chadwick, upon visiting Browning at Casa Guidi, noticed a tapestry on the wall and asked Browning if the "miserable horse" depicted in the fabric was "the beast of the poem." Browning said that it was (BRO, 1020); but there is no horse in the tapestry that fits the grotesque description here of a "still blind horse, his every bone a-stare," and I question the accuracy of the Chadwick anecdote. The tapestry was one of seven that were sold out of Casa Guidi in 1913, and the Sotheby Catalogue lists the one specifically associated with Browning's poem as no. 1385 (KEL, 524, item H667; SOT, 159). The tapestry shows Hermes driving the cattle of Apollo off to Pylos and Apollo piping among his herds. All of the horses in the scene look healthy and idealized. Tapestry no. 1386 is a companion piece to no. 1385, and the two of them may be seen in the Vizcaya Museum, in Miami, Florida. No. 1386, like no. 1385, has no "miserable horse" in it and does nothing to support the present text (see illustrations in KEL, Pl. 27, items H667 and H668). I have not seen the other five tapestries described in the Sotheby Catalogue, but I doubt if they depict the horse in question. Nos. 1387, 1388, and 1389 are described in the catalogue as rural or hunting scenes with horses included in them, but they are probably idyllic scenes, like tapestries nos. 1385 and 1386, and have only idealized horses in them. Nos. 1390 and 1391 are not described in the catalogue as having horses in them at all and raise no hope for any correspondence with the text. No. 1390 is a scene depicting Christ appearing to Mary, and no. 1391, along with no. 1390, shows the Medici coat of arms. On the other hand, as a possible explanation for the Chadwick anecdote, Philip Kelley suggests that Browning owned tapestries other than those sold by Sotheby in 1913. But where these tapestries are today—if they do exist—I am not prepared to say. For another reference to tapestries nos. 1390 and 1391, in connection with the Medici coat of arms, see *The Ring and the Book*, I.1-4, 15-17, in the Supplement to Citations and Notes.

31:181-84

> What in the midst lay but the Tower itself?
>> The round squat turret, blind as the fool's heart,
>> Built of brown stone, without a counterpart
> In the whole world.

Browning, in a letter to A. W. Hunt (NEW, 229), describes the "Tower" in the present passage as

>> . . . a strange solitary little tower I have come upon more than once in Massa-Carrara, in the midst of low hills. . . [;]

yet no one has identified this structure, which, according to Browning, should be in the "low hills" rising up from the coast of the Tirrano Sea in the area combining the Italian cities of Massa and Carrara. My own observations, however, lead me to believe that the proper source here is the "solitary little tower" below the Malaspina Castle, in Massa, just south of Carrara. (Continued under this reference in the Supplement to Citations and Notes.)

CHRISTMAS-EVE (*Easter-Day* under separate entry)

10:526-76

> And what is this that rises propped
> With pillars of prodigious girth?
> Is it really on the earth,
> This miraculous Dome of God?
> . . .
> Columns in the colonnade
> With arms wide open to embrace
> The entry of the human race
> To the breast of . . . what is it, yon building,
> Ablaze in front, all paint and gilding,
> With marble for brick, and stones of price
> For garniture of the edifice?
> . . .
> Forever, in pictures, thus it looks,
> . . .
> . . . how these fountains play,
> Growing up eternally
> Each to a musical water-tree,
> Whose blossoms drop . . .
> . . .

To the granite lavers underneath.

. . .

The whole Basilica alive!
Men in the chancel, body and nave,
Men on the pillars' architrave,
Men on the statues, men on the tombs
With popes and kings in their porphyry wombs,
All famishing in expectation
Of the main altar's consummation.

. . .

. . . the taper-fires
Pant up, the winding brazen spires
Heave loftier yet the baldachin;

. . .

. . . the organ blatant
Holds his breath. . . .

In and around the Church of St. Peter, in Rome, the "columns," "colonnade," "fountains," "statues," "baldachin," and "organ" are all as Browning describes (Figs. 133 and 134). For other references to the Church of St. Peter, see above under "Abt Vogler," 2-4, 13-26; "The Boy and the Angel," 47-52; and below under *Easter-Day*, 26:798-802; "The Pope and the Net," 13-15; *Prince Hohenstiel-Schwangau, Saviour of Society*, 861-65; and *The Ring and the Book*, III. 566-72.

Compare this image of the "colonnade / With arms open to embrace / The entry of the human race" (Fig. 133) with the negative image of the colonnade as outstretched scorpion claws, entered below under *Prince Hohenstiel-Schwangau*, 861-65.

11:678-82

. . . filthy saints rebuked the gust
With which they chanced to get a sight
Of some dear naked Aphrodite
They glanced a thought above the toes of,
By breaking zealously her nose off.

This is an allusion to an unspecified statue of "Aphrodite" damaged by Christian priests. For a reference to Aphrodite as the *Cnidian Venus*, see below under *The Ring and the Book*, IX.169-71.

12:749-52

But, now and then, [the artist] bravely aspires to consummate
A Colossus by no means so easy to come at,
And uses the whole of his block for the bust,
Leaving the mind of the public to finish it. . . .

This is an allusion to the famous bronze Colossus of Rhodes, built by Chares in the harbor of Rhodes. It depicted Helios, god of the sun, and was destroyed by an earthquake in 224 B.C. (KRY, 140).

CLEON

51-54

> The image of the sun-god on the phare,
> Men turn from the sun's self to see, is mine;
> The Poecile, o'er-storied its whole length,
> As thou didst hear, with painting, is mine too.

Cleon, Browning's imaginary Greek poet, painter, and philosopher, attributes to himself here an unspecified architectural design and a painting—or paintings—on the Stoa "Poecile." The "image of the sun-god on the phare" means the design of a sun-god on a lighthouse. In reference to the lighthouse, Porter and Clarke state (POR, V, 297):

> The French authority, Allard, . . . says that though there is no mention in classical writings of any light-house in Greece proper; it is probable that there was one at the port of Athens as well as at other points in Greece. There were certainly several along both shores of the Hellespont, besides the famous father of all light-houses, on the island of Pharos, near Alexandria. Hence the French name for light-house, phare.

Whether or not Browning had any particular lighthouse in mind, however, is an open question.

The "Poecile" is the Stoa Poecile, which was painted by Polygnotus of Thasos (5th century B.C.) and others. It was a porch, or covered colonnade, in Athens, where Zeno, the founder of the Stoics, taught (hence the word "stoa" produced the name "Stoics"). The description of the Stoa Poecile "o'er-storied its whole length . . . with painting" means that its columns were covered with pictures of mythological and historical events (thus the use of the name "Poecile," which means "many colored"). But how the pictures were actually related to the columns is not known. The Stoa Poecile has not been excavated, yet Paul Mackendrick thinks that if we judge from findings of excavations near the Stoa Poecile, it may be that the columns had pins inserted in them upon which hung frames for holding the paintings (MAC, 255).

82-88

> See, in the chequered pavement opposite,
> Suppose the artist made a perfect rhomb,
> And next a lozenge, then a trapezoid—
> He did not overlay them, superimpose
> The new upon the old and blot it out,
> But laid them on a level in his work,
> Making at last a picture; there it lies.

A likely source for this "chequered pavement" is the famous pavement in the Duomo of Siena. Fig. 22 shows the exterior of the Duomo, and Fig. 23 illustrates Giovanni Ricciarelli's floor plan for the pavement, which is housed in the Museo dell' Opera del Duomo di Siena. The floor plan makes "a picture" in the form of a Latin cross comprised of bas-relief scenes and decorative designs set in various geometrical shapes. All the shapes are there that Browning describes: a "rhomb, / And next a lozenge, then a trapezoid." Finally, mention should be made that five years before publishing his poem Browning lived two miles outside of Siena for two weeks during the late summer of 1850 (DEVA, 215). That he did not see the Cathedral and the checkered pavement while residing near Siena is inconceivable.

Symbolically, the Latin cross design of the floor plan foreshadows the discussion of Christianity in the last seventeen lines of the poem.

174-80

>   "... what survives myself?
> The brazen statue to o'erlook my [Cleon's] grave,
> Set on the promontory which I named.
> And that—some supple courtier of my heir
> Shall use its robed and sceptred arm, perhaps,
> To fix the rope to, which best drags it down.
> I go then: triumph thou, who dost not go!"

A possible source for Cleon's "statue" is entered under this reference in the Supplement to Citations and Notes.

287-88

>   ... if I paint,
> Carve the young Phoebus, am I therefore young?

See above under 51-54 for another reference to a sun-god.

Fig. 22
Cathedral and Piazza del Duomo
Siena

Fig. 23
Giovanni Ricciarelli
Floor Plan of the Pavement in the Duomo of Siena
Museo dell' Opera del Duomo di Siena
Siena

CRISTINA AND MONALDESCHI

5-14ff

> . . . there they are—"*Quis*
> *Separabit*?"—plain those two
> Touching words come into view,
> Apposite for me and you. . . .
>
> Since they witness to incessant
> Love like ours: King Francis, he—
> Diane the adored one, she—
> Prototypes of you and me.
> Everywhere is carved her Crescent
> With his Salamander-sign. . . .

According to Jean-Pierre Samoyault, curator of Fontainebleau
Palace, the words "*Quis Separabit*"—"who shall separate?"—are
imaginary and may be found nowhere in Fontainebleau Palace
to represent the constancy of the love between King Francis I and
Diane de Poitiers.   "Her crescent / With his Salamander-sign,"
however, may be seen throughout the palace as Browning
describes.   The crescent sign is part of the decor in the Ballroom,
and the salamander sign decorates the Gallery of Francis I and
the exterior walls of the palace (Figs. 24, 25, and 26; SAM).

81-88

> Me as standing, you as stooping,—
> Who arranged for each the pose?
> Lest men think us friends turned foes,
> Keep the attitude you chose!
> Men are used to this same grouping—
> I and you like statues seen.
> You and I, no third between
> Kneel and stand! That makes the scene.

There is no group sculpture in the Palace of Fontainebleau
showing Monaldeschi "stooping" before a "standing" Queen
Cristina.   But there is a painting in the palace that could be a
source for this "grouping . . . like statues seen."   In the Gallery of
Diane, situated directly above the Gallery of the Deer (see 105-12
below), hangs a portrait by Madame Haudebourg-Lescot, which
represents Diane de Poitiers asking King Francis I to pardon her
father, who in 1523 was involved in the Duke of Bourbon's
treason.   In the painting (Fig. 27) Francis is sitting and leaning
forward to raise Diane by the right hand.   King Francis I and

Fig. 24
Fontainebleau Palace, central entrance
Fontainebleau

Fig. 25
Crescent signs in the decor in the Ballroom
Fontainebleau Palace
Fontainebleau

Fig. 26
Salamander sign in the decor in the Gallery of Francis I
Fontainebleau Palace
Fontainebleau

Fig. 27
Madame Haudebourg-Lescot
Diane de Poitiers Asks Grace from Francis I for Her Father
Gallery of Diane
Fontainebleau Palace
Fontainebleau

Diane de Poitiers are "Prototypes of you and me" (see above under 5-14ff), that is, prototypes of the crown-subject relationship between Queen Cristina and Count Monaldeschi. Both the painting of Diane de Poitiers kneeling before King Francis and the imaginary group sculpture of Count Monaldeschi stooping before Queen Cristina emphasize the obeisance of the subjects before the crown figures. In addition, it should be pointed out that the portrait by Madame Haudebourg-Lescot was rendered in 1812 (SAM) and that Browning visited Fontainebleau in 1872 (KELL, 496; IRV, 472-73), eleven years before publishing his poem in 1883. Thus Browning could have seen the painting during his visit to Fontainebleau and could have been influenced by it in this context.

105-12

> See, where Juno strikes Ixion,
>> Primatice speaks plainly! Pooh—
>> Rather, Florentine Le Roux!
>> I've lost head for who is who—
> So it swims and wanders! Fie on
>> What still proves me female! Here
>> By the staircase!—for we near
>> That dark "Gallery of the Deer."

No painting showing that "Juno strikes Ixion" may be found in the Palace of Fontainebleau, although much work of "Primatice" (Primaticcio) and "Le Roux" (Il Rosso or Rosso Fiorentino) exists in the Palace (SAM). The "Gallery of the Deer," where Cristina actually had Monaldeschi executed, is on the lower east floor of the palace (Fig. 28).

121-28

> What if to the selfsame place in
>> Rustic Avon, at the door
>> Of the village church once more,
>> Where a tombstone paves the floor
> By that holy-water basin
>> You appealed to—"As, below.
>> This stone hides its corpse, e'en so
>> I your secrets hide"? What ho!

As Browning describes it, Monaldeschi's tomb is in the "village church"—the Parish Church—of Avon (Fig. 29) and is located in the pavement "stone" near the "Holy-water basin" (Fig. 30).

Fig. 28
Gallery of the Deer
Fontainebleau Palace
Fontainebleau

Fig. 29
Parish Church
Avon, France

Fig. 30
Tomb of Count Monaldeschi
Parish Church
Avon, France

DEAF AND DUMB: A GROUP BY WOOLNER

1-8

> Only the prism's obstruction shows aright
> The secret of a sunbeam, breaks its light
> Into the jewelled bow from blankest white;
> So may a glory from defect arise:
> Only by Deafness may the vexed Love wreak
> Its insuppressive sense on brow and cheek,
> Only by Dumbness adequately speak
> As favored mouth could never, through the eyes.

In the Borough Cemetery, Tunbridge Wells, England, there is a group sculpture by Thomas Woolner depicting Arthur and Constance, the deaf and dumb children of Sir Thomas Fairbairn (Fig. 31). The group was exhibited in the International Exhibition of 1862, but these lines that Browning wrote for it did not appear in the exhibition catalogue (DEVA, 316).

For another reference to Woolner, see below under "A Face," 1-3, 11-13.

EASTER-DAY (*Christmas-Eve* under separate entry)

26:798-802

> ... think, now
> What pomp in Buonarroti's brow,
> With its new palace-brain where dwells
> Superb the soul, unvexed by cells
> That crumbled with the transient clay!

The dome—the "palace-brain"—of the Church of St. Peter, in Rome, was designed by Michelangelo "Buonarroti" (Fig. 133). See above under *Christmas-Eve*, 10:526-76, and below under *Prince Hohenstiel-Schwangau, Saviour of Society*, 861-65.

Fig. 31
Thomas Woolner
Deaf and Dumb
Borough Cemetery
Tunbridge Wells, England

AN ENGLISHMAN IN ITALY: PIANO DI SORRENTO

207-38

... there slumbered
  As greenly as ever
Those isles of the siren, your Galli;
  No ages can sever
The Three, nor enable their sister
  To join them,—halfway
On the voyage, she looked at Ulysses—
  No farther to-day,
Though the small one, just launched in the wave
  Watches breast-high and steady
From under the rock, her bold sister
  Swum halfway already.
Fortù, shall we sail there together
  And see from the sides
Quite new rocks show their faces, new haunts
  Where the siren abides?
Shall we sail round and round them, close over
  The rocks, though unseen,
That ruffle the gray glassy water
  To glorious green?
Then scramble from splinter to splinter,
  Reach land and explore,
On the largest, the strange square black turret
  With never a door,
Just a loop to admit the quick lizards;
  Then, stand there and hear
The birds' quiet singing, that tells us
  What life is, so clear?
—The secret they sang to Ulysses
  When, ages ago,
He heard and he knew this life's secret
  I hear and I know.

The "square black turret" is a tower built by King Robert of
Naples in 1330. It is on the largest of the three "isles of the siren,
your Galli," which are grouped together off the Amalfian Coast
facing Positano, to the west. A fourth island, a "sister" to "The
Three," lies a little apart from the main group. King Robert's
Tower was built over a cistern as a refuge for seafarers against
pirates (DOU, 28). Observation reveals that the tower is part of a
network of other towers which dot the Amalfian Coast and that
each tower is visible to the next in line as part of a signaling
system. Except for King Robert's Tower, which, as Fig. 32 shows,
has been restored with windows and a door for modern living,

Fig. 32
Tower of King Robert of Naples
Galli Islands
Italy

each of the other towers, still being in their original condition, answers accurately to Browning's description of a "turret / With never a door, / Just a loop to admit the lizards," that is, with just a slit to safeguard the seafarers and to admit and remit the signal lights.

That Browning took a personal, symbolic interest in King Robert's Tower is clear from biographical evidence. In October, 1844, Browning, as the text indicates, was to "Reach land and explore, / On the largest [island], the strange square black turret." A year later he sent a copy of "An Englishman in Italy" to Elizabeth Barrett (DEVA, 157-58); and in that same year Walter Savage Landor sent to Browning the sonnet "To Robert Browning," which ends as follows:

> Beyond Sorrento and Amalfi, where
> The Siren waits thee singing song for song.

Concurrently, Browning picked up the siren motif in his 1845-1846 correspondence with Elizabeth Barrett when they were planning their marriage and elopement to Italy, for recurrent in Browning's letters of this period is the expression "our Siren song" (KIN, I, 273). Finally, Browning certainly would have been aware that King Robert of Naples associates with his own name of Robert.

260-91

> To-morrow's the Feast
> Of the Rosary's Virgin, by no means
> Of Virgins the least,
> As you'll hear in the off-hand discourse
> Which (all nature, no art)
> The Dominican brother, these three weeks,
> Was getting by heart.
> Not a pillar nor post but is dizened
> With red and blue papers;
> All the roof waves with ribbons, each altar
> Ablaze with long tapers;
> But the great masterpiece is the scaffold
> Rigged glorious to hold
> All the fiddlers and fifers and drummers
> And trumpeters bold,
> Not afraid of Bellini nor Auber,
> Who, when the priest's hoarse,
> Will strike us up something that's brisk
> For the feast's second course.

And then will the flaxen-wigged Image
    Be carried in pomp
Through the plain, while in gallant procession
    The priests mean to stomp.
All round the glad church lie old bottles
    With gunpowder stopped,
Which will be, when the Image re-enters,
    Religiously popped;
And at night from the crest of Calvano
    Great bonfires will hang,
On the plain will the trumpets join chorus,
    And more poppers bang.
At all events, come. . . .

The "flaxen-wigged Image" here is unquestionably a wood statue of the Madonna of the Rosary in the Church of the Santissima Trinità in the Italian town of Piano di Sorrento. The town is indicated in the subtitle of the poem and is not to be confused with Sorrento proper, which is two miles west of Piano di Sorrento. The statue is the only one of its kind in Piano di Sorrento and has probably been in the Church of the Santissima Trinità since the 18th century, shortly after the Madonna of the Rosary was coronated in 1773. As Fig. 33 shows, the Madonna is "flaxen-wigged," that is, upon closer examination, seen to be made with the hair of vegetable fibers. The "procession" in which the statue was used is, with one or two exceptions, described accurately by Browning. The "Dominican brother" might well have been participating on the occasion, for the Madonna of the Rosary has traditionally been the protectress of the Dominican order, though the Church of the Santissima Trinità is not Dominican. Dominicans, however, have been known to participate in the procession in order to promulgate a devotion to the Madonna of the Rosary. Furthermore, the wood statue probably was originally in the Convent of San Vincenzo, a Dominican order formerly outside of nearby Sorrento. Each "post" or "pillar" in the Church of the Santissima Trinità was "dizened" or decorated with "red" and "blue papers" and—as Browning omits—yellow papers besides. Each "altar" was "Ablaze with long tapers." A band of "fifers and drummers / And trumpeters" led the procession from the "glad church" (Fig. 34). The "fiddlers," who would not have been used in the procession, were possibly used during the church service before the procession. "Old bottles / with gun-powder stopped," that is, firecrackers inside of empty cylinders were discharged to

Fig. 33
Madonna of the Rosary
Church of the Santissima Trinità
Piano di Sorrento
Italy

Fig. 34
Church of the Santissima Trinità
Piano di Sorrento
Italy

announce when the statue left—not "when the Image re-enter [ed]"—the church. And "at night from the crest of Calvano"— Mount Vicoalvano or Mount Vicalvano as it is called today— "Great bonfires" could be seen from its "crest," upon which is mounted a large cross. (The mountain is illustrated in Fig. 35 because it is an integral part of the procession.) The procession, which is part of the Feast of St. Peter today, has probably been observed every year during the last week in June since Browning's time (ESP). Browning, however, having been in or around

Piano di Sorrento in October (DEVA, 158) and not June of 1844, no doubt did not view the procession first hand and probably obtained his information from local inhabitants and/or by watching other Catholic processions, most of which, I am told, employ a procedure similar to that described above (ESP).

Fig. 35
Mount Vicoalvano
Piano di Sorrento
Italy

AN EPISTLE . . . OF KARSHISH

122-25

> He listened not except I spoke to him,
> But folded his two hands and let them talk,
> Watching the flies that buzzed: and yet no fool.
> And that's a sample how his years must go.

Joseph A. Dupras puts forth the following points in maintaining that the *Lazarus Triptych*, a painting by the fifteenth-century French painter Nicolas Froment, may be a source for this poem: the three-part structure of the poem corresponds with the three-panel form of the *Triptych*; the development of the character of Karshish in the poem corresponds with the developing character of Peter in the *Triptych*; and the incident in the passage here where Lazarus is "Watching the flies that buzzed" corresponds with the panel in the *Triptych* where Lazarus is pointing to a group of flies on the corner of the dinner table.   Furthermore, Dupras notes that the painting has been in the Uffizi Gallery since 1841 (Map F:8H) and that Browning could have seen it there prior to publishing his poem in 1855 (DUP, 50-56, including illustrations).

EURYDICE TO ORPHEUS: A PICTURE BY LEIGHTON

1-8

> But give them me, the mouth, the eyes, the brow!
> Let them once more absorb me! One look now
>   Will lap me round forever, not to pass
> Out of its light, though darkness lie beyond:
> Hold me but safe again within the bond
>   Of one immortal look! All woe that was,
> Forgotten, and all terror that may be,
> Defied,—no past is mine, no future: look at me!

Frederic Leighton's picture *Orpheus and Eurydice* hangs in the Leighton House, in London (Fig. 36). Browning's poem, although published without metrical divisions in the Royal Academy Catalogue of 1864, was later published as it is here (DEVA, 316-17).

Fig. 36
Frederic Leighton
Orpheus and Eurydice
Leighton House
London

Of further interest in association with Leighton's painting and the legend of Orpheus and Eurydice is the tomb of Elizabeth Barrett Browning, which was designed by Leighton and placed in the Protestant Cemetery in Piazza Donatello, Florence (Fig. 37).

Fig. 37
Frederic Leighton
Tomb of Elizabeth Barrett Browning
Protestant Cemetery, Piazza Donatello
Florence

DeVane tells us that the present poem was meant to memorialize the death of Elizabeth, since in a later edition of poems it was placed after "Prospice," a poem well known to be a personal commemoration of the death of Elizabeth; and he informs us that in *Balaustion's Adventure* Leighton's painting *Hercules*

Wrestling for the Body of Alcestis was also employed in order to commemorate the death of Elizabeth (DEVA, 316). From these connections Elizabeth's tomb comes to mind, since the tomb, like the two paintings mentioned above, was designed by Leighton and since Browning's life, just as the two poems mentioned above are biographical, was associated with the story of Orpheus and Eurydice. After the death of Elizabeth, Browning left Florence for good in 1861 and Elizabeth's tomb was completed between 1863-1864 (ORMO, 76). Thus Browning never looked back on Elizabeth, so to speak, for, unlike Orpheus who cast a forbidden look on Eurydice and lost her, Browning never returned to Florence to look upon the tomb of Elizabeth.

For other references to Lord Leighton and his work, see elsewhere in this study under *Balaustion's Adventure*, 2672-97, and "Yellow and pale as ripened corn."

A FACE

1-3, 11-13

> If one could have that little head of hers
> Painted upon a background of pale gold,
> Such as the Tuscan's early art prefers!
>
> . . .
>
> Then her lithe neck, three fingers might surround,
> How it should waver on the pale gold ground
> Up to the fruit-shaped, perfect chin it lifts!

This poem was written as a memorial to the beauty of Mrs. Coventry Patmore, the first wife of Coventry Patmore and the inspiration for his 1854 poem "The Angel in the House." Two possible sources for "A Face" are suggested by DeVane: an 1851 portrait of Mrs. Coventry Patmore by John Everett Millais (see Fig. 38, a copy reproduced from CHA, facing p. 116) and a medallion of her by Thomas Woolner, done about the same time as the Millais portrait (see Fig. 39, a copy reproduced from CHA, facing p. 118). DeVane maintains that the poem was written in 1852 (DEVA, 305), but whether or not Browning was aware that Millais and Woolner had rendered their portraits of Mrs. Patmore while he was writing the poem depends largely on the possibility that Browning knew both Millais and Woolner as early as 1852. Elizabeth Barrett Browning records in a letter of

Fig. 38
John Everett Millais
Emily Augusta Patmore (copy of the painting)
Fitzwilliam Museum
Cambridge
England

Fig. 39
Thomas Woolner
Emily Augusta Patmore (copy of the medallion)
Location unknown

October 5-6, 1852, that Pen gave one of his drawings to Millais (OG, 85), and DeVane in his *Handbook* states that Browning and Woolner might have met at Coventry Patmore's home early in 1852 (DEVA, 316). Today, the Millais painting is no. 37, a very small oil in the Fitzwilliam Museum, Cambridge. The medallion by Woolner is presently unlocated.

FIFINE AT THE FAIR

35:536-37, 549-51

The Rafael faces me, in fine, no dream at all,
My housemate, evermore to glorify my wall.
. . .

> Next year, I saunter past with unaverted eyes,
> Nay, loll and turn my back [to the Raphael]:
>   perchance to overlook
> With relish, leaf by leaf, Doré's last picture-book.

The painting by Raphael that Don Juan describes as presumably in his possession is unspecified. "Doré's last picture-book" may refer to *Les Idylles du Roi*, which is translated from the English and includes 36 designs. DeVane dates the genesis of Browning's poem to 1871-72 (DEVA, 364), while Doré's picture book was published in 1869 (JER, 415).

52:757-59, 777-79

> I' the palace-gallery, the corridor beyond,
> Upheaves itself a marble, a magnitude manshaped
> As snow might be....
>   ...
> Of Michelagnolo takes elemental shape?
> I think he meant the daughter of the old man o' the sea,
> Emerging from her wave, goddess Eidotheé....

Michelangelo is not known to have fashioned a marble statue of the "goddess Eidothée," yet Korg thinks that the *Prisoners* of Michelangelo could be sources for a figure struggling to set itself free as if it were "emerging from her wave." Four of these supposedly unfinished statues are in the Accademia of Florence (Map F:7I), and the other two are in the Louvre (KO, 199). Specifically, it appears to me that the *Awakening Captive*, as shown in Fig. 238, gives the best impression of emergence—emergence from stone rather than water.

107:1846

> ...Venice' Square, Mark's Church...

Also see stanzas 94, 95, 104, 117; below under *Sordello*, I. 820-21, III. 136-37; and "A Toccata of Galuppi's," 5-8. For illustrations of the Church of St. Mark, see Figs. 201 and 216.

121:2044-45ff

> ...see the very thing, and save my tongue describe
> The Druid monument which fronts you.

The "Druid monument" is the group of ruins near Pornic, in Loire-Atlantique, France (POR, III, 302; Fig. 40).

Fig. 40
Druid Monument (detail)
Pornic, Loire-Atlantique
France

FILIPPO BALDINUCCI ON THE PRIVILEGE OF BURIAL: A REMINISCENCE OF A.D. 1676

31:241-44ff

> On just the side
> They drew their purse-strings to make quit
> Of Mary,—Christ the Crucified
> Fronted them now....

In this poem, Ludovico Buti, a painter of the Florentine Movement, is specifically mentioned in connection with two of his paintings, a *Madonna* and a *Crucifixion*. Filippo Baldinucci, whose *Notizie dei professori del disegno* is the literary source for the poem, recounts the anecdote employed by Browning involving Buti's paintings. Briefly, the anecdote is about the desecrating of a Jewish cemetery near Porta San Frediano, in Florence. Opposite the cemetery a Christian shrine was mounted displaying Buti's *Madonna*. When the Jews complained about the shrine, the *Madonna* was removed to the other side of the shrine and replaced with Buti's *Crucifixion*, much to the anger of the Jews (COOKE, 139-40). It is noted in the Thieme-Becker *Lexikon*, which is in accord with Baldinucci, that Buti's *Crucifixion* was located near the Porta San Frediano (THI, V, 300), in a shrine that Baldinucci places in a corner of the outside wall adjoining the Porta San Frediano. But part of the wall south of the portal was removed to allow for modern traffic, and the shrine was no doubt taken down during construction work. Where the *Madonna* and *Crucifixion* of Buti are today I have been unable to ascertain. The Jewish cemetery, however, may be seen over the chained gate at 16 Viale L. Ariosto, at the intersection of Via dell' Orto, where the south wall has been removed (Fig. 230; Map F:8F indicates the Via dell' Orto; KO, 203; HAR, 205).

Other poems by Browning which draw from Baldinucci's *Notizie* are discussed under "Beatrice Signorini," "Of Pacchiarotto, and How He Worked in Distemper," and "Parleying with Francis Furini."

FRA LIPPO LIPPI

7-8

> The Carmine's my cloister: hunt it up,
> Do,—harry out, if you must show your zeal. . . .

Lippi served in the Church of Santa Maria del Carmine, in Florence. The church was consecrated in 1422 (Fig. 41; Map F:8F). See below under 90-91 and 138-41.

Fig. 41
Church of the Carmine
Florence

14-18

>   Who am I?
> Why, one, sir, who is lodging with a friend
> Three streets off—he's a certain . . . how d' ye call?
> Master—a . . . Cosimo of the Medici,
> I' the house that caps the corner.

The "house that caps the corner" is the Palazzo Medici-Riccardi,
located on Via Cavour (Fig. 42; Map F:7H). It was built by
Michelozzo from 1440 to 1460 by order of Cosimo the Elder. For
other references to Cosimo the Elder and/or the Medici family,
see below under 28-29, 47-49, 78-79, 98-101, and 226-30. For other
references to the Palazzo Medici-Riccardi, see below under 61-67
and 226-30; *The Ring and the Book*, I.38-52; and "The Statue and
the Bust," 32-34.

Fig. 42

Left:	Palazzo Medici-Riccardi
Right front:	Palazzo Panciatichi
	Florence

25-26

> He's Judas to a tittle, that man is!
> Just such a face!

Lippi did not render a Judas, but the allusion here could be to the figure of Judas in Leonardo da Vinci's *Last Supper*, in the Church of Santa Maria delle Grazie, in Milan (Fig. 43).   Allan Dooley attributes this to an anecdote in Vasari's account of Leonardo's life.   Dooley's argument is that just as Leonardo fashioned his Judas after one of his tormentors, a prior in the Church of Santa Maria delle Grazie, so too Lippi equates one of his tormentors—a street guard—with the face of Judas (DO, 51).

28-29

> Drink out this quarter-florin to the health
> Of the munificent House that harbors me....

The "munificent House that harbors" Lippi is Palazzo Medici-Riccardi and the Medici family under Cosimo the Elder.   For other related references, see above under 14-18 and below under 47-49, 78-79, 98-101, and 226-30.

31-36

> I'd like his face—
> His, elbowing on his comrade in the door
> With the pike and lantern—for the slave that holds
> John Baptist's head a-dangle by the hair
> With one hand ("Look you, now," as who should say)
> And his weapon in the other, yet unwiped!

Under 194-98 below is the reference to the fresco in the Duomo of Prato long identified as Lippi's *Feast of Herod* (WOR, II, 253; DEV, 194-95; Figs. 52 and 53).   More recently identified is the *Decapitation of John the Baptist*, the continuing fresco on the left wall adjoining the *Feast of Herod*, in the chancel of the same Duomo (ALL, 207).   The *Decapitation of John the Baptist* is also by Lippi (MAR, 210, no. 46) and, as the text indicates, depicts "the slave that holds / John Baptist's head a-dangle by the hair / With one hand ... / And his weapon in the other" (Fig. 44).

Fig. 43
Leonardo da Vinci
Last Supper (detail)
Church of Santa Maria delle Grazie
Milan

Fig. 44
Left: Filippo Lippi
          Decapitation of John the Baptist
Right: *Feast of Herod* (detail)
          Duomo
          Prato

Fig. 45
Filippo Lippi
Seven Saints, Sacred Conversation
National Gallery
London

47-49

And I've been three weeks shut within my mew,
A-painting for the great man, saints and saints
And saints again.

The "mew" is the Palazzo Medici-Riccardi, described above under 14-18 and 28-29, and below under 61-67; the "great man" is Cosimo the Elder, described above under 14-18 and 78-79, and below under 226-30. (Continued under this reference in the Supplement to Citations and Notes.)

61-67

> Into shreds it went,
> Curtain and counterpane and coverlet,
> All the bed-furniture—a dozen knots,
> There was a ladder! Down I let myself,
> Hands and feet, scrambling somehow, and so dropped,
> And after them. I came up with the fun
> Hard by Saint Laurence, hail fellow, well met. . . .

After making his escape from the Palazzo Medici-Riccardi, Lippi quickly finds himself "Hard by Saint Laurence," which is the Church of San Lorenzo, in Piazza San Lorenzo (Fig. 141; Map F: 7H). The church is literally "hard by," that is, diagonally across the piazza from the northeast corner where the palace is situated. In the Old and New Sacristies and in the Cappella de' Principi are the tomb monuments of the Medici family. For other references to the Church of San Lorenzo, see below under *The Ring and the Book*, I.38-52; and "The Statue and the Bust," 217-19. For references to Palazzo Medici-Riccardi and/or the Medici family, see above under 14-18, 28-29, 47-49, and below under 98-101, 226-30; *The Ring and the Book*, I.38-52; and "The Statue and the Bust," 32-34.

70-75

> And so as I was stealing back again
> To get to bed and have a bit of sleep
> Ere I rise up to-morrow and go work
> On Jerome knocking at his poor old breast
> With his great round stone to subdue the flesh,
> You snap me of a sudden.

Numerous paintings of St. Jerome are catalogued by Marchini as Lippi's own (MAR, 205-13). These include a panel from the *Four Fathers of the Church*, in the Accademia Albertina, Turin (no. 24); a sketch of St. Jerome on the reverse side of the *Madonna with the Christ Child*, in the Palazzo Medici-Riccardi, Florence (no. 40); the *Death of St. Jerome* (no. 44), in the Museo dell' Opera del Duomo, in Prato (KING, V, 365-66); a *St. Jerome*, in the Lindenau Museum, in Altenburg (no. 45; Fig. 46); the *Adoration of the Christ Child*, in the Uffizi Gallery, Florence (no. 48), which shows St. Jerome in the background (ORM, opposite 199; Fig. 47); the *Trinity and Saints*, in the National Gallery, London (no. 51); a *Suffering Christ among St. Francis and St. Jerome*, in the Palazzo Arcivescovile, Florence (no. 52); and *Three Saints*, in the Fogg Art Museum, in Cambridge, Massachusetts (no. 53). Several of these paintings show a correspondence with the text here. The sketch of St. Jerome on the verso of the *Madonna with the Christ Child* and the *St. Jerome* correspond in that they were done for Cosimo the Elder, with whom Lippi is residing in the poem; while the *Adoration of the Christ Child*, the *Suffering Christ Among St. Francis and St. Jerome*, and the *Three Saints* correspond in that they depict "Jerome knocking at his poor old breast / With his great round stone to subdue the flesh." Browning most likely saw the *Adoration of the Christ Child* in the Uffizi (Map F:8H), the *Suffering Christ Among St. Francis and St. Jerome* in the Palazzo Arcivescovile (Map F:7H), and the sketch of the St. Jerome that is in Palazzo Medici-Riccardi. Vasari considered the *St. Jerome* lost in his time, but Marchini identifies it now with the one in Altenburg, where it has been since 1848 (MAR, 210, no. 45; AL, 377, note 80; VAS, II, 74). The probability that Browning was familiar with three of the above five versions of St. Jerome that correspond with the text—either by showing a connection with Palazzo Medici-Riccardi or indicating actual flagellation with a stone—leads me to believe that Browning drew upon a conflation of several St. Jeromes by Lippi.

In addition, the painting called the *Penitent St. Jerome*, described below under "Old Pictures in Florence," stanza 24, may be considered part of this composite theory. Marvin Eisenberg, who attributes the painting to Toscani, demonstrates that this was the Jerome Browning owned and had hanging in his Florentine residence Casa Guidi. Moreover, Eisenberg states that Browning may have had the *Penitent St. Jerome* in mind while writing the present passage. Certainly the dating to 1855 of both "Old Pictures in Florence" and "Fra Lippo Lippi," as Eisenberg indicates, bears out the correspondence (EIS, 280, 283, PS, and n27; cf. DELA, 7-8); and, as obviously may be seen in accordance with the text, the *Penitent St. Jerome* corresponds as it shows "Jerome knocking at his poor old breast / With his great round

Fig. 46
Filippo Lippi
St. Jerome
Lindenau Museum
Altenburg, East Germany

Fig. 47
Filippo Lippi
Adoration of the Christ Child (detail)
Uffizi Gallery
Florence

stone to subdue the flesh" (see DELA, cover, for a color illustration, and EIS, 281, or KEL, Pl.16, item H22, for a black and white
version).

Finally, for a probable literary source in this context, see
the reference to St. Jerome above under "Bishop Blougram's
Apology," 704-07.

78-79

> If Master Cosimo announced himself,
> Mum's the word naturally....

For other references to Cosimo the Elder, see above under 14-18,
28-29, 47-49, and below under 98-101, 226-30.

90-91

> ... along the wall, over the bridge,
> By the straight cut to the convent.

Geographically, the "straight cut to the convent," the monastery
Santa Maria del Carmine, is over the Ponte alla Carraia, the
"bridge" across to the bank of the Arno where the Carmine is
located almost directly in line with the bridge (Map F:8G). The
bridge was first built of wood in 1218 and subsequently of wood
on stone piers. In 1334 Giotto supervised its construction in
stone, and in 1337 it was completed. It was repaired in 1559 by
Ammanati, extended in 1867, destroyed in 1944 by the Germans,
and later reconstructed (MARTI, 126).

For other references to the Monastery—or Church—of
Santa Maria del Carmine, see 7-8 above and 138-41 below.

98-101

> I did renounce the world, its pride and greed,
> Palace, farm, villa, shop, and banking-house,
> Trash, such as these poor devils of Medici
> Have given their hearts to—all at eights years old.

For other references to the Medici family, see above under 14-18,
28-29, 78-79, and below under 226-30.

138-41

> What if at last we get our man of parts,
> We Carmelites, like those Camaldolese

And Preaching Friars, to do our church up fine
And put the front on it that ought to be!

As Fig. 41 shows, the façade—or "front"—of the Church of Santa Maria del Carmine—the "Carmelites"—is still unfinished. For other references to the Church—or Monastery—of the Carmine, see 7-8 and 90-91 above. The reference to "those Camaldolese / And Preaching Friars" ties in with 234-37 below, that is, with the reference to the monk-painters Lorenzo Monaco (ca. 1370-ca. 1423/24) and Fra Angelico (ca. 1400-1455). Lorenzo was associated with the Order of the Camaldolese, in the Monastery of Santa Maria degli Angeli, in Piazza Brunelleschi, in Florence (Fig. 48; Map F:7I); and Fra Angelico was a member of the Order of the Dominicans (the "Preaching Friars"), in the Monastery of San Marco, in Piazza San Marco, also in Florence (Fig. 49; Map F:6I).

Fig. 48
Church of Santa Maria degli Angeli
Florence

Fig. 49
Church of San Marco
Florence

145-63

First, every sort of monk, the black and white,
I drew them, fat and lean: then, folk at church,
From good old gossips waiting to confess
Their cribs of barrel-droppings, candle-ends,—
To the breathless fellow at the altar-foot,
Fresh from his murder, safe and sitting there
With the little children round him in a row
Of admiration, half for his beard and half
For that white anger of his victim's son
Shaking a fist at him with one fierce arm,
Signing himself with the other because of Christ
(Whose sad face on the cross sees only this
After the passion of a thousand years)
Till some poor girl, her apron o'er her head,
(Which the intense eyes looked through) came at eve
On tiptoe, said a word, dropped in a loaf,
Her pair of earrings and a bunch of flowers
(The brute took growling), prayed, and so was gone.
I painted all. . . .

As a possible source for the "fat and lean" figures here, Walter Leisgang nominates Lippi's fresco *La conferma della regola carmelitana*—*The Innovation of the Rule of the Carmelites*—in the Monastery of the Carmine, in Florence (LEI, 23-24; Map F:8F). Fig. 50 shows that one of the monks in the fresco is indeed fat, but Leisgang does not mention that Browning could not have seen the painting at the time of publishing the poem in 1855. Browning's friend Seymour Kirkup began the research which brought about the removal of whitewash in the monastery, and in 1860 the wash was removed and the painting revealed to modern eyes (MAR, 198, no. 3). But whether or not Kirkup conveyed any information about the fresco to Browning at an earlier date is not known. At present, the detached fresco is housed in one of the rooms of the monastery. For other references to whitewashing and Kirkup, see below under "Old Pictures in Florence," 24:185-92, and "A Soul's Tragedy." Kirkup is specifically mentioned below in stanza II, line 12, under "Of Pacchiarotto, and How He Worked in Distemper." Also, Kirkup drew the original sketch, reproduced in Fig. 189, of the Franceschini coat of arms, which is described below under *The Ring and the Book*, XI.2159-64 and XII.818-20.

Johnstone Parr, on the other hand, advances Masaccio's lost fresco of the Consecration as a possible source for the "fat

Fig. 50
Filippo Lippi
Innovation of the Rule of the Carmelites (detail)
Monastery of the Carmine
Florence

and lean" figures. Parr maintains that Browning probably read in Vasari that Masaccio's painting "distinguishes the short and stout man from the tall and slender figure" (PARR, 278-79; VAS, I, 238). The painting was originally in the Monastery of the Carmine but was destroyed in 1600 (BERT, 79); yet sketches by other artists have been made of the painting, and they show the variety of physiques in the original painting (see BERT, plates 43-48, for sketches of the *Consecration*). For a direct reference to Masaccio in the poem, see below under 276-80.

Next, the reference to Lippi's drawing of "Christ . . . on the cross" calls to mind Crucifixions by Lippi and the School of Lippi that could be sources for the drawing. One Crucifixion by Lippi is the *Trinity and Saints*, which was painted in collaboration with Pesellino and is now in the National Gallery of London (MAR, 212-13, no. 51, plate 149). Another is the *Crucifixion and Saints*, a small sketch in the British Museum, also in London (see MAR, 218, plate 180). And a third, from the school of Lippi, is the statue called *Crucifixion and Saints*, in the Church of San Gaetano, in Florence (see MAR, 248, item F, plates 208, 209). Which, if any, of these works Browning was aware of, however, I have not determined. The *Trinity and Saints* was in private hands until obtained by the National Gallery in 1945; the provenance of the sketch *Crucifixion and Saints* is not traced by Marchini; and the statue *Crucifixion and Saints* by the School of Lippi, though possibly seen by Browning in Florence, might or might not have been connected by him with Lippi himself. None of the Crucifixions is mentioned in Vasari.

As for the "breathless fellow at the altar . . . Fresh from his murder," this appears to be an imaginary drawing, yet Browning's reading in Vasari could, I think, have been the influence here. In the chapter on Andrea del Castagno and Domenico Veneziano, Vasari records the presumed murder of Domenico by Castagno (VAS II, 89-90). The fact that this chapter closely follows the chapter on Filippo Lippi might have suggested to Browning a murder as a suitable subject for Lippi to draw, just as Lippi drew the sanguine murder of John the Baptist, described above under 31-36 and below under 194-98.

As a possible source suggesting the mixed image of Christ and a group of agitated children, David DeLaura nominates a passage from Ruskin's *The Stones of Venice II*, which describes a scene in front of the façade of St. Mark's (DELA, 10; RUS, X, 84-85):

> And in the recesses of the porches, all day long, knots of men of
> the lowest classes, unemployed and listless, lie basking in the
> sun like lizards; and unregarded children,—every heavy glance
> of their young eyes full of desperation and stony depravity, and
> their throats hoarse with cursing,—gamble, and fight, and
> snarl, and sleep, hour after hour, clashing their bruised centesi-
> mi upon the marble ledges of the church porch. And the images
> of Christ and His angels look down upon it continually.

DeLaura goes on to point out that if Browning has this passage
in mind, it determines the dating of his poem as later than the
summer of 1853 because *Stones II* did not come out until late
July of that year. For further corroboration of this dating see
below under 323-32 and above under "By the Fireside," stanzas
14ff, 18. Under these references it is noted that Browning was in
Prato during the summer of 1853, where he no doubt saw the
several paintings in the Duomo of Prato that tie in with the
poems "Fra Lippo Lippi" and "By the Fireside."

Finally, the "poor girl . . . On tiptoe" is, according to
Walter Leisgang, a reference to paintings of two figures by Lippi,
both of whom are tiptoeing and carrying baskets on their heads.
One of the figures is in the painting *Madonna and Child and the
Life of St. Anne*, in the Palazzo Pitti, in Florence (Fig. 51; Map
F:9G), and the other is part of the scene in the *Birth of St.
Stephen*, a fresco in the Duomo of Prato (LEI, 23, 31n). Both of
these paintings, we may be sure, were seen by Browning while in
Florence and Prato. For other references to paintings in the
Duomo of Prato, see above under 31-36, below under 194-98, 323-
32, and above under "By the Fireside," 14:66-68ff, 18:86-90. (Con-
tinued under this reference in the Supplement to Citations and
Notes.)

189-90

> Here's Giotto, with his Saint a-praising God,
> That sets us praising,—why not stop with him?

Turner identifies this passage with the fresco *St. Francis Glori-
fied in Heaven*, in the Lower Church of San Francesco, in Assisi
(TUR, 319-19). Although the fresco was attributed in Browning's
time to Giotto, it is presently given to a follower of Giotto (EISE).
My own insight into the passage, however, follows Dooley's line
(KING, V, 366-67). Turner is probably correct in assuming that
St. Francis is intended here as the subject for the "Saint a-

Fig. 51
Filippo Lippi
Madonna and Child and the Life of St. Anne (detail)
Palazzo Pitti
Florence

praising God," for Browning visited Assisi two years prior to publishing his poem in 1855 (KELL, 493). But if we define "a-praising" as praying or preaching, then a number of frescoes attributed to Giotto in the *Upper* Church of San Francesco, in Assisi, serve as more appropriate candidates for the passage. The scenes involving St. Francis at prayer are *The Crucifix at St. Damiano Speaks to St. Francis*, which renders the occasion when St. Francis praying before the crucifix hears a voice from the cross; *Vision of the Thrones*, which shows a friar's vision in heaven while St. Francis is praying; *St. Francis in Ecstasy*, which depicts the saint in ecstasy after praying fervently; *Vision of the Fiery Chariot*, which honors the occasion when St. Francis is praying in one room as the friars in another room have a vision of St. Francis glowing in a fiery chariot; *Death of the Knights of Celano*, which celebrates the occasion when St. Francis prays for the soul of the dying Cavalier; and *The Stigmatization*, which shows the saint receiving the stigmata after praying on Mount Verna. The scenes depicting St. Francis preaching are *St. Francis Preaches to the Birds* and *The Saint Preaches before Honorius III*.

194-98

> Rub all out, try at it a second time.
> Oh, that white smallish female with the breasts,
> She's just my niece . . . Herodias, I would say,—
> Who went and danced and got men's heads cut off!
> Have it all out!

The painting referred to here by the Prior is Lippi's fresco the *Feast of Herod*, in the Duomo of Prato. In 1907 Basil Worsfold mentioned that Lippi painted frescoes illustrating the history of St. John the Baptist (WOR, 253), but he did not coordinate this information with the proper references in the poem. DeVane, as far as I can determine, in his 1935 edition of *A Browning Handbook*, was the first to do this (DEV, 194-95). Turner points out that it was Salome of course, not her mother Herodias, who dances (Fig. 52), and he explains the mistake as either a way to show that the Prior does not know his Bible or as misinforma-tion copied from Vasari (TUR, 319; VAS, II, 73). Herodias is represented in the *Feast of Herod* in the scene described by Marchini as *La presentazione della testa a Erodiade—The Presentation of the Head to Herodias* (Fig. 53; MAR, 210, no. 46). For a reference to the *Decapitation of John the Baptist* on the wall adjoining the *Feast of Herod*, see 31-36 above.

Fig. 52
Filippo Lippi
Salome Dancing
from the *Feast of Herod*
Duomo
Prato

Fig. 53
Filippo Lippi
*Presentation of the Head
of John the Baptist to Herodias*
from the *Feast of Herod*
Duomo
Prato

226-30

> I'm my own master, paint now as I please —
> Having a friend, you see, in the Corner-house!
> Lord, it's fast holding by the rings in front—
> Those great rings serve more purposes than just
> To plant a flag in, or tie up a horse!

The "Corner-house" is identified above under 14-18, 47-49, and 61-67 as the Palazzo Medici-Riccardi. The "friend" is Lippi's benefactor Cosimo the Elder, identified above under 14-18, 28-29,

78-79, and 98-101.   When Lippi says that the "rings in front" of
the palazzo "serve more purposes than just / To plant a flag in,
or tie up a horse," he is probably referring to one of the rings as
part of the makeshift ladder he devises for furtively leaving and
re-entering the palace.   Under 61-67 above, the ladder is described
as curtains and bedclothes made into a rope, which is no doubt
suspended from either the second or third story of the palace
(Fig. 42).   Since the cloth ladder is probably too short, Lippi can
gain support at the farthest point down by using one of the
numerous rings attached to the outside wall a few feet above
street level (Fig. 54).

Fig. 54
Ring on the façade
of Palazzo Medici-Riccardi
Florence

234-37

> You're not of the true painters, great and old;
> Brother Angelico's the man, you'll find;
> Brother Lorenzo stands his single peer:
> Fag on at flesh, you'll never make the third!

The idea of contrasting the formal religious art of Fra Angelico and Lorenzo Monaco with the realistic humanism of Filippo Lippi in all probability derives from the critical writings of Mrs. Anna Jameson, with whom Browning was well acquainted before writing the poem. Johnstone Parr identifies Mrs. Jameson's writings as a series of essays published in Knight's *Penny Magazine*, in 1843, and then reprinted in *Memoirs of the Early Italian Painters*, in 1845, ten years prior to the publishing of Browning's poem (PARR, 280; cf. DEL, 374, and TUR, 319). For another —though implied—reference to Fra Angelico and Lorenzo Monaco, see above under 138-41; for references to Fra Angelico and Lorenzo Monaco in other contexts, see *The Ring and the Book*, XI.2114, and "Old Pictures in Florence," 26:208 and 26:201-04, in the Supplement to Citations and Notes.

245-46

> ... there's pretty sure to come
> A turn, some warm eve finds me at my saints. ...

A possible source for these "saints" Lippi is painting is described above under 47-49.

265-69

> For me, I think I speak as I was taught;
> I always see the garden and God there
> A-making man's wife: and my lesson learned,
> The value and significance of flesh,
> I can't unlearn ten minutes afterwards.

Lippi himself did not do a Creation of Eve; nevertheless, what he might "always see," to gain a "lesson learned," is the subject as rendered by one of his contemporaries, one who showed the "value and significance of flesh" by executing Eve in the nude. Strictly speaking, the contemporary who could properly have "taught" Lippi would have lived during the first half of the fifteenth century, during the formative years of Lippi's career. But "taught" does not necessarily mean formal training, and in the present context probably more accurately means setting an example for Lippi to follow. As I read Berenson, there was only one painter of the Florentine school who rendered a Creation of Eve during the first half of the fifteenth century, and that was Paolo Uccello, who executed a fresco on the subject for the Green Cloister of Santa Maria Novella, in Florence (BERE, 290; Map F:7G). Two other Florentine painters of the early fifteenth century, however, should also be mentioned, even though their treatment of the subject does not exactly fit the text here. One is Masolino, who fashioned a fresco of The Temptation (Fig. 55), and the other is Masaccio, who did a fresco of The Expulsion (Fig. 223). These works were done for the Brancacci Chapel in Santa Maria del Carmine, the church and monastery where Lippi lived and worked during his early years. In the field of sculpture, mention should be made of the bas-relief of the Creation of Eve that Ghiberti did sometime between 1425 and 1452 for the famous bronze doors of the Baptistery of Florence (Fig. 56; Map F:7H). Lippi undoubtedly could "always see" the three frescoes and preparatory models for the relief while in Florence, and Browning assuredly familiarized himself with these works while reading Vasari (VAS, I, 182-83, 210-11) and residing in Florence. Of additional interest in this context is a possible source suggested by Professor Marvin Eisenberg, of the Department of History of Art at the University of Michigan. This is Jacopo della Quercia's *Creation*, a marble bas-relief on the left pilaster of the main portal of the Church of St. Petronius, in Bologna (EISE; Fig. 226). Although I am not aware of any evidence that Filippo Lippi was ever in Bologna, where he could have learned from Quercia's *Creation*, Browning probably saw it when he was in Bologna in 1851, four years before publishing "Fra Lippo Lippi" (KELL, 493; OG, 207), and he no doubt re-enforced the image in his mind while reading about Quercia's work in Vasari (VAS, I, 154).

For other references to the Church of Santa Maria del Carmine, see above under 7-8, 90-91, and 134-41. For another reference to Masaccio, see below under 276-80.

276-80

> His name is Guidi—he'll not mind the monks—
> They call him Hulking Tom, he lets them talk—
> He picks my practice up—he'll paint apace,
> I hope so—though I never live so long,
> I know what's sure to follow. You be judge!

Fig. 55
Masolino
The Temptation
Church of the Carmine
Florence

Fig. 56
Ghiberti
Creation of Eve (detail)
East door, Baptistery
Florence

"Guidi," or "Hulking Tom" as he is referred to here, is Tommaso Guidi, more commonly called Masaccio (1401-1428). The anachronism of placing Lippi (c. 1406-1469) ahead of Masaccio in development—"He picks my practice up"—Browning probably took from misinformation in the editorial footnotes in the Milanesi edition of Vasari's *Lives* (PAR, 197-201; cf. TUR, 319; VA).

286-90
             Do you feel thankful, ay or no,
For this fair town's face, yonder river's line,
The mountain round it and the sky above,
Much more the figures of man, woman, child,
These are the frame to?

A perusal of Marchini's book reveals that Lippi used landscape extensively as a background or "frame to" his pictures (MAR, illus. nos. 4, 12, 26, 39, 46, 48, 57, 59, 60, 66, 75, 77, 98, 107, 115, 124, 130, 143, 144, 147, 151, 153, 155, 156, 157, 160, 162, 163, 166, 171, 172, 174). None of the backgrounds, however, specifically shows Florence, "this fair town's face." (Continued under this reference in the Supplement to Citations and Notes.)

323-32

> I painted a Saint Laurence six months since
> At Prato, splashed the fresco in fine style:
> 'How looks my painting, now the scaffold's down?'
> I ask a brother: 'Hugely,' he returns—
> 'Already not one phiz of your three slaves
> Who turn the Deacon off his toasted side,
> But's scratched and prodded to our heart's content,
> The pious people have so eased their own
> With coming to say prayers there in a rage:
> We get on fast to see the bricks beneath.'

The most likely source for this painting is the *Martyrdom of St. Lawrence*, a painting in the Duomo of Prato by Mario Balassi (1604-1667) and Carlo Dolci (1616-1687). In an article I argue this by showing that the painting closely follows the present text (see Fig. 57), that Browning undoubtedly had seen the painting "At Prato" in the summer of 1853, and that no other known painting of Lippi fits the text by depicting St. Lawrence roasting on a gridiron (THO, 45-51). Marchini (MAR, 199-209) identifies a St. Lawrence in Lippi's *Madonna Enthroned with Angels and Saints* (no. 5); *Sacred Conversation and Donor* (no. 7); *St. Lawrence Enthroned among St. Cosmas, St. Damian, and Donors, with St. Benedict and St. Anthony Abate* (no. 28); and *Seven Saints, Sacred Conversation* (no. 30). But these paintings only show St. Lawrence sitting or posed with a gridiron, not being "turn[ed] . . . off his toasted side." As for the damage done to the painting of St. Lawrence by the congregation of Prato, who presumably "scratched and prodded it," this is probably Browning's invention, for the Balassi-Dolci source, as Fig. 57 shows, is in a good state of preservation. Or, if the description is not Browning's invention, it is, as Eisenberg believes, based on his observations of other Italian frescoes or panels of predellas depicting martyrdom that were commonly desecrated in the same way (EISE). (Continued under this reference in the Supplement to Citations and Notes.)

Fig. 57
Mario Balassi and Carlo Dolci
Martyrdom of St. Lawrence
Duomo
Prato

345-87

> I shall paint a piece
> ... There's for you. Give me six months, then go, see
> Something in Sant'Ambrogio's! Bless the nuns!
> They want a cast o' my office. I shall paint
> God in the midst, Madonna and her babe,
> Ringed by a bowery, flowery angel-brood,
> Lilies and vestments and white faces, sweet
> As puff on puff of grated orris-root
> When ladies crowd to Church at midsummer.
> And then i' the front, of course a saint or two—
> Saint John, because he saves the Florentines,
> Saint Ambrose, who puts down in black and white
> The convent's friends and gives them a long day,
> And Job, I must have him there past mistake,
> The man of Uz ... [and]
> ...
> I, caught up with my monk's-things by mistake,
> My old serge gown and rope that goes all round. ...
> ...
> ... Could Saint John there draw—
> His camel-hair make up a painting-brush?
> We come to brother Lippo for all that,
> *Iste perfecit opus!* ...
> ...
> ... Thus I scuttle off
> To some safe bench behind, not letting go
> The palm of her, the little lily thing
> ...
> ... Saint Lucy, I would say.

Lippi's painting the *Coronation of the Virgin* was, in keeping with the text here, originally located in the Church of "Sant' Ambrogio," in Florence. Today it is in the Uffizi (Fig. 58; Map F:8H), although from 1813-1919 it was in the Accademia, in Florence (MAR, 202), where Browning certainly saw it before publishing his poem in 1855. With varying degrees of accuracy Browning describes the figures in the painting. "Saint John" the Baptist is seen on the lower right dressed in "camel-hair," "Saint Ambrose" is on the lower left wearing his mitre, and "Job" is standing between them wearing a shoulder band with his name on it. There is, however, no "Saint Lucy" as line 387 indicates (MAR, 201-02). In the early edition of Vasari's *Lives*, the figure identified in line 346 with the words "*Iste perfecit opus*" ("This is the one who caused it to be done") was presented as a self-portrait, and Browning picked up this identification and used it

Fig. 58
Filippo Lippi
Coronation of the Virgin
Uffizi Gallery
Florence

in the text. But today the figure in question is not known to be a self-portrait of Lippi; rather, it is the benefactor for the painting, the Rev. Francesco Maringhi, of the Church of St. Ambrose (DEVA, 218; MAR, 201-02). If there is a self-portrait in the picture, it is possibly what Montgomery Charmichael identifies as "the rather disdainful young Carmelite leaning his chin on one hand, in the left foreground of the picture" (DEVA, 218n). Of "God in the midst, Madonna and her babe" there is the question of the babe, who does not appear in the central scene of the coronation along with God and the Virgin. (Continued under this reference in the Supplement to Citations and Notes.)

THE GLOVE

189-90

Venienti occurrite morbo!
With which moral I drop my theorbo.

Louise Schultz Boas, with the concurrence of DeVane, thinks that Browning probably got the name and the idea of the "theorbo" from the Invocation in Francis Quarles's picture book *Emblems, Divine and Moral* (BOA; DEVA, 183). The opening lines to the Invocation read,

> Rouse thee, my soul, and drain thee from the dregs
> Of vulgar thought; screw up the heightened pegs
> Of thy sublime theorbo.

The emblem picture accompanying the verse shows the theorbo, a seventeenth-century lute with its double neck and two sets of tuning pegs (Fig. 59). For another reference to Quarles's book, see above under "Andrea del Sarto," 97-98. The copy of Quarles's book that was owned by Browning is in the Berg Collection of the New York Public Library.

GOLD HAIR: A STORY OF PORNIC

15:71-75

> At little pleasant Pornic church,
>   It chanced, the pavement wanted repair,
> Was taken to pieces: left in the lurch,
>   A certain sacred space lay bare,
> And the boys began research.

In 1762, gold was found under the "pavement" in the Church of St. Giles, in Pornic, Loire-Atlantique, France. DeVane observes that the church was razed in 1865 to clear the way for the construction of a new one (DEVA, 287). Fig. 60, taken from the *Album du Baigneur*, by Charpentier, shows a general view of Pornic before 1865. Only the roof and bell tower of the Church of St. Giles are visible in the view (NA).

Fig. 59
Francis Quarles
Emblem for the Invocation
from *Emblems, Divine and Moral*

GOLDONI

1-2

Goldoni—good, gay, sunniest of souls,—
Glassing half Venice in that verse of thine....

This sonnet was written to commemorate the unveiling of
Goldoni's bronze statue, which in 1883 was erected in Piazza San

Bartolommeo, just off the east side of the Rialto Bridge, in Venice. The poem is not inscribed on the statue but is inserted as a preface to a civic album honoring Goldoni (DEVA, 564-65). Fig. 61, which illustrates the statue in profile, would, if shown from the front, reveal Goldoni smiling. Browning picks up this expression where he says that the playwright is "good, gay, sunniest of souls."

Fig. 60
Church of St. Giles (center)
Pornic
Loire-Atlantique
France

Fig. 61
Goldoni Monument
Piazza San Bartolommeo
Venice

A GRAMMARIAN'S FUNERAL
(See the Supplement to Citations and Notes.)

THE GUARDIAN ANGEL: A PICTURE AT FANO

36-37

> Guercino drew this angel I saw teach
> (Alfred, dear friend!)—that little child to pray....

This poem describes the painting *L'Angelo Custode*, by Giovanni Francesco Barbieri, also called "Guercino." The painting was formerly in the Church of Sant' Agostino, in Fano, but is now lodged in the Civic Museum of Fano (Fig. 62).

A possible collateral painting in the present context has been noted by F. Davies at the Dulwich Picture Gallery, in London. The painting is called *Child and Guardian Angel* and is identified with the French school in the Dulwich catalogue (DULW, 19, item 313; Fig. 63). According to Davies, the painting was acquired by the gallery in 1811 and was undoubtedly seen there by Browning. Davies points out that these lines referring to Alfred Domett recall Browning's early days when Domett accompanied the poet on tours of the Dulwich Gallery. Through emphasis on the words "this" and "that," the lines read as if the angel of the painting at the Dulwich gallery—recalled as the name "Alfred" is mentioned—is juxtaposed with the angel that Guercino painted, as if Guercino "drew," that is, copied the painting at the Dulwich Gallery—"*This* angel"—and was inspired to paint from the copy his angel at Fano teaching "*that* little child [the child in Guercino's painting] to pray" (italics mine; DAV, 692).

HELEN'S TOWER

12-13

> But thine, Love's rock-built Tower, shall fear no change:
> God's self laid stable earth's foundation so....

This 1870 sonnet commemorates the construction of a tower in Clandeboye, Ireland, in honor of Helen, Lady Dufferin and Countess of Gifford (DEVA, 559-60). Situated about 8 miles east

Fig. 62
Guercino
The Guardian Angel
Civic Museum
Fano

Fig. 63
Child and Guardian Angel
French School
Dulwich Picture Gallery
London

of Belfast and about 3 1/2 miles south of Bangor, Clandeboye is celebrated for its sylvan beauty, especially in Redmond O'Neale's lament in Sir Walter Scott's 1813 poem *Rokeby*, V.10:258-59, 68-69:

> Ah, Clandeboye! thy friendly floor
> Slieve Donard's oak shall light no more;
> . . .
> And now the strangers enjoy
> The lovely woods of Clandeboye!

The tower itself was constructed in 1850 and stands on a solitary site in the woods (Fig. 64). Many poets have commemorated the tower in verse, notably Tennyson, who writes of it in the first two lines of "Helen's Tower," from his 1885 volume, *Tiresias and Other Poems*:

> Helen's Tower, here I stand,
> Dominant over sea and land.

Browning's poem, along with those of other poets, is inscribed within the tower (PRA, 64-65).

HOLY-CROSS DAY

2:12, 9:52

> Stand on a line ere you start for the
>   church!
> . . .
> . . . spurred through the Corso, stripped
> to the waist. . . .

This poem recreates the historical practice of forcing Jews to gather in the Church of Sant' Angelo in Pescheria, Rome, to listen to a Christian sermon (DEVA, 260-61). The "church" is toward the end of the "Corso" near the Ponte Sisto (Fig. 65; Map R:8H). In 1843 a papal bull abolished the practice of Holy-Cross Day. See below under "Imperante Augustus Natus Est . . .," 56-58, for a reference to the Portico of Octavia, inside of which, as Fig. 65 shows, the Church of Sant' Angelo in Pescheria was built.

Fig. 64
Helen's Tower
Clandeboye
Northern Ireland

Fig. 65
Foreground: Portico of Octavia
Inside of portico: Church of Sant' Angelo in Pescheria
                         Rome

"HOW THEY BROUGHT THE GOOD NEWS FROM GHENT TO AIX."

17

And from Mecheln church-steeple we heard the half-chime. . . .

The bell-tower of the Cathedral of St. Rombold, in "Mecheln,"— Mechelen— Belgium, to which the "church-steeple" here refers, is 324 feet high. In the bell-tower an especially large bell, La Banclocque, was known to sound the alarm for fires and the approach of the enemy (ROL, 164; MIC, 34; Fig. 66).

40-41

> 'Neath our feet broke the brittle bright
> stubble like chaff;
> Till over by Dalhem a dome-spire sprang
> white. . . .

The "dome-spire" has been identified as the Octagon in Aix-la-Chapelle—Aachen today—in West Germany (ROL, 164; KING, IV, 377; Fig. 67). "Dalhem" is a village in Belgium close to Aachen but not close enough for the Octagon to be visible from Dalhem (OFF).

Symbolically, there is a rescue motif between the architecture, the legendary name Roland, and the heroic horse and rider in Browning's poem. The paladin Roland, as is well known, was the nephew of Charlemagne and was one of the twelve peers in Charlemagne's court. Charlemagne, as tradition has it, is buried in the Octagon. Thus Browning's horse and rider represent the knightly Roland, and the architectural landmarks mentioned in Browning's poem reinforce the rescue motif. The ringing of La Bancloche in the Church of St. Rombold, as described above under line 17, signals the approaching enemy and sets up the presumed rescue mission of Roland's rider (the enemy is not specified because, as noted in DEVA, 154, the poem has no historical basis); and the arrival at Aix-la-Chapelle, where the Octagon is located, highlights the chivalric act of the horse Roland completing the mission and the rider announcing the "good news" that "they brought."

Of course, a comparison of knight-errantry should be made with the later poem "Childe Roland to the Dark Tower Came," which is described above and in the Supplement to Citations and Notes.

"IMPERANTE AUGUSTO NATUS EST—"

31-40

> Caius Octavius Caesar the August—
> Where was escape from his prepotency?
> I judge I may have passed—how many piles
> Of structure dropt like doles from his free hand
> To Rome on every side? Why, right and left,
> For temples you've the Thundering Jupiter,
> Avenging Mars, Apollo Palatine:
> How count Piazza, Forum—there's a third

> All but completed. You've the Theatre
> Named of Marcellus—all his work, such work!

The historical source for the architecture in Rome described in these lines is set forth in the chapter on Augustus (paragraph 29)

Fig. 66
Cathedral of St. Rombold
Mechelen
Belgium

Fig. 67
Octagon
Aachen (Aix-la-Chapelle)
West Germany

in the *Lives of the First Twelve Caesars,* by Suetonius (DEVA, 546).   The Temple of "Thundering Jupiter" is located by Suetonius on the Capitoline Hill.   All that remains of the original 6th-century B.C. temple are some very large, roughly-fashioned gray stones that are visible in openings in the Gallery of the Roman Wall (Passaggio del Muro Romano) in the New Museum of the Conservatori, on the Capitoline Hill, or the

Piazza del Campidoglio, as it is called today (Fig. 69; Map R:8H,8I).   The ruins of the Temple of the "Avenging Mars"—Mars Ultor—are in the Forum of Augustus, near Piazza Venezia (Fig. 68, Map R:8I).   The Temple of "Apollo Palatine" was on the Palatine Hill, next to the Palace of Augustus, but was completely destroyed during the great fire of 363.   The Theater of "Marcellus" is just to the south of the Capitoline Hill and is still fairly well preserved (Fig. 20; Map R:8H,9H).   And the "Forum— there's a third / All but completed" is probably a reference to the Forum of Augustus mentioned above.   Suetonius (paragraph 26) explains that the Forum of Augustus was constructed because the people had "need of a third"—a third one, he no doubt means, in addition to the Roman Forum (Fig. 68) and the Forum of Caesar.   Compare 56-58 below.

56-58

> ... but Rome itself
> All new-built, 'marble now, brick once,' he boasts:
> This Portico, that Circus.

The famous quotation from Suetonius in his chapter on Augustus (paragraph 28) more accurately reads, "where he [Augustus] found it [Rome] built of brick, he left it all of marble." Regarding a "Portico" and "Circus," Suetonius does not speak of a circus but he does mention a "Portico of Livia and Octavia" (paragraph 29).   The Portico of Livia, which used to be near the Coliseum on the Esquiline Hill, is defunct; while the ruins of the Portico of Octavia may be seen close to the Theater of Marcellus (Michelin, *Rome*, 1985, pp. 14-15).   As Fig. 65 shows, the pediment and columns of the façade of the Portico of Octavia still remain (Map R:8H).   Inside the portico was built the Church of Sant' Angelo in Pescheria, which is part of the setting for the poem "Holy-Cross Day" described above (Map R:8H,9H). Browning's mention of a "Circus" could be a reference to improvements made by Augustus on the Circus Maximus, which is near the Porta Capena.   For another reference to architecture built by Augustus, see above under 31-40.

Fig. 68
Above: Roman Forum
Below: Forum of Augustus

92-94, 100-01

> ... yon gold shape
> Crowned, sceptred, on the temple opposite—
> Fulgurant Jupiter ...
>
> ...
> Our Holy and Inviolable One,
> Caesar, whose bounty built the fane above!

The Temple of Thundering Jupiter on the Capitoline Hill, described above under 31-40, may correspond with the "temple" of "Fulgurant Jupiter" in these lines, for in both instances it is Augustus "Caesar, whose bounty built the fane."

139-42, 157-60

> There's meaning in the fact
> That whoso conquers, triumphs, enters Rome,
> Climbing the Capitolian, soaring thus
> To glory's summit ...
>
> ...
> Was it for nothing the gray Sibyl wrote
> "Caesar Augustus regnant, shall be born
> In blind Judæa"—one to master him,
> Him and the universe? An old-wife's tale?

These references to the "Capitolian" and the "gray Sibyl" allude to the Altar to the Legend of Augustus in the Church of Santa Maria d'Aracoeli, in Rome. According to medieval legend, the Sibyl appeared to Augustus showing him a vision of the Madonna and Child, and then Augustus had an altar built on the Capitoline Hill commemorating the vision. Berdoe identifies the altar in this context and points out that in the ninth century the Church of Santa Maria d'Aracoeli was built over the altar (BER, 214; Figs. 69 and 70; Map R:5H,6H). The name "Aracoeli" appropriately means "altar in the sky," that is, high on the Capitoline Hill.

IN A GONDOLA

1-7

> I send my heart up to thee, all my heart
> In this my singing.

For the stars help me, and the sea bears part;
The very night is clinging
Closer to Venice' streets to leave one space
Above me, whence thy face
May light my joyous heart to thee its dwelling place.

When Browning was originally asked to write a few lines illustrating *The Serenade*, by Royal Academy painter D. Maclise, he submitted these lines.   Later, when Browning saw the painting for the first time, he said that he "thought the Sere-nader somewhat too jolly" for his original conception of the painting, and he went on to work the poem in his own manner. The result was the addition of 226 lines to the original 7 and the

Fig. 69
Left: Church of Santa Maria d'Aracoeli
Right: Piazza del Campidoglio
            Rome

Fig. 70
Altar to the Legend of Augustus
Church of Santa Maria d'Aracoeli
Rome

poem as we know it today (DEVA, 114-15). The painting is hanging in the Hankamer Treasure Room of the Armstrong Browning Library at Baylor University (Fig. 71).

43-48

> Past we glide, and past, and past!
>   Why's the Pucci Palace flaring
> Like a beacon to the blast?
>   Guests by hundreds, not one caring
> If the dear host's neck were wried:
>   Past we glide!

Since no known "Pucci Palace" exists in Venice, I believe that Browning could have confused the residence of the Pucci family in Florence with this imaginary Venetian setting. On Via de' Pucci at Via de' Servi, in Florence, is the large palace of the still-existing Pucci family. The structure, which was substantially rebuilt in the seventeenth century by Falconiere, still retains a loggia and windows originally designed by Ammanati (VAU, 282; Fig. 72; Map F:7H). In 1842, when the poem was first published, Browning had not been to Florence, yet it is possible that he had read the more than full-column account of the ancient Pucci family in his *Biographie Universelle* (BIO, XXXIV, 498-99) and confusedly placed the Florentine palazzo of the family in Venice. DeVane tells us, relying on the testimony of Mrs. Orr, that Browning, owing much of the poem to his trip in 1838 to Venice, admitted later that his first impressions of the city were not accurate (DEVA, 115).

183-99

> And how your pictures must descend
> To see each other, friend with friend!
> Oh, could you take them by surprise,
> You'd find Schidone's eager Duke
> Doing the quaintest courtesies
> To that prim saint by Haste-thee-Luke!
> And, deeper into her rock den,
> Bold Castelfranco's Magdalen
> You'd find retreated from the ken
> Of that robed counsel-keeping Ser—
> As if the Tizian thinks of her,
> And is not, rather, gravely bent
> On seeing for himself what toys
> Are these, his progeny invent,
> What litter now the board employs
> Wheron he signed a document
> That got him murdered!

Fig. 71
D. Maclise
The Serenade
Hankamer Treasure Room
Armstrong Browning Library
Baylor University
Waco, Texas

Fig. 72
Palazzo Pucci
Florence

Bartolommeo "Schidone's eager Duke" and the "prim saint by Haste-thee-Luke," that is, by Luca Giordano, are probably either imaginary or unspecified paintings because their titles are too indefinite to be specifically identified. Titian's "counsel-keeping Ser—" (Messer) is also too vague to be identified readily and may be considered either imaginary or unspecified. "Castelfranco's Magdalen," as I view it, is possibly just an imaginary painting, for there is no clear evidence that Castelfranco—Giorgione as he is usually called—ever rendered a Magdalen. But a source for the Magdalen could be, I think, one of Titian's famous versions of the same subject, inasmuch as Titian's name—"Tizian"—is in close proximity with the reference to the painting (the Magdalen is mentioned in line 190; Titian's name, in line 193). Perhaps Browning saw Titian's *Magdalen* in the Hermitage (Fig. 73) when he visited St. Petersburg in 1834. Later, by the time the poem was published in 1842, he could have confused Titian's name with Castelfranco's. Another version of Titian's *Magdalen* may be seen in the Pitti Palace, in Florence (Map F:9G). Also, a copy of the work is in the Capodimonte National Gallery of Naples. (Continued under this reference in the Supplement to Citations and Notes.)

THE INN ALBUM

I.34-37

> On a spring-pattern-papered wall there brays
> Complaint to sky Sir Edwin's dripping stag;
> His couchant coast-guard creature corresponds;
> They face the Huguenot and Light o' the World.

Four nineteenth-century English paintings have been identified here: "Sir Edwin" Landseer's "dripping stag," that is, his *The Hunted Stag*, in the Tate Gallery, in London (Fig. 74); Landseer's "couchant coast-guard creature," properly known as *A Distinguished Member of the Humane Society* (Fig. 75), also in the Tate Gallery; *The Huguenot*, by John Everett Millais (Fig. 76), presently owned by T. Agnew and Son, London, with a water color version in the Drawing Room of the Fogg Art Museum, in Cambridge, Massachusetts; and *The Light of the World*, by William Holman Hunt, in the Chapel of Keble College, Oxford

Fig. 73
Titian
St. Mary Magdalen in Penitence
Pitti Palace
Florence

Fig. 74
Landseer
The Hunted Stag
Tate Gallery
London

Fig. 75
Landseer
A Distinguished Member of the Humane Society
Tate Gallery
London

Fig. 76
Millais
The Huguenot
T. Agnew and Sons
London

Fig. 77
William Holman Hunt
The Light of the World
St. Paul's Cathedral
London

(POR, IX, 297; CROW, 59). A larger version of *The Light of the World*, also painted by Hunt, is in the south aisle of St. Paul's Cathedral, London (Fig. 77).

I.76-77

> Painters are more productive, stop a week,
> Declare the prospect quite a Corot....

Crowder speculates that the "prospect" in this passage is similar to that around Ville d'Avray, the inspiration for many of Corot's paintings (CRO, 249).

I.353-54

> ...that Gainsborough
> Sir Richard won't sell...

The painting by Gainsborough referred to here is unspecified.

I.392-93

> ...they say your brother closets up
> Correggio's long lost Leda....

Correggio's "long lost" *Leda and the Swan* was stolen out of Italy by the Swedes in 1648. When it was returned to Rome by Queen Cristina of Sweden, it became the property of the Duke of Bracciano and the Regent Orléans. The son of the regent, Louis d'Orléans, then condemned the nude Leda as indecent and had the heads of Leda and her nurse cut from the canvas. It was Jacob Schlesinger (1792-1855) who repainted the heads as they look today (CRO, 249; Fig. 78). For another reference to this painting, see below under *The Ring and the Book*, IV.888-89.

III. 5-7

> ...islanded in lawn
> And edged with shrubbery—the brilliant bit
> Of Barry's building that's the Place....

Sir Charles Barry, who designed the Houses of Parliament, also fashioned "brilliant" houses for the wealthy (CROW, 57, 59). This one, presumably belonging to the rich aunt of the Younger Man, is unspecified.

Fig. 78
Correggio
Leda and the Swan
Staatliche Museen, Gemäldegalerie
Berlin-Dahlem

THE ISLE'S ENCHANTRESS

1-5

Wind wafted from the sunset, o'er the swell
Of summer's slumbrous sea, herself asleep
Come shoreward, in her iridescent shell
Cradled, the isle's enchantress. You who keep
A drowsy watch beside her,—watch her well!

These five lines were written to accompany Felix Moscheles's picture of the same name, which was probably painted in 1889 (DEVA, 574). The poem is reproduced here from F. G. Kenyon's edition of the *New Poems* (NE, 60). To my knowledge the painting has not been traced.

THE ITALIAN IN ENGLAND

73-75

> ... carry safe what I shall write
> To Padua, which you'll reach at night
> Before the duomo shuts; go in. ...

The setting for this passage is the Cathedral or "duomo" of "Padua." Compare lines 215-16 from Shelley's "Lines Written Among the Euganean Hills":

> Many-domed Padua proud
> Stands, a peopled solitude. ...

Of the several churches in Padua that have domes, even multiple domes, the Duomo, as Fig. 79 shows, features a large one.

IVÁN IVÁNOVITCH

414-18, 421-25

>   Iván Ivànovitch
> Knelt, building on the floor that Kremlin rare and rich
> He deftly cut and carved on lazy winter nights.
> Some five young faces watched, breathlessly, as, to rights,
> Piece upon piece, he reared the fabric nigh complete.
> ...
> Ivàn's self, as he turned his honey-colored head,
> Was just in act to drop, 'twixt fir-cones,—each a dome,—
> The scooped-out yellow gourd presumably the home
> Of Kolokol the Big: the bell, therein to hitch,
> —An acorn-cup—was ready. ...

Fig. 79
Duomo
Padua

As Iva`n Iva`novitch is playing with his children and using
natural objects as toys to reconstruct architectural features of the
"Kremlin," he designates "fir cones,—each a dome"—to represent the various domes of the churches in the Kremlin; an
"acorn-cup" to stand for "Kolokol the Big," the largest bell in the
world; and a "yellow gourd" to represent the "home", that is, the
housing for the Kolokol Bell (POR, XI, 316).   In actuality, the
Kolokol weighs 200 tons, stands 26' 4" high, is 671" in circum-
ference, and has a thickness of 28." In 1733-1735 it was cast and
hung in a pavilion beside the belfry of Ivan the Great, in the
Kremlin.   But during the fire of 1737 the bell dropped, and in
1836 it was mounted on its present pedestal beside the belfry. On
the upper part of the bell may be seen the bas-relief figures of
Tsar Alexis and Empress Anne, and on the scroll below the figures are representations of the Savior, the Holy Virgin, and the
Four Evangelists surrounded by cherubim (MURR, 136; Fig. 80).

The depiction of imperial and Christian personages on the
Kolokol Bell symbolizes the contrast between secular and
religious justice as respectively portrayed in Browning's poem by
Pomeschi`k, the "Lord of the Land" (lines 300-19), and the old
priest, the "Pope" (lines 320-90).

JAMES LEE'S WIFE

VIII.27-32

> 'T is a clay cast, the perfect thing,
>   From Hand live once, dead long ago:
> Princess-like it wears the ring
>   To fancy's eye, by which we know
> That here at length a master found
>   His match, a proud lone soul its mate. . . .

A possible source for the "clay cast . . . From Hand live once" is
the *Clasped Hands of the Brownings*, rendered by Harriet
Hosmer.   Since the original plaster cast of the hands was formed
in 1853, and since the present poem was not published until
1864, Browning might have been thinking about Hosmer's work
on the hands while writing the poem over the intervening
eleven years.   The original plaster cast of 1853, which was made
from a mold formed while the Brownings were in Rome, is
reproduced in CARR, opposite page 92.   This cast is now housed

at Radcliffe College, in Cambridge, Massachusetts. A subsequent mold was probably made much later, for another plaster cast exists stamped with a copyright date of 1895. This cast is at Scripps College, in Claremont, California. Of the many bronze casts that were made by Hosmer, on two or more occasions,

Fig. 80
Kolokol Bell
Kremlin
Moscow

about thirty-five exist. Examples of these may be seen at the Armstrong Browning Library (Fig. 81); the Boston Public Library; the National Portrait Gallery, London; the Wellesley College Library; and the Dominican College of San Rafael, California (WHI, 152-53; CARR, 92; ORMOND, 73-74; KEL, 514, item H538). Also see VIII.43-48 under this poem and "Prospice," 27-28, in the Supplement to Citations and Notes.

For a possible collateral source, compare Hawthorne's *The Marble Faun*, published four years before Browning's poem. In Chapter XIII, paragraph 26, reference is made to "Harriet

Fig. 81
Harriet Hosmer
Clasped Hands of the Brownings
Armstrong Browning Library
Baylor University
Waco, Texas

Hosmer's clasped hands of Browning and his wife, symbolizing the individuality and heroic union of two high poetic lives." Also mentioned in the same paragraph is "Loulie's hand with the baby-dimples" (Fig. 239), which was sculptured by Loulie's father, Hiram Powers, who was a friend of the Brownings, in Florence. A third sculptured hand, a literary hand, which is the focus of Chapter XII in Hawthorne's book, is Kenyon's white marble hand of Hilda. As possible composite sources, the three sets of hands described by Hawthorne relate to the hand in the present passage as symbols of marriage and/or maternity—marriage, of course, being the central concern of Browning's poem. The first version of Loulie's Hand—about forty were made—was given by Powers to his wife (WI, 158), clearly honoring the birth of their child. The *Clasped Hands of the Brownings*, as interpreted above by Hawthorne, obviously expresses matrimony. And both Kenyon's marble hand of Hilda and the clay cast in the present text that "wears the ring" given by a "master [who] found / His match," represent sculptors—Kenyon marries Hilda—who marry their models. For other references to *The Marble Faun*, see above under "Cenciaja," 15-29, and below under "Prospice," 27-28, and *The Ring and the Book*, I.896-903.

VIII.71-76

> ... I [Leonardo] might reproduce
> One motive of the powers profuse,
> Flesh and bone and nerve that make
> The poorest coarsest human hand
> An object worthy to be scanned
> A whole life long for their sole sake.

These lines, presumably spoken by Leonardo da Vinci, suggest to my mind Leonardo's famous drawing *Two Hands*, in the Royal Library at Windsor Castle (Fig. 82). Although graceful and not like the "poorest coarsest human hand" described here, the hands of Leonardo's drawing coordinate with the text in that they represent Leonardo's intense interest in anatomical studies.

JUBILEE MEMORIAL LINES

> Fifty years' flight! wherein should he rejoice
>   Who hailed their birth, who as they die decays?
> This—England echoes his attesting voice;
>   Wondrous and well-thanks Ancient Thou of days.

Fig. 82
Leonardo da Vinci
Two Hands
Windsor Castle
Windsor

These four lines are reproduced from the *Browning Society Papers*, II, page 234, edited by F. J. Furnivall (London: Trübner Co., 1881-1891). According to DeVane, they were written late in 1887 for a window by Clayton and Bell in St. Margaret's Church, Westminster—close to Westminster Abbey—in London. DeVane goes on to describe the window as follows (DEVA, 574):

> [It] contains a full length figure of the Queen, bearing the orb and sceptre, with scenes from the coronation and the jubilee service, the arms of the colonies, and other details.

But the window was either destroyed along with many others during the blitz, or it was not mounted in the church at any time. Concerning the latter point, I am told by Rev. John A. Baker, Canon at St. Margaret's, that there are no records in the church archives to indicate that the window was ever in the church.

KING VICTOR AND KING CHARLES

The general setting for this play, as indicated in the stage directions of Part I, is Palazzo Rivoli, which is located about eight miles west of Turin (Fig. 83). The palace was the favorite residence of King Victor Amadeus II (1666-1731).

Fig. 83
Palazzo Rivoli
Turin (environs)

King Charles. II.77-79

> *D'Ormea.*   At midnight, only two hours since, at Turin,
> He rode in person to the citadel
> With one attendant, to Soccorso gate. . . .

The Soccorso Gate used to be an entrance to the fortified city of Turin. The gate is not standing today, and although King maintains that a Contrada del Soccorso leads to the Piazza Carlina in the city (KING, III, 256), I have not been able to verify this claim.

LA SAISIAZ

The name of this poem is also the name of a chalet situated a little over a mile from the French village of Collonges-sous-Salève, in the Savoyard Mountains some five miles southwest of Geneva. In 1877 Browning stayed in the chalet (Fig. 84), and in that same year Anne Egerton Smith, who is commemorated in the poem, died in the chalet.

Fig. 84
La Saisiaz Chalet
Geneva (environs)

THE LAST RIDE TOGETHER

6:65-66

> They scratch his name on the Abbey-stones.
> My riding [with a loved one] is better, by their leave.

The biographical association here is with Browning and Westminster Abbey, in London (Fig. 85). Browning's name is actually "on the Abbey-stones," although of course he did not know at the time that he would be buried there. His name is embedded in the pavement over his tomb, which is in the Poets' Corner, in the south transept.

For another reference to Westminster Abbey, see above under "Bishop Blougram's Apology," 3-9.

A LIKENESS

22-23, 42-43, 49-50, 60-61

> ... prints—Rarey drumming on Cruiser,
> And Sayers, our champion, the bruiser. . . .
> . . .
> I keep my prints, an imbroglio,
> Fifty in one portfolio.
> . . .
> [We] Talk about pencil and lyre,
> And the National Portrait Gallery. . . .
> . . .
> 'By the by, you must take, for a keepsake,
> That other, you praised, of Volpato's.'

"Rarey drumming on Cruiser" refers to a print of the horse Cruiser being whipped by J. S. Rarey in Rarey's book *Art of Taming Horses* (PET, I,1162). DeVane tells us that Browning, in his correspondence, requested this book from his publisher (DEVA, 306; KNI, 106). The copy owned by Browning is presently in the collection of the Ohio Historical Society, in Columbus, Ohio (KEL, 163, item A1927).

"Sayers, our champion, the bruiser" is an unspecified print of Tom Sayers, who gained the British prizefighting championship in 1857. He retired from the ring after fighting to a draw with the American fighter Heenan, "the Benecia Boy," on

Fig. 85
Westminster Abbey
London

April 17, 1860. For a direct reference by Browning to the Benecia Boy, see "Mr. Sludge, 'the Medium,'" line 1269.

"Talk about . . . the National Portrait Gallery," in London, calls to mind associations between the Brownings and the holdings of the Gallery. Included among the portraits of the Brownings are the famous pair of canvases by Gordigiani. Also housed in the gallery is a bronze cast of the *Clasped Hands of the Brownings* by Harriet Hosmer. For a complete list of portraits of the Brownings in the gallery, see ORMOND, I, 73-74. For more about the *Clasped Hands of the Brownings*, see above under *James Lee's Wife*, VIII. 27-32.

The print of "Volpato's" is possibly a copy of the etching *Perseus and Andromeda*, which might have been one of the prints that Browning's father owned "Fifty in one portfolio." For a further discussion of this possibility, see below under *Pauline*, 656-67.

LOVE AMONG THE RUINS

No source study has appeared with a thoroughly convincing case advancing one particular site for the ruins in this poem. To date, the site has been variously identified as Nineveh, Babylon, Thebes, Jerusalem, Tarquinia, the Roman Campagna, and Syracuse (SIR).

LURIA

I.67-73

> Brac.   And, when we visit Florence, let you pace
> The Piazza by my side as if we talked,
> Where all your old acquaintances may see:
> You'd die for me, I should not be surprised.
> Now then!
> Sec.   Sir, look about and love yourself!
> Step after step the Signory and you
> Tread gay till this tremendous point's to pass. . . .

The council that will decide the fate of Luria is the "Signory"— the Signoria—that meets in the Palazzo Vecchio in the "Piazza" —the Piazza della Signoria, in Florence (KING, IV, 348; Fig. 86; Map F:8H).

Fig. 86
Piazza della Signoria
Florence

I.121-26

Brac. (*Looks to the wall of the tent.*) Did he draw that?
Sec.   With charcoal, when the watch
       Made the report at midnight; Lady Domizia
       Spoke of the unfinished Duomo, you remember;
       That is his fancy how a Moorish front
       Might join to, and complete, the body,—a sketch. . . .

Ernest Radford maintains that Luria's sketch of a Moorish façade
for the unfinished Duomo of Florence is based on an 1822 design
by the architect Giovanni Silvestri. Radford reports a description
of a project on exhibit in 1833 in the Museum of the Duomo in
Florence. In translation the description reads (RAD, 251n):

> Project for the façade of the Metropolitan Church of Florence
> conceived and executed in 1822 by the Architect Giovanni
> Silvestri and sent to the I. R. Academy of Fine Arts.
> —Giovanni Silvestri and Felice Francolini, Architects, dedi-
> cate it to their fellow citizens. 1833.

But there is no archival record in Florence of Silvestri's design
(IST), and Browning, as Radford tells us, knew nothing about the
design when he wrote the poem in 1846 (RAD, 252). Consequently, as of now, we can only assume on the authority of Radford
what the design actually looked like. Specifically, all that I can
glean from Radford's description is that Silvestri's design
seemed oriental because of "small pinnacles or minarets on the
shoulders of the façade" (RAD, 252).

I. 297-300

Lur.   'Gainst the glad heaven, o'er the white palace-front
       The interrupted scaffold climbs anew;
       The walls are peopled by the painter's brush;
       The statue to its niche ascends to dwell.

This "white palace-front" being painted is not specified. No
medieval palace front in Florence that I am aware of was painted
white, and the two that flourished during the siege of Pisa by the
Florentines in 1405 and 1406—the dating for Browning's play—
were certainly not painted white. These medieval buildings, as
seen today in their original, rough-hewn state, are the Bargello
and the Palazzo Vecchio. Perhaps in this passage Luria is meant
to be thinking of painting done on the interior rather than the

exterior of one of these palaces.   For another reference to the
Palazzo Vecchio, see above under I.67-73.

The "statue to its niche" that "ascends to dwell" has been
identified with the Church of Orsanmichele (Fig. 87; Map F:8H),
which has niches in the exterior walls where great bronze and
marble Florentine statues are mounted (KING, IV, 348).   The

Fig. 87
Church of Orsanmichele
Florence

church was completed in 1404, a year before the seige of Pisa began, and the statues, which are by Renaissance sculptors, were mounted after the seige. The sculptures, commissioned by various Florentine guilds, include the *John the Baptist* by Ghiberti, the *Four Crowned Saints* by Nanni di Banco, and the *St. George* of Donatello (original now in the Bargello; Map F:8H,8I).

THE "MOSES" OF MICHAELANGELO

1-14

> And who is He that, sculptured in huge stone,
>> Sitteth a giant, where no works arrive
>> Of straining Art, and hath so prompt and live
> The lips, I listen to their very tone?
> Moses is he—Ay, that, makes clearly known
>> The Chin's thick boast, and brow's prerogative
>> Of double ray: so did the mountain give
> Back to the world that visage, God was grown
> Great part of! Such was he when he suspended
>> Round him the sounding and vast waters; such
> When he shut sea on sea o'er Mizraïm
> And ye, his hordes, a vile calf raised, and bended
>> The knee? This Image had ye raised, not much
> Had been your error in adoring Him.

This sonnet is an undated translation of a sonnet by Giambattista Felice Zappi (1667-1719). The *Moses* that is described is the famous statue by Michelangelo in the Church of San Pietro in Vincoli, in Rome (DEVA, 557; Fig. 88). The sonnet is reproduced here from F. G. Kenyon's edition of *New Poems* (NE, 27).

MY LAST DUCHESS: FERRARA

1-4

> That's my last Duchess painted on the wall,
> Looking as if she were alive. I call
> That piece a wonder, now: Frà Pandolf's hands
> Worked busily a day, and there she stands.

Although "Frà Pandolf" has long been considered an imaginary painter, scholars are generally agreed that the historical personages serving as models for the Duke and Duchess in this

Fig. 88
Michelangelo
Moses
Church of San Pietro in Vincoli
Rome

poem are Alfonso II, fifth Duke of Ferrara, and Lucrezia de' Medici, his first wife (FRI, 658-84; DEVA, 107-09; KING, IV, 371-72). From this assumption, R. J. Berman lists various pictures and medals with portraits of Lucrezia de' Medici as possible sources for the Duke's "last Duchess." The pictures of Lucrezia are either by the Renaissance painter Agnolo Bronzino or his pupil Alessandro Allori. Two of them, one a miniature, are in the Uffizi Gallery, in Florence (Map F:8H); one is in the Pitti Palace, in Florence (Fig. 222; Map F:9G); one is in the Villa del Poggio Imperiale, just outside of Florence; and another is in the Kunsthistorisches Museum, in Vienna (BERM, 106-08, with an illustration of the portrait in Vienna on p. 107). The medals are nos. 473-476 by Pastorino da Siena (1508-1592), in the Department of Coins and Medals in the British Museum; a bronze medal by Francesco Salviati (1410-1563), in the Herberden Coin Room of the Ashmolean Museum, Oxford; and a medal by Domenico Poggini, in the Ashmolean and National Gallery of Art, Washington (BERM, 108-11, with an illustration of the medal by Pastorino da Siena on p. 110). Berman, however, in listing these pictures and medals, only describes them; he makes no case to prove that any of them was known to Browning and is thus a viable source for the portrait of the Duchess in the poem. In particular, as regards the paintings, there are several reasons why it is difficult to make a case for them. Browning did not visit Florence or Vienna prior to publishing his poem in 1842. Vasari's *Lives* lists no entry for Bronzino or Allori. And the entries in the *Biographie Universelle* are not specific enough to be useful. The entry on Allori—there is none on Bronzino— simply mentions that Allori specialized in portraits but does not spell out the name of Lucrezia de' Medici as a subject for one of the portraits; and the entry on the Este family, which DeVane maintains is a probable historical source for the poem (DEVA, 107-08), lists no portrait of the Medici family. Perhaps, as Berman suggests, Browning saw a reproduction of one of these portraits (BERM, 106), but, at the present time, this is only conjecture.

    C. E. Carrington, on the other hand, nominates *A Young Lady*, a painting identified with the Italian School in the Dulwich Picture Gallery, in London (CAR; DULW, 25, item 254; Fig. 89). To support his case, Carrington points out that Browning undoubtedly saw the painting while spending many of his younger days viewing the Dulwich Gallery, and that there are several resemblances between Browning's portrait in the

Fig. 89
A Young Lady
Italian School
Dulwich Picture Gallery
London

poem and the one in the Dulwich Gallery: first, the face of *A Young Lady* has, in keeping with the fate of the Duchess, a melancholy expression; second, a mantle—or some sort of garment—"laps / Over my lady's wrist too much" (16-17); and third, a "faint / Half-flush . . . dies along her throat" (18-19). The flush, as it has been checked in the original color version of the portrait, may be seen as heightened coloring on the right cheek just above the ruffle (BAN). Carrington's case, I should add, is further strengthened by references in Browning's poetry to other possible sources in the Dulwich Gallery. For these references, see the nine other entries under the Dulwich Picture Gallery in the Index of Sources with Locations. The difficulty with Carrington's case, however, is that the Young Lady from the Italian School obviously has nothing to do with the historical model described above, Lucrezia de' Medici.

For a literary source relating to the portrait of Browning's Duchess, see the note on the statue scene in Shakespeare's *The Winter's Tale* above under "Bishop Blougram's Apology," 513-16.

47-48

>   Will 't please you rise? We'll meet
> The company below, then.

The setting for the Duke of Ferrara and the emmisary as they view a portrait of the Duke's previous Duchess and then descend a staircase past a statue of Neptune is most likely a composite of two places: the Castel Estense, the castle of the Este family in Ferrara (Fig. 90; see above under 1-4), and the Ducal Palace, or Palace of the Doges, in Venice (Figs. 201, 204, and 216). Built in the fourteenth century, the Castel Estense best represents Ferrara, the locale designated by the subtitle of the poem. No doubt there were other structures in Ferrara that were used by the Este family during the Renaissance era, but the Castel Estense, as the center of court activity, was the most appropriate place for Browning's Duke, Alfonso II, to officially receive an emmisary from another state in general "company" with other dignitaries. But, by itself, the Este Castle is not an entirely satisfactory choice for the locale, since in the castle there is neither a portrait of Lucrezia de' Medici, Alfonso's first wife, nor any statue of Neptune, and there is no statue of any kind placed at the top of or on the way down a staircase in the castle. In the

Fig. 90
Castel Estense
Ferrara

Ducal Palace of Venice, however, there is Jacopo Sansovino's large statue of Neptune posed at the top of the Giant Staircase, which leads down to the courtyard of the palace. Furthermore, the Ducal Palace coordinates as a joint setting with the Este Castle because both the palace and the castle were official meeting places for visiting dignitaries. For the reference to this Neptune statue by Sansovino, see below under 54-56, paragraph seven.

54-56

> Notice Neptune, though,
> Taming a sea-horse, thought a rarity,
> Which Claus of Innsbruck cast in bronze for me!

Studies proposing various art objects as sources for this statue of Neptune by the imaginary "Claus of Innsbruck" begin with L. Robert Stevens's claim that Browning had in mind a model by Scopas taken from classical antiquity. To support this proposal Stephens quotes from one of Browning's favorite reference books, Wanley's *Wonders of the Little World* (STE, 26):

> Scopas deserveth praise for his worthy workmanship, in which most account is made of those images in the chapel of Cn. Domitius in the cirque of Flaminius; viz., Neptune, Thetis, and her son Achilles; the Sea-nymphs, or Nereids, mounted upon dolphins, whales, and mighty sea-horses....

But notwithstanding Browning's familiarity with Wanley's book, the weakness of Stevens's proposal, as Berman points out, is that Scopas was a classical figure and cannot be related to the Renaissance character of Browning's poem (BERM, 113). Today, the copy of Wanley's book that was owned by Browning is in the Armstrong Browning Library, at Baylor University.

Next, Berman on his own part describes several statuettes of Neptune which could be sources, but, as with the medals of Lucrezia de' Medici described above under 1-4, Berman makes no case to prove that Browning was familiar with any of them. The statuettes are all about 18 inches from the base to the top of Neptune's trident and are variously attributed to The Master of the Dragon and to Severo da Ravenna, a sixteenth-century Paduan. The statuettes may be found in the Frick Collection, in New York; the National Gallery of Art, in Washington; the Museo Nazionale, in Florence; the Kunsthistorisches Museum, in Vienna; and the Blumka Collection, in New York. In addition, Berman describes a 19-inch bronze attributed to Alessandro Vittoria (1525-1608); it was acquired by the Victoria and Albert Museum in 1910, but its earlier history is unknown. That Browning knew the work seventy years earlier is conjec-. tural. Another possibility mentioned by Berman is a Neptune statue that was owned by Isabella d'Este in Mantua or Ferrara during the sixteenth century. But again, as with the candidates above, Berman presents no evidence to prove that Browning knew about this model, and this is in face of the fact that Browning did not visit Mantua or Ferrara prior to publishing "My Last Duchess" (BERM, 111-13, with an illustration of the statuette by Vittoria on p. 112).

A more recent consideration of a source for the Neptune statue is by Raymond Fitch, who, in discussing Browning's sculptor "Claus of Innsbruck," points out that during the first half of the sixteenth century Innsbruck was probably the most important center in Europe for the making of bronze statuary. At that time, the Emperor Maximilian of Germany commissioned a tomb-monument of bronze for the Court Church of Innsbruck, with a private foundry set up for the project. The monument depicts members of the Hapsburg house cast in over lifesize bronze statues along with small bronze figures of Roman emperors and saints of the Church (KING, IV, 372). Of course this information says nothing about the subject at hand, the Neptune statue, yet from these facts arise the following possibilities, and, as William Janes, of Leroy, Texas, has called to my attention, the consequent need for further research: (1) Browning considered Innsbruck the logical place for the fashioning of a statue in bronze during the sixteenth century; (2) Browning intended Claus of Innsbruck to be the foundryman who "cast in bronze" the Neptune statue rather than the artist who designed it; and (3) Claus of Innsbruck might have been modelled after one of the actual foundrymen who was commissioned by Emperor Maximilian to execute the bronzes for the Court Church of Innsbruck. For more on Innsbruck as a source for bronze statuary, see the following discussion and below under *Pippa Passes*, II.49-55.

My own view on the Neptune statue is that Browning formed his idea of it from impressions that he received during his trip to Europe in 1838. Along his itinerary through Trieste, Venice, Trent, Innsbruck, and Munich, Browning might have seen various pieces of sculpture that could have formed a composite model for his Duke's imaginary statue. In Trieste, in the Piazza della Borsa, there is a stone statue of Neptune rendered by Giovanni Mazzolan da Bergamo. In Venice, at one time in Palazzo Rezzonico, there was a bronze statuette of Neptune by Jacopo Sansovino; and, mounted on the top of the Giant Stairway of the courtyard of the Palace of the Doges, there is another Neptune statue by Sansovino, this one in marble. In Trent, in the Piazza del Duomo and the Palazzo Municipale, there are the two parts of a marble fountain of Neptune by the eighteenth-century sculptor Giongo. In Innsbruck, in the Court Church of Innsbruck, there are the bronze statues of the Hapsburg house mentioned above. And in Munich, in the Residenz, there is a small chalice surmounted by a figure of Neptune. None of these possible sources in and of itself completely fits Browning's description of a "rarity . . . cast in bronze" showing "Neptune, taming a sea horse," but between them they combine to form the model Browning possibly had in mind.

The statue in Trieste is not in bronze and is not small as I think a "rarity" should be, but it has a sea horse that Neptune is dominating if not "taming," and the statue is prominently posed in the Piazza della Borsa, where the statue might have been the first on Browning's itinerary to suggest the subject of Neptune to Browning (Fig. 221). The name of the sculptor, Giovanni Mazzolan da Bergamo, is engraved on the base of the statue along with his birthdate, 1755, which means, of course, that the statue could have been seen during Browning's visit to Trieste in 1838.

The statuette by Sansovino that was in the Palazzo Rezzonico was recommended to me as a possible source by Professor Marvin Eisenberg, of the Department of the History of Art at the University of Michigan (EISE). The statuette does not show Neptune in the taming process (Fig. 91), but it is in bronze and, as a statuette 37 inches tall (DAR), is small enough to be considered a "rarity." Whether or not the statuette was in the palace during Browning's time, however, is not known. Before Palazzo Rezzonico was turned over to the city of Venice, the furniture in the palace was sold, and no record was kept of when the *Neptune* left the palace (ROM). We know that for an unspecified period of time the statuette was in the possession of the now defunct Portalès family, but for how long before it was obtained in 1949 by its present owner, The Detroit Institute of Arts, the Institute cannot determine (DAR). If the statuette was

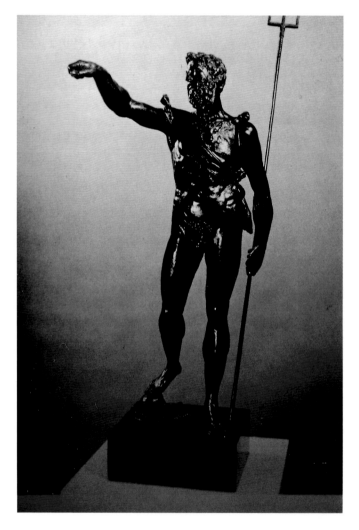

Fig. 91
Jacopo Sansovino
Neptune
The Detroit Institute of Arts
Detroit

in Palazzo Rezzonico during Browning's first trip to Venice in 1838, there is a strong possibility that Browning saw it, for the fact that Browning died in Palazzo Rezzonico suggests that Browning might have been familiar with the palace as early as 1838.

As regards Sansovino's large marble statue of Neptune surmounting the Giant Stairway in the courtyard of the Palace of the Doges, there can be no doubt that Browning, in 1838, saw this very prominent attraction (Fig. 201). Although the statue is not small or made of bronze or taming a sea horse, its position fits in with the setting of the poem. As Browning's Duke and emissary are accompanying each other down the stairway to "meet / The company below" (47-48), the Duke points out his statue of Neptune to the emissary. And so, too, Browning might have passed the Sansovino *Neptune* while descending the Giant Stairway of the Palace of the Doges and, in so doing, might have conceived the position for the statue in the poem. For another possible source for the interior setting of the poem, see the note on the Castel Estense above under 47-48.

The fountain statue of Neptune in Trent is important as a possible source because of its prominent site, the presence of two sea horses as part of the fountain complex, and because Trent is a pertinant locale. Originally fashioned in marble in the eighteenth century by Giongo, the statue of Neptune was removed from the rest of the fountain in 1942, mounted in the courtyard in the Palazzo Municipale, and replaced with the bronze version that now surmounts the rest of the marble fountain complex (TON; Fig. 92). Thus the version that stood in Browning's time was marble, not bronze; yet because of the prominent position of the fountain in the Piazza del Duomo, Browning undoubtedly saw the fountain and probably retained an impression of it. And this impression was no doubt reinforced by the presence of the two sea horses—each ridden by a Triton—that are placed below the dominant figure of Neptune. The importance of Trent as a locale derives from the fact that Alfonso d'Este II, the historical personage associated with Browning's Duke (see above under 1-4), originally planned to marry *in* Trent Barbara of Austria, his second wife and the historical model for the "fair daughter" (line 52) who succeeds the Duke's first Duchess (FRI, 638).

Innsbruck, of course, is important because of the reference in the text to the presumed sculptor "Claus of Innsbruck," who supposedly formed the Duke's statue of Neptune. As detailed

Fig. 92
Giongo
Fountain of Neptune
Trent

above under 54-56, there are numerous bronze statues of the Hapsburgs in the Court Church of Innsbruck that might have suggested to Browning the city of Innsbruck as the center for a foundry that had an artisan with possibly a real name of Claus, who "cast in bronze," but did not necessarily design, the Neptune statue.

And the chalice in the Residenz in Munich should be noted on two counts: first, it is indeed a rarity in that it is small, and, second, of all the possible sources mentioned above, it best depicts Neptune taming a sea horse.   It is entered in *The Treasury of the Residenz Munich* as item 393, a

> shallow drinking vessel: Onyx, enamelled gold mount, diamonds, rubies, Milan c. 1570.

The vessel features Neptune sitting on top of the rim.   In front of him are two sea horses, one of which has a whole body including a fish tail, the other, a partial body that is emerging from the inside of the cup.   Neptune is looking and pointing his prong at the sea horses.   In his left hand are two chains that are separately attached to the bodies of the sea horses (Fig. 240).   That Browning saw the chalice is highly probable, for elsewhere in this study it is evident that he visited the major museums in Munich—the Residenz included—and referred to art objects in them.   In "Old Pictures in Florence," he unquestionably refers to the statue *Paris*, which is in the Glyptothek (see below under Old, 13:97-104).   In "Andrea del Sarto," he probably alludes to Raphael's *Madonna of the Palazzo Tempi*, which is in the Alte Pinakothek (see above under And, 104-13); and in *Pippa Passes*, he specifically refers to Canova's *Psiche-fanciulla*, which in Browning's time was either in the Biederstein Castle or the Residenz (see below under Pip, I.375-94).

Finally, as an emendation to the foregoing composite theory of Neptune sculpture that Browning probably saw during his 1838 trip through northern Italy, Austria, and Germany, I would add one prominent example from the field of painting: Tiepolo's *Venice Receives the Homage of Neptune* (Fig. 241). While Browning was at the Palace of the Doges in Venice, he no doubt saw Tiepolo's well known work in conjunction with the Sansovino *Neptune* statue described above.   The painting was formerly in the Hall of the Four Doors and is presently on an easel in the Hall of the Squires.   The painting depicts Neptune pouring out a cornucopia of riches to a woman personifying Venice, and the idea of Venice, a notable seaport, being identified with Neptune, the Roman god of the sea, reinforces the importance of Venice and, for that matter, Trieste, another seaport mentioned above, as appropriate places for Browning to vividly fix in mind Neptune imagery.

NED BRATTS

278

... a death-like hush sealed up the old Mote House.

According to the Bedfordshire County Librarian, the "old Mote House" was the Moot Hall, in Bedford, sometimes known as the Guildhall, and the *Oxford English Dictionary* tells us that "mote hall" and "moot hall" were synonymous in the nineteenth century as terms for a courthouse. The Guildhall is no longer in existence but was in St. Paul's Square facing the High Street as marked on John Sneed's 1611 map of Bedford (BED).

328

... Bunyan's Statue stands facing where stood his Jail.

John "Bunyan's Statue" is a bronze by Joseph Edgar Boehm (1834-1870). It was given to the town of Bedford in 1874 by the Duke of Bedford and placed at the corner of Dame Alice and Broadway Streets in front of the Church of St. Peter de Meron (Fig. 93). Two blocks away from the statue is "where stood his Jail," that is, the jail where Bunyan was incarcerated between the years 1660-1667 and again in 1675. On the corner of Silver and Broadway Streets, embedded in the sidewalk, is a marker locating the jail. Fig. 94 shows one of the jail doors, which is now housed in Moot Hall, in Elstow, the town where Bunyan was born. Another door is kept at the Bunyan Meeting House, in Bedford.

William DeVane and Frances Bolton believe that Browning personally saw Boehm's statue, but only Bolton offers a reason to support her opinion. She thinks that Browning went to Bedford to attend a Bunyan festival and the unveiling of the

Fig. 93
Joseph Boehm
John Bunyan
Bedford

Fig. 94
A door of the Bedford Jail
Moot Hall
Elstow

statue on June 10, 1874, four years prior to the writing of the poem. The festival was a continuation of the 1872 festival, which celebrated the release of Bunyan from prison (BOL, 33ff; DEVA, 444). The claim of DeVane and Bolton can be corroborated by observing the position of the statue in relation to the marker locating the jail, for the topographical accuracy of the text —indeed "Bunyan's Statue stands facing where stood his Jail" two blocks away—strongly suggests an actual visit to Bedford.

If we assume that Browning personally viewed Boehm's statue, then the problem of determining the identity of Bunyan's "Book" in the poem (lines 110, 188, 194, 208) resolves itself. According to DeVane's exposition of the problem, the book was given to the Brattses presumably when Bunyan was in jail, and its contents influenced the conversion of the Brattses. Browning's poem overtly refers to the book as *Pilgrim's Progress* by detailing episodes from it that affected the Brattses, and Ned Bratts even identifies himself with Master Faithful by tracing his progress from the city of Destruction to Vanity Fair. But the difficulty with this interpretation is that historically *Pilgrim's Progress* could not have been given to the Brattses while Bunyan was in prison, for the book was not published until 1678, three years after Bunyan's last incarceration. Thus DeVane thinks that Browning created an anachronism in the poem, and he goes on to attribute the anachronism to misinformation Browning took from Southey and other early Bunyan biographers; whereas, in point of time, the book that would have been given to Bratts, DeVane avers, is *Grace Abounding to the Chief of Sinners*, which was published in 1666 and which, appropriate to Browning's theme, deals with Bunyan's own religious experiences (DEVA, 443-44). But despite the problem of anachronism in the poem, *Pilgrim's Progress* is indeed an appropriate book for making converts and should be considered the proper reference for the "Book" in the poem. This conclusion, I believe, is strengthened by the four scenes taken from *Pilgrim's Progress* that surround the four sides of the pedestal of Boehm's statue of Bunyan. Three of the scenes are illustrated on bronze plates, and the fourth is described in an inscription. Fig. 93 shows the front plate, which illustrates Christian's fight with Apollyan. On the right of this scene is a plate depicting the three Shining Ones pointing out to Christian the Celestial City. And on the left is a plate showing the Evangelist directing Christian to the wicket gate. The inscription is on the back of the pedestal and is an adaptation of a scene in the Interpreter's house. Thus the scenes, depicted in bronze or inscribed in stone on the pedestal of the statue, in conjunction with the descriptions of Christian's and Master Faithful's progress in the poem, suggest that Browning indeed intended *Pilgrim's Progress* to have had an effect on the conversion of the Brattses.

OLD PICTURES IN FLORENCE

13:97-104

> You would fain be kinglier, say, than I am?
>   Even so, you will not sit like Theseus.
> You would prove a model? The Son of Priam
>   Has yet the advantage in arms' and knees' use.
> You're wroth—can you slay your snake like Apollo?
>   You're grieved—still Niobe's the grander!
> You live—there's the Racers' frieze to follow:
>   You die—there's the dying Alexander.

The six pieces of idealized sculpture here, that is, sculpture in the classical style, are most likely the "Theseus"—also known as the *Dionysus*—on the east pediment of the Parthenon, now in the British Museum (BER, 291; POR, IV, 370; TUR, 354; COOKE, 220; COR, 225-26; Fig. 95); the "Son of Priam," the *Paris* of the Aeginetan Sculptures, now in the Glyptothek, in Munich (COOKE, 220; COR, 225-26; POR, IV, 370; Fig. 96); the "Apollo," a copy of the *Omphalos Apollo,* in the British Museum (Fig. 97; see discussion below); the "Niobe," the *Niobe* mourning the death of her children, in the Uffizi Gallery (BER, 291; COOKE, 221; COR, 225-26; POR, IV, 371; TUR, 355; Fig. 98; Map F:8H); the "Racers' frieze," the procession of horsemen on the frieze of the Parthenon, in the British Museum (BER, 291; COOKE, 221; POR, IV, 371; TUR, 355; Fig. 99); and the "dying Alexander," which is either the bust of that name in the Uffizi (BER, 291; COOKE, 221; COR, 225-26; POR, IV, 371; Fig. 100) or, as Turner thinks, the *Alexander Sarcophagus,* in the Istanbul Museum (TUR, 355; RIC, Fig. 800). Of these two possibilities I am inclined to go along with the bust in the Uffizi for two reasons: first, the bust was no doubt seen by Browning during his stay in Florence, while the sarcophagus in the Istanbul Museum was unquestionably not viewed by Browning during his travels; and, second, the expression on the face of the bust in the Uffizi is truly "dying," as the text and Fig. 100 indicate, while the expression on the face of Alexander on the bas-relief frieze of the sarcophagus in the Istanbul Museum is, as illustrated in Richter (RIC, Figs. 184 and 800), robustly displayed in the heat of battle.

Fig. 95
Theseus (Dionysus)
from the east pediment of the Parthenon
British Museum
London

Fig. 96
Paris
from the Aeginetan sculptures
Glyptothek
Munich

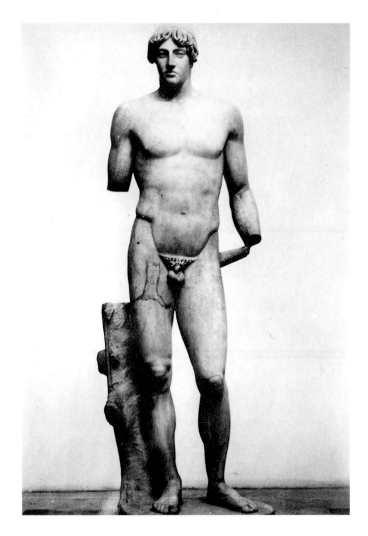

Fig. 97
Omphalos Apollo (copy)
British Museum
London

Fig. 98
Niobe
Uffizi
Florence

Fig. 99
Racers' Frieze (detail)
British Museum
London

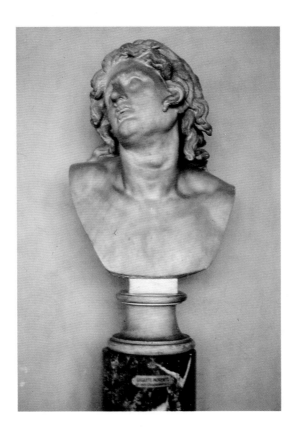

Fig. 100
Dying Alexander
Uffizi
Florence

Regarding the above identification of the *Omphalos Apollo*, we have Browning's seminal statement naming the *Apollo Alexikakos* as the proper source for the statue (COOKE, 220; POR, 370-71):

> A word on the line about Apollo the snakeslayer, which my friend Professor Colvin condemns, believing that the god of the Belvedere grasps no bow, but the agis, as described in the 15th Iliad. . . . The conjecture of Flaxman that the statue was suggested by the bronze Apollo Alexikakos of Kalamis, mentioned by Pausanius, remains probable; though the 'hardness' which Cicero considers to distinguish the artist's workmanship from that of Muron is not by any means apparent in our marble copy, if it be one.—Feb. 16, 1880.

In a study by Richter, the *Apollo Alexikakos* is presently connected with the *Omphalos Apollo* (RIC, 160), and since Browning refers to "our marble copy," he is probably indicating that he had seen a reproduction of the *Apollo Alexikakos*, or what we now call the *Omphalos Apollo*. Furthermore, inasmuch as Browning made the above statement in 1880 while living in London, he had probably seen the copies of the *Omphalos Apollo* in the British Museum. Arthur Hamilton Smith's museum catalogue lists these as nos. 209, 210, and 211 in the Archaic Room of the Department of Greek and Roman Antiquities. One of the pieces is the Choiseul-Gouffier statue (Fig. 97), which has been housed in the British Museum since 1818 (BAI), and the other two are heads from a temple of Apollo in Cyrene (SMI, 34, item 96). The original *Omphalos Apollo* is in the National Museum of Athens.

24:185-92

> Their ghosts [the artists] still stand, as I said before,
>   Watching each fresco flaked and rasped,
> Blocked up, knocked out, or whitewashed o'er:
>   —No getting again what the church has grasped!
> The works on the wall must take their chance;
>   "Works never conceded to England's thick clime!"
> (I hope they prefer their inheritance
>   Of a bucketful of Italian quick-lime.)

The idea of "each fresco . . . whitewashed o'er," presumably by a bucket of "Italian quick-lime," calls to mind one of the paintings uncovered from whitewash, the *Portrait of Dante*, attributed to Giotto (EISS, 82-83). The portrait, which is discussed below under *A Soul's Tragedy* (Figs. 209 and 210), was restored in 1840 by the authorities in Florence fifteen years before Browning's poem was published. The whitewash which covered the fresco was painted over it during the plague of 1620 (MARTI, 122, item 164). This means that the fresco was probably covered with the type of "Italian quick-lime" Browning mentions.

According to David DeLaura, Browning may be making an allusion here to Mrs. Jameson when he speaks of "each fresco flaked and rasped . . . Works never conceded to England's thick clime." In her *Sketches of Art, Literature, and Character,* Mrs. Jameson says (JAMES, 303; DELA, 9):

> It has been said that fresco-painting is unfitted for our climate, damp and sea-coal fires being equally injurious; but the new method of warming all large buildings, either by steam or heated air, obviates, at least, this objection.

(Continued under this reference in the Supplement to Citations and Notes.)

26:201-08; 27:209-16; 28:217-24

> Not that I expect the great Bigordi,
>   Nor Sandro to hear me, chivalric, bellicose;
> Nor the wronged Lippino; and not a word I
>   Say of a scrap of Frà Angelico's:
> But are you too fine, Taddeo Gaddi,
>   To grant me a taste of your intonaco,
> Some Jerome that seeks the heaven with a sad eye?
>   Not a churlish saint, Lorenzo Monaco?
>
> Could not the ghost with the close red cap,
>   My Pollajolo, the twice a craftsman,
> Save me a sample, give me the hap
>   Of a muscular Christ that shows the draughtsman?
> No Virgin by him the somewhat petty,
>   Of finical touch and tempera crumbly—
> Could not Alesso Baldovinetti
>   Contribute so much, I ask him humbly?
>
> Margheritone of Arezzo,
>   With the grave-clothes garb and swaddling barret,
> (Why purse up mouth and beak in a pet so,
>   You bald old saturnine poll-clawed parrot?)
> Not a poor glimmering Crucifixion,
>   Where in the foreground kneels the donor?
> If such remain, as is my conviction,
>   The hoarding it does you but little honor.

Four artists are mentioned here probably in reference to paintings possessed by Browning and which were reportedly given away before or sold at the Sotheby Sale in 1913 (cf. TUR, 353; COOKE, 222; BROW, 169; ORM, 199; COR, 232). The "Jerome," presumed here as one by "Gaddi," is undoubtedly the painting the *Penitent St. Jerome*, presently attributed to Toscani and now housed in the Princeton Art Museum. It shows St. Jerome standing with his hand to his breast, his Cardinal's hat at his feet, and an upturned head that "seeks the heaven with a sad eye" (EIS, 275-83; KEL, 473, item H20; SOT, 17, item 66; DELA, 7-8, with a color illustration on the cover). The "muscular Christ" by "Pollajolo" is assuredly the *Christ at the Column* currently in the Harewood House, Yorkshire (ORM, 199n; Fig. 101). The Harewood House catalogue identifies the painting with the school of Antonio Pollaiuolo (BOR, 24), but this listing should be compared with the view of Leopold D. Ettlinger, who judges that it was not possible for Browning's picture to be identified with Pollaiuolo (DELA, 8-9). The "Virgin" presumably by Alesso Baldovinetti is possibly a *Virgin and Child* that was given by Browning to Rossetti (ORM, 199n). And the "Crucifixion" by "Margheritone of Arezzo" is possibly a painting from the Tuscan School that hung in Casa Guidi as the center of a triptych (KEL, 473, item H23; SOT, 16, item 64; purchased in 1913 by Bacri Fréres, Paris). The placement of the *Penitent St. Jerome* and the *Christ of the Column* may be seen in George Mignaty's painting the *Drawing Room at Casa Guidi* (Fig. 149). The *Penitent St. Jerome* is over the fireplace on the middle right-hand side, and the *Christ at the Column* is on the wall to the left of the fireplace in the upper left-hand corner. For another reference to Mignaty's painting, see below under *The Ring and the Book*, I.472-83. (Continued under the separate stanzas of this reference in the Supplement to Citations and Notes.)

30:233-40, 31:241-44

> . . . Giotto, you,
> Have you allowed, as the town-tongues babble it,—
> Oh, never! it shall not be counted true—
> That a certain precious little tablet
> Which Buonarroti eyed like a lover—
> Was buried so long in oblivion's womb
> And, left for another than I to discover,
> Turns up at last! and to whom?—to whom?

I, that have haunted the dim San Spirito,
     (Or was it rather the Ognissanti?)
Patient on altar-step planting a weary toe!
     Nay, I shall have it yet!

Fig. 101
Antonio Pollaiuolo (attributed to school of)
Christ at the Column
Harewood House
Yorkshire, England

The "precious little tablet" that Michelangelo "Buonarroti eyed like a lover" ties in with the references to the Florentine churches of "San Spirito" (Fig. 102; Map F:8G) and "Ognissanti" (Fig. 103; Map F:7G). The tablet is the painting *Death of the Virgin*, by Giotto (Fig. 104), which, as Ormond points out, was lost from the Church of Ognissanti but was eventually recovered. After passing from the Rev. Davenport Bromley to the

Fig. 102
Church of Santo Spirito
Florence

Fig. 103
Church of Ognissanti
Florence

Fig. 104
Giotto (attributed to)
Death of the Virgin (detail)
Staatliche Museen, Gemäldagalerie
Berlin-Dahlem

Langton Douglas Collections, the painting was housed in the
Kaiser Friedrich Museum, now the Gemäldegalerie of the
Staatliche Museen, in West Berlin.   Browning, however, in a
letter to Hiram Corson, mistakenly reads Vasari and identifies
the painting as a *Last Supper* by Giotto and claims that it disap-
peared from the Church of Santo Spirito (ORM, 200; VAS, I, 70-
71; COR, frontispiece; MARTI, 126).   (Continued under this
reference in the Supplement to Citations and notes.)

33:257-58

> This time we'll shoot better game and bag 'em hot—
> No mere display at the stone of Dante....

Korg thinks that the "stone of Dante" is Pazzi's marble statue of Dante in Piazza Santa Croce, in Florence (KORG, 273). But engraving on the statue indicates that it was placed in the piazza in 1864, on the sixth centennial of Dante's birth (also see HAR, 82). This is nine years after the poem was published and means that the statue could not be the stone of Dante referred to in the poem. Actually, the "stone" is a block of marble embedded a few feet above the street in the façade of a building on the south side of the Piazza del Duomo between the Via dello Studio and the Piazza delle Pallottole (Map F:7H). In Fig. 105 the name on the stone is given in Italian as "Sasso di Dante" (also see BAR, 112-13). Wordsworth describes the stone in his *Poems, at Florence* as follows:

> Under the shadow of a stately Pile,
> The dome of Florence, pensive and alone,
> Nor giving heed to aught that passed the while,
> I stood, and gazed upon a marble stone,
> The Laurelled Dante's favourite seat.

And Elizabeth Barrett Browning refers to the block of stone in her *Casa Guidi Windows*, I.601-07, written five years before "Old Pictures in Florence" was published:

> On the stone
> Called Dante's,—a plain flat stone scarce discerned
> From others in the pavement,—whereupon
> He used to bring his quiet chair out, turned
> To Brunelleschi's church, and pour alone
> The lava of his spirit when it burned:
> It is not cold to-day.

That Browning was familiar with Wordsworth's account seems probable, and that he knew about Elizabeth's version is certain (MARKUS, 51). Furthermore, since the block of stone is commonly called "stone"—or *sasso* in Italian—the name of the object fits in with Browning's text.

Fig. 105
Stone of Dante
Piazza del Duomo
Florence

35:278-80; 36:281-88

Thy great Campanile is still to finish. [17:136]

. . .

The Campanile, the Duomo's fit ally,
Shall soar up in gold full fifty braccia,
     Completing Florence, as Florence Italy.

Shall I be alive that morning the scaffold
     Is broken away, and the long-pent fire,
Like the golden hope of the world, unbaffled
     Springs from its sleep, and up goes the spire

> While "God and the People" plain for its motto,
> Thence the new tricolor flaps at the sky?
> At least to foresee that glory of Giotto
> And Florence together, the first am I!

Fig. 106, right, shows the "great Campanile," the Bell-tower of Florence, as it stands today without a spire. Fig. 106, left, shows the design for the Bell-tower as completed with a spire. The drawing, which is now in the Museo dell' Opera del Duomo di Firenze (Map F:7I), probably represents, for the most part, Giotto's original conception of the Bell-tower. Ghiberti avers that Giotto was definitely the one who designed the Bell-tower and that he supervised the construction of the lower order of bas-reliefs. Gioseffi claims that the design for the lower order of the Bell-tower corresponds with the design, measurement, and color of that actually built. The rest of the tower, however, Gioseffi thinks represents the alterations of the later architects Andrea Pisano and Francesco Talenti (MARTI, 126). Browning, no doubt, got his information regarding the spire from Vasari (DEVA, 251-52; VAS, I, 71-72). As a symbol of the Risorgimento, the tricolored Italian flag that Browning would like to have attached to the spire, had it been completed, roughly corresponds in hue with the red, white, and green marble which covers the Bell-tower as it stands today.

Compare Elizabeth Barrett Browning's description of Giotto's Bell-tower in *Casa Guidi Windows*, I.68-72. Mrs. Browning's poem, it should be noted, antedates her husband's by five years (MARCUS, 52-54).

ONE WORD MORE

2:5-17; 3:18-25; 4:26-31; 5:32-34

> Rafael made a century of sonnets,
> Made and wrote them in a certain volume
> Dinted with the silver-pointed pencil
> Else he only used to draw Madonnas:
> These, the world might view—but one, the volume.
> Who that one, you ask? Your heart instructs you.
> Did she live and love it all her lifetime?
> Did she drop, his lady of the sonnets,
> Die, and let it drop beside her pillow
> Where it lay in place of Rafael's glory,
> Rafael's cheek so duteous and so loving—
> Cheek, the world was wont to hail a painter's
> Rafael's cheek, her love had turned a poet's?

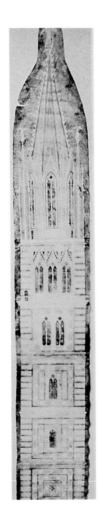

Fig. 106
Left: Giotto (attributed to)
         Design for the Bell-tower of Florence
Right: Bell-tower of Florence

You and I would rather read that volume,
(Taken to his beating bosom by it)
Lean and list the bosom-beats of Rafael,
Would we not? than wonder at Madonnas—
Her, San Sisto names, and Her, Foligno,
Her, that visits Florence in a vision,
Her, that's left with lilies in the Louvre—
Seen by us and all the world in circle.

You and I will never read that volume.
Guido Reni, like his own eye's apple
Guarded long the treasure-book and loved it.
Guido Reni dying, all Bologna
Cried, and the world cried too, "Ours, the treasure!"
Suddenly, as rare things will, it vanished.

Dante once prepared to paint an angel:
Whom to please? You whisper "Beatrice."
While he mused and traced it and retraced it. . . .

Of Raphael's "century of sonnets," only four are claimed by
Browning scholars to be extant (POR, V, 299; HAR, 162; DEVA,
277). One of these sonnets is written on some sketches for
Raphael's fresco of the *Disputa*, in the Vatican. These sketches
with the sonnet are in the Department of Prints and Drawings in
the British Museum. According to the museum catalogue on
Raphael, the center group of the sketches is a study for the two
right-hand foreground figures who, in the completed composition, are standing next to the door (POU, 26-28; Fig. 107).
Richardson's translation of the sonnet is included in the catalogue as follows (POU, 28; Richardson's full name is not given):

Sweet Remembrance! Hour of Bliss
When we met, but Now the more
I Mourn, as when the Sailor is
Star-less, distant far from Shore.

Now Tongue, tho' 'tis with Grief, relate
How Love deceiv'd me of my Joy;
Display the Unaccustom'd Cheat,
But Praise the Nymph, and Thank the boy.

It was when the declining Sun
Beheld Another Sun arise;
And There where Actions should be done,
No Talking, only with the Eyes.

> But I tormented by the Fire
> That burnt within, was overcome:
> Then when to speak we most desire
> The More we find we must be Dumb.

The original Italian version of the sonnet is also reproduced in the catalogue and, more conveniently, in Berdoe (BER, 297). Evidence that the rest of the 100 sonnets by Raphael existed is summarized by DeVane, who points out that Guido Reni possessed the sonnets, as the poem indicates, and that they were subsequently lost (DEVA, 277n). (Continued under this reference in the Supplement to Citations and Notes.)

Fig. 107
Raphael
Sketch for the *Disputa*
British Museum
London

In stanza 2, line 10, "that one" is probably Raphael's "Lady of the sonnets," his famous loved one who was the subject for many of his paintings. These are *La Velata*, in the Palazzo Pitti, in Florence; *La Fornarina*, in the Palazzo Barberini, in Rome; the *Sistine Madonna*, formerly in Piacenza and now in the Dresden Gallery; the Mary Magdalen in the *St. Cecilia*, in the Pinacoteca Nazionale, in Bologna; the *Phrygian Sibyl*, in the Church of Santa Maria della Pace, in Rome; and the *Portrait of a Lady*, in the Kestner Museum, in Hannover (DUS, 32). Harrington believes that the reference "that one" is to the painting *La Fornarina* (HARR, 162), while Porter and Clarke think that the same reference is to both *La Fornarina* and *La Velata* (POR, V, 299). But on several counts I would support the choice of *La Velata* (Fig. 108). First, of all the likenesses of Raphael's loved one only *La Velata* may be found in Florence, which is the main setting in the poem. Second, Browning probably read in Vasari's *Lives* that the painting of La Velata was considered by Vasari as a close likeness of Raphael's loved one (VAS, III, 184). And third, although we cannot be sure that Browning was aware of the fact, the original *La Velata* depicted St. Catherine (DUS, 32), a religious subject more in keeping with the reverent tone of Browning's poem than the sensual semi-nude *La Fornarina* (Fig. 231). Korg, on the other hand, nominates the *Sistine Madonna* because it is mentioned in the present text under stanza 3, line 22 (KO, 136).

Altogether, in stanza 3, lines 22-25, Browning refers to four Madonnas painted by Raphael. Clearly "Her, San Sisto names" is the *Sistine Madonna*, in the Staatliche Kunstsammlungen, in Dresden (Fig. 109), and "Her, Foligno," is the *Madonna of Foligno*, now in the Vatican Museum (Fig. 110; POR, V, 299). For the one that "visits Florence in a vision" (Fig. 111) and the one with the "lilies in the Louvre" (Fig. 112), we have Browning's own testimony to Rolfe (ROL, 196):

> The Madonna at Florence is that called del Granduca, which represents her 'as appearing to a votary in a vision'—so say the describers; it is in the earlier manner, and very beautiful . . . about the one in the Louvre I think I meant La Belle Jardiniere —but am not sure—from the picture in the Louvre.

Other Madonnas by Raphael in Florence are the *Madonna of the Baldacchino*, the *Madonna of the Sedia*, and the *Madonna of the Impannata*, all in the Palazzo Pitti along with the *Madonna del*

Fig. 108
Raphael
La Velata
Palazzo Pitti
Florence

Fig. 109
Raphael
Sistine Madonna
Staatliche Kunstsammlungen
Dresden

Fig. 110
Raphael
Madonna of Foligno
Picture Gallery
Vatican

Fig. 111
Raphael
Madonna del Granduca
Palazzo Pitti
Florence

Fig. 112
Raphael
La Belle Jardinière
Louvre
Paris

Granduca mentioned above (Map F:9G); and the *Madonna of the Cardellino,* in the Uffizi (Map F:8H). In the Louvre there are also the *Madonna of Loreto,* the *Madonna with the Diadem,* the *Holy Family of Francis I,* and the Madonna in a group called the *Holy Family.*

In stanza 5, line 32, the "angel" that Dante drew is the mysterious "Beatrice" described in his poetry. We may surmise from Dante's own account, as given in DeVane, that Dante actually drew the angel, but there is no evidence that the drawing still exists (DEVA, 277), and Browning, in stanza 7, line 53, states that "You and I will never see that picture." (Continued under this reference in the Supplement to Citations and Notes.)

    15:144-52; 16:164

> ... Lo, the moon's self!
> Here in London, yonder late in Florence,
> Still we find her face, the thrice-transfigured.
> Curving on a sky imbrued with color,
> Drifted over Fiesole by twilight,
> Came she, our new crescent of a hair's-breadth.
> Full she flared it, lamping Samminiato,
> Rounder 'twixt the cypresses and rounder,
> Perfect till the nightingales applauded.
> ...
> [One side of the moon is]
> Blind to Galileo on his turret. ...

"Samminiato," the Church of San Miniato al Monte, is located on a hill southeast of Florence (Fig. 113). Near the church Galileo could have made astronomical experiments "on his turret" from Il Gioiello, his villa at Arcetri, on the outskirts of Florence. Of the four other Florentine residences illustrated in Maria Bonelli and William Shea's book *Galileo's Florentine Residences* (Florence: Istituto e Museo di Storia della Scienza, n.d., pp. 16, 21, 22, 30, 51), only Il Gioiello has a tower (Fig. 114). And Villa Gioiello, according to Professor Paolo Galluzzi, director of the above-mentioned historical institute and museum of science in Florence, was most likely the one open to tourists in Browning's time, just as it is the only one open to the public today. Barfucci, on the other hand, illustrates the Villa Torre al Gallo as the tower used by Galileo for his experiments (BAR, 276). The villa is near Il Gioiello and is the most conspicuous structure silhouetting the skyline on top of the hill above San Miniato. Pettigrew's idea that the turret from which Galileo

Fig. 113
Church of San Miniato al Monte
Florence

made his experiments is the Bell-tower—the Leaning Tower—of Pisa is true in point of fact (PET, 1147), but it is not, it seems to me, consistent with the Florentine setting of the poem.

Fig. 114
Il Gioiello
Galileo's Villa at Arcetri
Florence (environs)

OF PACCHIAROTTO, AND HOW HE WORKED IN DISTEMPER

2:5-19

> He [Pacchiarotto], pupil of old Fungaio,
> Is always confounded (heigho!)
> With Pacchia, contemporaneous
> No question, but how extraneous
> In the grace of soul, the power
> Of hand,—undoubted dower
> Of Pacchia who decked (as *we* know,
> My Kirkup!) San Bernardino,
> Turning the small dark Oratory
> To Siena's Art-laboratory,
> As he made its straitness roomy
> And glorified its gloomy,
> With Bazzi and Beccafumi.
> (Another heigho for Bazzi:
> How people miscall him Razzi!)

Giacomo di Bartolommeo Pacchiarotto (1471-1540), the pupil of "Fungaio," that is, Bernardino Fungai (1460-1516), was a Sienese painter and political reformer. The artistic contemporaries of Pacchiarotto were "Pacchia" (1477-1535), "Beccafumi" (1488-1551), and "Bazzi," the last more commonly known as Sodoma (1477-1549). Frescoes by these contemporaries are in the famous "Oratory" of "San Bernardino," in Siena (Fig. 115). Frescoes in the oratory by Pacchia are the *Nativity of the Virgin, St. Bernardine,* the *Announcing Archangel Gabriel,* and the *Annunciation.* Those by Beccafumi are the *Marriage of the Virgin,* the *Virgin in Glory with Saints,* and the *Translation of the Virgin.* And those by Sodoma are *San Lodovico,* the *Presentation of the Virgin in the Temple, St. Anthony of Padua,* the *Assumption, St. Francis of Assisi,* and the *Coronation of the Virgin.* For another reference to Browning's friend "My Kirkup," see below under *A Soul's Tragedy.*

5:64-75

> So, the painter Pacchiarotto
> Constructed himself a grotto
> In the quarter of Stalloreggi—
> As authors of note allege ye.
> And on each of the whitewashed sides of it
> He painted—(none far and wide so fit
> As he to perform in fresco)—

He painted nor cried *quiesco*
Till he peopled its every square foot
With Man—from the Beggar barefoot
To the Noble in cap and feather;
All sorts and conditions together.

Fig. 115
Oratory of San Bernardino
Siena

"As authors of note allege," that is, as Vasari and Baldinucci record it (DEVA, 397), the painter Pacchiarotto had a house in the "quarter of Stalloreggi," in Siena, and the house contained frescoes depicting men in "All sorts and conditions together," that is, in all stations of life. Investigation reveals, however, that although the street Via Stalloreggi still exists on the south side of Siena, the house and the frescoes no longer are standing (SOS).

14:233-37

> These Spare-Horses forthwith assembled:
> Neighed words whereat citizens trembled
> As oft as the chiefs, in the Square by
> The Duomo, proposed a way whereby
> The city were cured of disaster.

For the "Square by / The Duomo"—the Piazza del Duomo, in Siena—see Fig. 22. For a reference to the pavement in the Duomo, see above under "Cleon," 82-88.

17:307-09

> Lately was coffered
> A corpse in its sepulchre, situate
> By St. John's Observance.

"St. John's Observance," or the Basilica dell' Osservanza, stands on a hill outside the Porta Ovile about a mile and a half north of Siena (Fig. 116). Pacchiarotto took sanctuary in the church for protection against political persecution (DEVA, 397-98).

PARLEYINGS WITH FRANCIS FURINI

1:3-7

> ... you [Francis Furini] walked Tuscan earth,
>   a painter-priest.
> Something about two hundred years ago.
> Priest—you did duty punctual as the sun
> That rose and set above Saint Sano's church
> Blessing Mugello. ...

Francis Furini (c. 1600-1649) was a Florentine painter who became a priest of the Church of Sant' Ansano—"Saint Sano" —in Borgo di San Lorenzo, in Mugello, north of Florence. Furini's life is described in Filippo Baldinucci's *Notizie de'*

Fig. 116
Basilica dell'Osservanza
Siena

professori del disegno (DEVA, 513), Browning's historical source for "Filippo Baldinucci on the Privilege of Burial," "Beatrice Signorini," and "Of Pacchiarotto, and How He Worked in Distemper." In 1903 a painting of Sant' Ansano, by Furini, was stolen from the Church of Sant' Ansano. In spite of severe earthquakes over the years, the church still stands "blessing Mugello" (SAN; Fig. 118).

Fig. 117
Adrian van Ostade
Boors Making Merry (detail)
Dulwich Picture Gallery
London

Fig. 118
Church of Sant' Ansano, bell-tower
Borgo di San Lorenzo
Mugello, Italy

3:141-43

> ... Andromeda—
> God's best of beauteous and magnificent
> Revealed to earth—the naked female form.

As noted in the Thieme-Becker *Lexikon,* Furini rendered a painting of "Andromeda" (THI, XII, 596), which could be associated with the present text. Also, compare the reference to *Perseus and Andromeda* below under *Pauline,* 656-67, the mention of Volpato above under "A Likeness," 60-61, and the discussion in DEVA, 515.

3:176-81

> ... mere lust
> Inspired the artist [Michelangelo] when his Night and Morn
> Slept and awoke in marble on that edge
> Of heaven above our awe-struck earth: lust-born
> His Eve low bending took the privilege
> Of life from what our eyes saw—God's own palm....

Porter and Clarke identify "Night and Morn" as two of the statues by Michelangelo in the Medici Chapel in the Church of San Lorenzo, Florence (Fig. 119, Map F:7H), and they identify "Eve" as one of the frescoes by Michelangelo in the Sistine Chapel of the Vatican (POR, XII, 350). These frescoes depicting Eve are the *Creation of Eve* (Fig. 120) and the *Temptation and Expulsion.* Also, compare the description here of the statues in the Medici Chapel with that of Elizabeth Barrett Browning in her earlier work *Casa Guidi Windows,* I.73ff.

11:601-07

> *Now as she fain would bathe, one even-tide,*
> *God's maid, this Joan, from the pool's edge she spied*
> *The fair blue bird clowns call the Fisher-king:*
> *And "'Las, sighed she, my Liege is such a thing*
> *As thou, lord but of one poor lonely place*
> *Out of his whole wide France: were mine the grace*
> *To set my Dauphin free as thou, blue bird!"*

DeVane tells us that these seven lines, before they were inserted into this poem, were written by Browning to accompany his son's painting *Joan of Arc and the Kingfisher,* which was exhibited in the Grosvenor Gallery in 1886 (DEVA, 514). The picture shows a female nude, as Joan of Arc, standing over the edge

Fig. 119
Michelangelo
Morn
Tomb of Lorenzo de' Medici (detail)
Medici Chapel
Church of San Lorenzo
Florence

Fig. 120
Michelangelo
Creation of Eve (detail)
Sistine Chapel
Vatican

of a pool watching a kingfisher flying over the water. At present, the painting is housed at Yaddo, the Trask family estate in Saratoga Springs, New York (KEL, 541, item K43).

PAULINE

656-67

> Andromeda!
> And she is with me: years roll, I shall change,
> But change can touch her not—so beautiful
> With her fixed eyes, earnest and still, and hair
> Lifted and spread by the salt-sweeping breeze,
> And one red beam, all the storm leaves in heaven
> Resting upon her eyes and hair, such hair,
> As she awaits the snake on the wet beach
> By the dark rock and the white wave just breaking
> At her feet; quite naked and alone; a thing
> I doubt not, nor fear for, secure some god
> To save will come in thunder from the stars.

The "Andromeda" that is "with me"—that is, with the speaker Browning—is most likely an etching that hung over Browning's writing desk while he was composing his early poems. The etching is a copy of Polidoro da Caravaggio's *Perseus and Andromeda*, a fresco which formerly adorned a garden wall in Palazzo Bufalo, in Rome (ORR, 21n; POR, I, 306; Fig. 121). Browning mentions the "great Caldara Polidore" in "Waring" (VI, 152), and in two letters to Elizabeth Barrett he speaks of "my Polidoro" and "my perfect Polidoro" (KIN, 27, 704). The etching has been claimed as the one done by Volpato in 1772 (Fig. 122), but no facts have been put forth substantiating the claim (DUF, i-ii). I believe that a case for this source can be made, however, by examining internal evidence in Browning's poem "A Likeness" in conjunction with one of the letters mentioned above. In "A Likeness," Browning speaks of "prints, an imbroglio, / Fifty in one portfolio" (42-43), one print of which appears to be "Volpato's" (61). Browning, as Griffin and Minchin phrase it, "rescued" prints from his father's collection (GRI, 123), and the reference in "A Likeness" to Volpato could very well be to the etching of *Perseus and Andromeda*. In the above-mentioned letter to Elizabeth dated February 26, 1845, Browning explains why he rescued what appears in the present context to be Volpato's etching of Polidoro's *Andromeda* (KIN, I, 27):

> I have not little insight to the feelings of furniture, and treat books and prints with a reasonable consideration—how some

Fig. 121
Polidoro da Caravaggio
Perseus and Andromeda
Museo di Roma
Rome

people use their pictures, for instance, is a mystery to me—very
revolting all the same: portraits obliged to face each other for
ever,—prints put together in portfolios . . . [sic] my Polidoro's
perfect Andromeda along with "Boors Carousing," by Ostade,—
where I found her,—my own father's doing, or I would say more.

The implication is, then, that just as Perseus rescues Andromeda
from her predicament, so too Browning rescues the Volpato
Perseus and Andromeda from the "imbroglio" of his father's

Fig. 122
Volpato
Perseus and Andromeda
British Museum

portfolios of prints—from the indignity of "Boors Carousing" in "face" of the Volpato—and then safely hangs the Volpato over his desk.

An impression of the etching by Volpato is housed today in the Department of Prints and Drawings in the British Museum, but whether or not this is the one Browning owned is not known, for the museum cannot account for its origin. The original fresco by Polidoro da Caravaggio, though in poor condition, may be seen in the Museo di Roma, in Rome. The garden wall in Palazzo Bufalo on which the fresco was originally painted has been torn down since Browning's time, but the Palazzo Bufalo itself still stands on Via Bufalo, which is near the Piazza San Silvestro (Fig. 123; Map R:7H,7I). For an illustration of the fresco on the wall with other frescoes, see MA, II, 135-36.

The original painting by Ostade is in the Dulwich Picture Gallery and is entered in the gallery's catalogue as no. 115, *Boors Making Merry*. It came to the gallery in the Bourgeois bequest of 1811 (DULW, 52) and so was no doubt seen by Browning during his many visits to the gallery (Fig. 117). Perhaps seeing the original painting is what gave Browning the idea of rescuing the Volpato from the Ostade while going through the prints in his father's portfolios, and/or there is the possibility that Browning's act of saving the Volpato was influenced by the following words of William Hazlett, which stress the inappropriate placing of the Ostade among other paintings in the Dulwich Gallery (HAZ, 46):

> *Boors Merry-Making*, by Ostade, is fine;
> but has no business where it is.

Fig. 123
Palazzo Bufalo
Rome

PICTOR IGNOTUS: FLORENCE, 15—

1-2

> I could have painted pictures like that youth's
> Ye praise so.

For the controversy as to whether or not Fra Bartolommeo is a model for the Pictor Ignotus, see J. B. Bullen's "Browning's 'Pictor Ignotus' and Vasari's 'Life of Fra Bartolommeo di San Marco'" (BUL, 313-19); Michael H. Bright's rebuttal, "Browning's Celebrated Pictor Ignotus" (BRI, 192-94); Bullen's reply, "Fra Bartolommeo's Quest for Obscurity" (BULL, 206-09); and Bright's rejoinder, "A Reply to Fra Bartolommeo's Quest for Obscurity" (BRI, 209-15).   Other commentators in the controversy are Ian Jack, David DeLaura, and Jacob Korg, who further support Bullen's theory (JAC, 208-13; DEL, 367-88; KO, 62-64).   The proponents of Fra Bartolommeo as a model for the Pictor Ignotus maintain that (1) although Fra Bartolommeo was a public figure during his lifetime, he did, at one point, seek anonymity; and (2) even though Fra Bartolommeo employed the technique of the naturalist school of painting characteristic of the early sixteenth century, he differed from the naturalists in his piety and his exclusive use of religious subjects for his paintings.   Central to this argument is the art treatise by Alexis François Rio, *De la poesie chrétienne*, which is mentioned by Bullen and fully developed by DeLaura as a source for the poem.

The "youth" mentioned here and at the end of the poem is commonly accepted as a reference to Raphael, who was personally known to Fra Bartolommeo and was a prime representative of the naturalist school of painting during the early 1500's (BUL, 315; DEVA, 156; BRI, 193; DEL, 372).

25-26, 31-33

> Nor will I say I have not dreamed (how well!)
> Of going—I, in each picture,—forth, [with]
> . . .
> Flowers cast upon the car which bore the freight,
> Through old streets named afresh from the event,
> Till it reached home. . . .

What the speaker has "dreamed" is no doubt based on an account from Vasari's biography of Cimabue (DEVA, 156; VAS, I,

9-10). The "freight" is Cimabue's supposed painting of the *Rucellai Madonna* (Fig. 124). The "going . . . forth" is the presumed bearing of the painting from Cimabue's studio to the Rucellai Chapel in the Church of Santa Maria Novella, in Florence, where Vasari claims the painting was mounted (Map F:7G). The "old" street supposedly "named afresh" from the "event" is Borgo Allegri, which still exists adjoining the Church of Santa Croce (VAS, I, 10n; Map F:8I).

But research in the last century indicates that Vasari's report of the event is false and that the *Rucellai Madonna* is by Duccio, not Cimabue (KO, 101; STU, I, 23; WH, 33). Vasari's account of the procession, presumably from Cimabue's studio to the Church of Santa Maria Novella, is probably based on early chronicles describing Duccio's *Maestà* as it was carried in procession and installed in the Cathedral of Siena (STU, 25, 26). And the street Borgo Allegri was probably named after the Allegri family (MUR, 230) rather than the felicitousness—thus the word "Allegri"—of the presumed procession from Cimabue's studio to the Church of Santa Maria Novella (DEVA, 156). In 1937 the *Rucellai Madonna* was exhibited at the Nostra Giottesca, and since 1948 the picture has been on loan from the Church of Santa Maria Novella to the Uffizi, where it hangs today (STU, 23).

38-41

> And then not go to heaven, but linger here,
> Here on my earth, earth's every man my friend,—
> The thought grew frightful, 't was so wildly dear!
> But a voice changed it.

The "voice" here is generally thought to be that of Savonarola, whose preaching inspired Fra Bartolommeo to become a Dominican monk (BRI, 193; BUL, 318; DEL, 372; KO, 63). In this context, Fra Bartolommeo's famous portrait of Savonarola comes to my mind as the image of how the visage attending the "voice" appeared to Bartolommeo (Fig. 225). The portrait may be seen by the public today in one of the cells of the Convent of San Marco, in Florence. Browning, if we can be sure that he went to Florence in 1844, as several commentators suggest he did (DEVA, 155; IRV, 142; MAJ, 23; KO, 62), probably saw the picture then and/or read about it in Vasari (VAS, III, 66) before his poem was published in 1845. For more about Fra Bartolommeo, see above under 1-2.

Fig. 124
Duccio
Rucellai Madonna
Uffizi
Florence

THE PIED PIPER OF HAMELIN

21-22

> ... the people in a body
> To the Town Hall came flocking. ...

The proper year for the legendary events in this poem is 1284 (DEVA, 130). At that time there was a "Town Hall," but what remained of it was destroyed during World War II (HUM).

146-47

> You should have heard the Hamelin people
> Ringing the bells till they rocked the steeple.

In 1284, there were two churches in Hamelin that had "bells" and a "steeple": the Church of St. Boniface, which was on the right bank of the Weser River, and the Church of St. Nicholas, which was in the center of town next to the market place. Both churches were leveled during the blitz (HUM).

153-54

> ... up the face
> Of the Piper perked in the market-place. ...

The site of the "market-place" in 1284 corresponded to the one today. It was in the center of town next to the Church of St. Nicholas (HUM). For other references to the Church of St. Nicholas, see above under 146-47 and below under 277-88.

216-17

> ... the Piper turned from the High Street
> To where the Weser rolled its waters. ...

A "High Street" has never existed in Hamelin. The two main streets are the Osterstrasse, which goes from the market place to the eastern gate, and the Bäckerstrasse, which extends from the market place to the west (HUM).

277-88

> The place of the children's last retreat,
> They called it, the Pied Piper's Street—
> Where any one playing on pipe or tabor
> Was sure for the future to lose his labor.
> Nor suffered they hostelry or tavern
>   To shock with mirth a street so solemn;
> But opposite the place of the cavern
>   They wrote the story on a column.
> And on the great church-window painted
> The same, to make the world acquainted
> How their children were stolen away,
> And there it stands to this very day.

There has never been a "Pied Piper's Street" in Hamelin. What Browning refers to is the "Bungelosestrasse," which as a word has been current since the 15th century. The word, when analyzed by its parts, means drum ("bunge")-less ("lose") street ("strasse"), that is, the drum-less street, where musicians were forbidden to play, or, as Browning puts it, "Where any one playing on pipe or tabor / Was sure for the future to lose his labor." The idea in the above passage that the story of the Pied Piper was written on a "column" is in accord with local tradition, but the actual existence of such a column has never been proven. The "great church-window painted" with the story of the Piper was in the Church of St. Nicholas sometime before 1571. In 1654, a certain Samuel Erich provided an inscription for the window, but in 1660 the window was replaced and subsequently lost (HUM). DeVane suggests that Browning either visited Hamelin in 1834 on his way to Russia in order to attend a celebration in Hamelin of the 550th anniversary of the visit of the Piper or that he passed through Hamelin in 1838 on his way home from Italy (DEVA, 130).

PIPPA PASSES

Intro. 89-90

>   . . .
> New-blown and ruddy as St. Agnes' nipple,
> Plump as the flesh-bunch on some Turk bird's poll!

Rolfe and Hersey venture that Pippa has in mind some picture
in the Duomo of Asolo which represents St. Agnes (ROL, 182).
But inquiry into local archives reveals that there is no painting
of the saint either in the Duomo of Asolo or in the environs of
Asolo (RIG).

Intro. 130-31

> For do not our Bride and Bridegroom sally
> Out of Possagno church at noon?

As Rolfe and Hersey point out, the "Possagno church" is
probably the Tempio, that is, the Temple of Possagno. Designed
by Canova, the Tempio represents the most suitable place for the
marriage of Jules, a fellow sculptor and admirer of Canova (ROL,
183; Fig. 125). For another reference to the work of Canova, see
below under I. 375-94.

Fig. 125
Canova
Temple of Possagno
Possagno
Italy

Intro. 171-73

> ... the evening walk
> Of Luigi and his mother, always ends
> Inside our ruined turret ....

The "ruined turret" is the old castle of Asolo, which overlooks the town (ROL, 183; Fig. 126). The turret is the setting for Act III.

Fig. 126
Right: Castle of Asolo
Left: Villa of Caterina Cornaro

Intro. 180-82

> ... why not have God's love befall
> Myself as, in the Palace by the Dome,
> Monsignor?

The "Palace by the Dome" is the Palazzo Governo, which is close to the "Dome," or Duomo, of Asolo (ROL, 183). The Palazzo Governo, as may be seen in Fig. 127, is the building that is covered with frescoes and has a portico. Today it serves as the Museo Civico of Asolo. In Act IV the palace provides a setting for the action. For another reference to the Duomo of Asolo, see below under I. 58-61.

Fig. 127
Center left foreground: Palazzo Governo
Center left rear :   Villa of Caterina Cornaro
                         Asolo

I.28-29

Otti.   Ah, the clear morning! I can see Saint Mark's;
         That black streak is the belfry.

From Asolo, Venice is indeed visible. In 1902 the "belfry" of the
Church of St. Mark collapsed and was rebuilt as shown in Figs.
201 and 216. For other references to the Church of St. Mark, see
above under *Fifine at the Fair*, 107:1846, and below under
Sordello, I.820-21, III.136-37, and "A Toccata of Galuppi's," 5-8.

I.58-61

Otti.   There trudges on his business from the Duomo
         Benet the Capuchin, with his brown hood
         And bare feet; always in one place at church,
         Close under the stone wall by the south entry.

Fig. 128 shows the "south entry" of the "Duomo" of Asolo as it
looks today. Also see above under the Intro. 180-82.

I.375-94

1st Stud.   Well, this
             Jules ... a wretched fribble—oh, I watched
             his disportings at Possagno, the other day!
             Canova's gallery—you know: there he marches
             first resolvedly past great works by the dozen
             without vouchsafing an eye: all at once he stops
             full at the *Psiche-fanciulla*—cannot pass that
             old acquaintance without a nod of encourage-
             ment—"In your new place, beauty? Then
             behave yourself as well here as at Munich—I
             see you!" Next he posts himself deliberately
             before the unfinished *Pietà* for half an hour
             without moving, till up he starts of a sudden,
             and thrusts his very nose into—I say, into—
             the group; by which gesture you are informed
             that precisely the sole point he had not fully
             mastered in Canova's practice was a certain
             method of using the drill in the articulation of
             the knee-joint—and that, likewise, has he mas-
             tered at length!

The 1st Student is describing Jules as he ranges through
Canova's gallery in Possagno, the Gipsoteca. The two sculptures
in the gallery examined by Jules are the *Psiche-fanciulla* and the
Pietà. As he is being quoted by the 1st Student speaking of the

Fig. 128
Duomo
Asolo
Italy

Psiche-fanciulla, Jules states, " . . . here as at Munich—I see you!" which means that he has seen both a version of the sculpture in Munich and "here," that is, here in the Gipsoteca in Possagno, from where he is quoted speaking. The version of the sculpture in the Gipsoteca is dated 1789 and is a plaster-of-Paris model of a head catalogued as a *Muse or Psyche* (GIP, 22). The version at Munich was one of two marble statues of the *Psiche-fanciulla* that were executed for private parties as late as 1796 (RIZ, 37). Morse Peckham places one of these statues in Munich, but he does not determine the present whereabouts of the statue (KING, III, 347). My own inquiries have led me to the Kunsthalle, in Bremen, where one of the marble statues is presently located. But the Kunsthalle informs me that because of inadequate records kept during World War II, they do not know if their statue is the one that was originally in Munich (GERK). My inquiries into state archives in Munich, however, verify that the *Psiche-fanciulla* in Bremen is actually the one that was in Munich. After Napoleon acquired the statue, he gave it to the Bavarian Queen Caroline in 1807. From that year to 1930 the statue was in Munich, at different times, in both the Biederstein Castle and the Residenz. In 1930, the statue was removed from the Biederstein Castle—which was demolished in 1934—and auctioned off by Helbing, in Munich. From Munich the statue went into the hands of a private collector in Bremen, and, in 1943, the statue was given to the Kunsthalle in Bremen as a gift (MILL; Fig. 129).

The *Pietà* is another plaster-of-Paris sculpture, though executed later in 1821 (Fig. 130). Canova intended to finish the model in marble but died before its completion. A bronze version was made from the model by Bartolommeo Ferrari in 1830 and placed in Canova's Tempio at Possagno (KING, III, 347). For a direct reference to Canova's Tempio, see above under the Intro. 130-31. Browning undoubtedly saw both models for the *Psiche-fanciulla* and the *Pietà* when he visited Possagno in 1838, three years prior to publishing *Pippa Passes*. Also, he probably viewed the finished marble version of the *Psiche-fanciulla* when he visited Munich in the same year. For other references to works of art that Browning probably saw in Munich at this time, see above under "Andrea del Sarto," 103-12, and "My Last Duchess," 54-56, paragraph 2.

Fig. 129
Canova
Psiche-fanciulla
Kunsthalle
Bremen
West Germany

Fig. 130
Canova
Pietà
Gipsoteca
Possagno
Italy

I.413-14

. . . somebody had seen his [Jules's] Tydeus at the
Academy, and my picture was nothing to it. . . .

This statue by Jules is imaginary.

II. 49-55

> ... better that will look
> When cast in bronze—an Almaign Kaiser, that,
> Swart-green and gold, with truncheon based on hip.
> This, rather, turn to! What, unrecognized?
> I thought you would have seen that here you sit
> As I imagined you,—Hippolyta,
> Naked upon her bright Numidian horse.

Morse Peckham thinks that a possible source for this imaginary bronze statue of an "Almaign Kaiser" is in Innsbruck, where Jules presumably stopped on his way to Italy from Munich (see above under I.375-94 for the reference to Munich). Browning, too, we know, stopped at Innsbruck during his trip in 1838, which was prior to the publishing of *Pippa Passes*. In the Court Church of Innsbruck are a sixteenth-century bronze monument in honor of Emperor Maximilian I and bronze statues of heroic size, a number of which are of German emperors (KING, III, 348). For the view that these bronze works are a possible source for the bronze statue of Neptune by the imaginary Claus of Innsbruck, see above under "My Last Duchess," 54-56. The statue of "Hippolyta" in the present passage is also imaginary.

II. 271-74

> Jules *resumes*.
> What name was that the little girl sang forth?
> Kate? The Cornaro, doubtless, who renounced
> The crown of Cyprus to be lady here
> At Asolo, where still her memory stays....

Caterina "Cornaro" (1454-1510) was Queen of Cyprus but was forced to resign after Cyprus was annexed by Venice. In 1489 she took up residence in Asolo and occupied the palace illustrated in Figs. 126 and 127, "where still her memory stays" (ROL, 187). Also, see "Inapprehensiveness," lines 3, 4, 12, and 13 for a reference to the tower of Queen Cornaro's Villa (DEVA, 533; added at publication time).

III. 162-63

> *Luigi.*   We were to see together
>   The Titian at Treviso.

Berdoe identifies this painting as the *Annunciation*, by Titian (Fig. 131), located in the Cathedral of Treviso, which is near Asolo, the locale for the play (BER, 353). Korg points out that

Fig. 131
Titian
Annunciation (detail)
Cathedral
Treviso
Italy

there is another Titian at Treviso, a portrait of Sperone Speroni in the Bailo Museum, but he allows only for the *Annunciation* in the present context because it is what he calls "an emblem of the joys of life that Luigi is giving up, and a measure of his sacrifice" (KO, 44). The portrait of Speroni, however, I think might also apply here, inasmuch as, pending future research, a connection might be shown between Luigi's patriotism and Speroni's humanism.

PONTE DELL' ANGELO, VENICE

7-12

> An angel visibly guards yon house:
> Above each scutcheon—a pair—stands he,
> Enfolds them with droop of either wing:
> The family's fortune were perilous
> Did he thence depart—you will soon agree,
> If I hitch into verse the thing.

The art object around which the plot of this poem revolves is located on the façade of the Soranzo Palace, at the Bridge of the Angel—Ponte dell' Angelo—just off Piazza San Marco, in Venice. It is an altar in the form of a marble sculpture in bas-relief on which is carved the figure of an angel whose wing tips hover over "each scutcheon," that is, over the two family shields below the wings (Fig. 132). According to the legend that the narrator relates, the devil had passed through a breach in the stonework which he had made when he escaped from the palace. The marble bas-relief with the angel on it was put over the breach in order to protect the inhabitants of the dwelling from the devil by preventing his return through the breach (DEVA, 540-42).

THE POPE AND THE NET

13-15

> And straightway in his palace-hall, where commonly is set
> Some coat-of-arms, some portraiture ancestral, lo, we met
> His mean estate's reminder in his fisher-father's net!

Fig. 132
Altar
Palazzo Soranzo (façade)
Venice

According to DeVane, Pope Sextus V is the prelate alluded to in the title of this poem (DEVA, 537-37). "His palace-hall," then, I think could be the Sistine Great Hall in the Palazzo Apostolico of the Vatican, which was built by Sextus in 1587.

PRINCE HOHENSTIEL-SCHWANGAU, SAVIOUR OF SOCIETY

6-8

> Suppose my Oedipus should lurk at last
> Under a pork-pie hat and crinoline,
> And, latish, pounce on Sphinx in Leicester Square?

The imaginary object here is a statue of a "Sphinx in Leicester Square," in London. For a reference to a real statue that existed in Leicester Square, see below under 184-87, 194-96.

184-87, 194-96

> No doubt, you, good young lady that you are,
> Despite a natural naughtiness or two,
> Turn eyes up like a Pradier Magdalen
> And see an outspread providential hand....
> . . .
> Well, I believe that such a hand may stoop,
> And such appeals to it may stave off harm,
> Pacify the grim guardian of this Square....

The female companion of the Prince is represented by a "Pradier Magdalen," an imaginary statue by the French sculptor James Pradier (1793-1852), who is not known to have fashioned a Magdalen. But a possible source for this statue may be, I think, Pradier's *Marriage of the Virgin*, a marble statue in the Church of the Madeleine, in Paris. DeVane dates the composition of *Prince Hohenstiel-Schwangau, Saviour of Society* to 1871 and notes that Browning's trips to Paris in 1851 and 1856 were opportunities to observe the political career of Napoleon III, the model for Prince Hohenstiel-Schwangau (DEVA, 358-63). Perhaps Browning, in recalling his trips to Paris fifteen to twenty years later in England, confused Pradier's 1837 sculpture of the Marriage of the Virgin with the name of the church where it is housed—the Church of the Madeleine—and assumed that Mary Magdalen, rather than the Virgin Mary, was the subject of the sculpture. The Church of the Madeleine, it should be noted, was consecrated in 1842, nine years before Browning's first trip to Paris.

In the passage "the grim guardian of this Square," the square is Leicester Square, identified above under 6-8. The "grim Guardian" may be what Allan Dooley conceives to be a real policeman (DOO, 14), or, according to the *Browning Society Papers*, what was a real statue of George I (BROW, II, 198).

Charles Knight tells us that the statue was "much knockt about" and is now destroyed (KNIG, VI, 71). John Timbs describes the statue as it looked in Leicester Square (TIM, 513):

> In the center [of Leicester Square], upon a sculptured stone pedestal, is an equestrian metal statue of George I, modelled by C. Buchard for the Duke of Chandos, and brought from Canons in 1747, when it was "finely gilt," and within memory was regilt, but its history has been much disputed. Over this statue was built a colossal Model of the Earth, which became one of the most intellectual exhibitions of the metropolis. This statue has also been described as that of the Duke of Cumberland, the hero of Culloden, which may have arisen from the Duke's birth at Leicester House in 1721.

For another reference to a presumed statue in Leicester Square, see above under 6-8.

850-55

>   ... what suspends
> The breath in them [the clergy] is not the plaster-patch
> Time disengages from the painted wall
> Where Rafael moulderingly bids adieu,
> Nor tick of the insect turning tapestry
> Which a queen's finger traced of old, to dust. ...

The "plaster-patch" paintings by "Rafael" are probably the frescoes in the Raphael Rooms in the Vatican, as described below under *A Soul's Tragedy* and above under "Andrea del Sarto," 185-87. The "tapestry" is most likely one of those by Raphael housed in the Vatican. They have been used to adorn the base of the walls in the Sistine Chapel on great occasions. Dussler tells us that a total of ten tapestries depicting scenes from the lives of Christ and the Apostles were commissioned for Raphael by Pope Leo X in 1513-14. The cartoons for the tapestries were sent to the workshop of Pieter van Aelst, in Brussels, and the first tapestry was completed in 1517. Browning's description of the tapestry as one "Which a queen's finger traced of old" possibly refers to one of the many copies that were made—that is, "traced"—from the tapestries. No "queen of old" that I know of had a hand—or, as the text puts it, "a finger"—in the copywork, but, as Dussler records, replicas of the tapestries were ordered for Prince Charles of England in 1619. They were made in Pieter van Aelst's workshop and were based on Cleyn's copy of the original cartoons.

Today they are housed in the Garde-Meuble, in Paris. In 1623 Prince Charles further made the purchase of seven of the original cartoons for the Royal Collection. They are now hanging in the Victoria and Albert Museum. Copies of the tapestries may be seen, among other places, in the Palazzo Ducale, in Mantua; the Palazzo Ducale, in Urbino; the Royal Palace, in Madrid; and the Museo della Santa Casa, in Loreto (DUS, 100-08).

861-65

"Stamp out the nature that's best typified
By its embodiment in Peter's Dome,
The scorpion-body with the greedy pair
Of outstretched nippers, either colonnade
Agape for the advance of heads and hearts!"

This image of a "greedy" church is based on an aerial view of the Basilica and colonnade of St. Peter's, in Rome (Fig. 133). From above, the main part of the church looks like a "scorpion-body," and the curving colonnade like a "pair / Of outstretched nippers."   "Peter's Dome" itself suggests that a papal tiara—which has the shape of a dome—surmounts the scorpion-body of the church. For a reference to and an illustration of a papal tiara, see below under *The Ring and the Book*, I.896-903, Figs. 154 and 155.   For another reference to a church in Rome—the Gesù —symbolizing a criticism of the Catholic Church, see below under *The Ring and the Book*, III. 103-04.   Also see above under *Christmas-Eve*, 10:526-76, and *Easter-Day*, 26:798-802; and below under *The Ring and the Book*, VI.702-07.

1184-89

... a statue, luckless like myself,
I saw at Rome once! 'T was some artist's whim
To cover all the accessories close
I' the group, and leave you only Laocoön
With neither sons nor serpents to denote
the purpose of his gesture.

The "Laocoön," the ancient Greek group sculpture that the speaker "saw at Rome," is housed today in the Vatican courtyard along with a more intact Roman copy (POR, IX, 292).   Another copy, by Baccio Bandinelli, can be seen in the Uffizi (Map F:8H). As can be imagined by looking at Fig. 135, the original Greek version, if "'T was some artist's whim / To cover all the accessories close / I' the group," that is, cover the statue so that "neither sons nor serpents" were visible, then the "purpose of his [Laocoön's] gesture" would have to be determined from the gesture of "only Laocoön" himself. That gesture, interpreted as a satire directed against Napoleon III, the acknowledged model for Browning's poem, is, in lines 1196-98,

> ... a yawn
> Of sheer fatigue subsiding to repose:
> The statue's 'Somnolency' clear enough!

signifying that Napoleon III lacked energy; or, if a more charitable appraisal of Napoleon III's political career is read into the text, the gesture "strives against some obstacle we [the critics of Napoleon III] cannot see" (1194-96).

Fig. 133
Church and Square of St. Peter
Vatican

Fig. 134
Chair and Balduchin
Church of St. Peter
Vatican

PROTUS

1-4

Among these latter busts we count by scores,
Half-emperors and quarter-emperors,
Each with his bay-leaf fillet, loose-thonged vest,
Loric and low-browed Gorgon on the breast. . . .

Fig. 135
Laocoön Group (original Greek version)
Courtyard
Vatican

On the lower floor of the Palace of the Capitoline Museum, halls 4-6, there are numerous portraits and "busts" of "Half-emperors and quarter-emperors" of the imperial era that Browning, I think, could be referring to.   Turner points out that many emperors were half-emperors, that is, they served in pairs. And at one time Diocletian, Maxian, Constantius, and Galerius served as quarter-emperors, that is, between 293-305 A.D. they all reigned simultaneously (TUR, 368).

55-57

> Here's John the Smith's rough-hammered head. Great eye,
> Gross jaw and griped lips do what granite can
> To give you the crown-grasper. What a man!

A possible source for the imaginary "John the Smith's rough-hammered head" is the colossal head of Constantine the Great, mounted in the courtyard of the Palace of the Conservatori, on the Capitoline Hill (Fig. 136; Map R:8H,8I). The portrait, which Browning no doubt saw during his residency in Rome a year or so before his poem was published in 1855, could well have inspired him to use the exaggerated expression "Great eye, / Gross jaw and griped lips."

RAWDON BROWN

6-8

> ... Venice! What a sky,
> A sea, this morning! One last look! Good-by,
> Cà Pesaro!

The architectural landmark in Venice described here is "Cà Pesaro"—Casa Pesaro—which was built by Baldassare Longhena in 1710 (Fig. 137). It is located by San Stae pier on the Grand Canal and today houses the Museum of Modern Art.

Fig. 136
Constantine the Great
Palace of the Conservatori (courtyard)
Capitoline Hill
Rome

Fig. 137
Cà Pesaro
Venice

RED COTTON NIGHT-CAP COUNTRY: OR TURF AND TOWERS

One of the towers indicated in this title is the belvedere (Fig. 138), which Monsieur Antoine Mellerio (known in the poem as Léonce Miranda) built as part of his château at Tailleville (known in the poem as Clairvaux), in Calvados, France. The other tower, which is also in the area and in view of the château from the top of the belvedere, is the steeple of the Church of La Délivrande (Fig. 139, known in the poem as the Church of La Ravissante).

Fig. 138
Château at Tailleville
Calvados, France

THE RING AND THE BOOK

I.1-4, 15-17

Do you see this Ring?

'T is Rome-work, made to match

Fig. 139
Church of La Délivrande
Calvados, France

(By Castellani's imitative craft)
Etrurian circlets found ...
. . .
... hammer needs must widen out the round,
And file emboss it fine with lily-flowers,
Ere the stuff grow a ring-thing right to wear.

The ring described here as "Etrurian," that is, as Etruscan, is
imaginary. But there are two real rings and one literary ring that
satisfy the present text and combine to form a likely composite

source. One of the real rings, the *Vis Mea* ring, entered below in the Supplement to Citations and Notes under XII.870-74, evidently originates from "Castellani's . . . craft" and is made of gold as the text specifies from line I.7 on (KI, 151-52). The other real ring I shall call the *fleur-de-lis* ring and shall present as the source for the design of "lily-flowers" or, as the design is again referred to in line 27, "lilied loveliness."

I uncovered the *fleur-de-lis* ring in the collection of Castellani jewelry in the National Museum of Villa Giulia, in Rome. It is identified in the catalogue of jewelry photographs as no. 772 and is located with other thirteenth-century rings in window panel no. 35. The ring is made of gold and, as Fig. 258 and the half title page show, has a lily design—a *fleur-de-lis*—on the middle of the face of the ring. On each side of the ring proper leading up to the face are circlets in the form of serpents. On the whole, the design on the face of the ring is an emblem of family nobility. The ring belonged to the Castellani family up to the time that Alfredo Castellani bequeathed the collection of jewelry to the National Museum of Villa Giulia in 1919, but when the Castellani family obtained the ring is not known, for the museum has no provenance for the ring. Browning, however, visited the Castellani shop in Rome and signed the Castellani guestbook for January, 1860. Thus, if the ring had been in the possession of the Castellani family by 1860, Browning could have seen it during his visit to the family's shop.

The above information has been corroborated in conversation with Dr. Gabriella Bordenache Battaglia and in conjunction with her article on the Castellani family in the *Dizionario biografico degli italiani* (DIZ, 590-605; the Castellani guestbooks are housed in the Villa Giulia). Dr. Bordenache Battaglia further informs me that she knows of no other ring with a lily design on it that belonged to the Castellani family. In addition, she maintains that the ring in the present passage is imaginary, in that neither proposed source for it is Etruscan in design and that, specifically, neither ring has what the text describes as "Etrurian circlets." She has examined her photograph of the *Vis Mea* ring and is in accord with Gerard Taylor's cataloguing of the ring as a "Roman" or classical type (see TAY, 90, no. 921, or KI, 154 and 159, note 10, for a complete description of the ring); and she has analyzed the "circlets" on the *fleur-de-lis* ring, as described above, and has determined that they too are not "Etrurian"— Etruscan—in style, that, on a whole, the *fleur-de-lis* ring, like the *Vis Mea* ring, is classical in style. But this stylistic deficiency is accounted for by the third ring—the literary ring.

The literary ring belongs to Godfrey Wentworth in Isa Blagden's book *Agnes Tremorne*, published in 1861 (London: Smith, Elder), seven years before *The Ring and the Book*. Kincaid introduces the source and quotes from the first volume, page 152, the passage that identifies the ring (KI, 156):

> Agnes looked up and saw a simple Etruscan ring, with the device *Vis Mea* on it.

The real *Vis Mea* ring was given to Browning by Isa Blagden around 1858, three years before her book was published (KI, 156-57). Having received the *Vis Mea* ring as a gift before having no doubt read about it in Isa Blagden's book, Browning was probably susceptible to associating the real *Vis Mea* ring with the Godfrey Wentworth literary *Vis Mea* ring in Etruscan style. Thus we have a conflation of three probable sources: the real *Vis Mea* ring, the literary Godfrey Wentworth ring, and the *fleur-de-lis* ring, which comprise the Castellani, Etruscan, and lilied elements necessary to round out the imaginary ring described at the beginning of Browning's poem. (Continued under this reference in the Supplement to Citations and Notes.)

I.38-52

> I found this book,
> Gave a *lira* for it, eightpence English just,
> (Mark the predestination!) when a Hand,
> Always above my shoulder, pushed me once,
> One day still fierce 'mid many a day struck calm,
> Across a Square in Florence, crammed with booths,
> Buzzing and blaze, noontide and market-time,
> Toward Baccio's marble,—ay, the basement-ledge
> O' the pedestal where sits and menaces
> John of the Black Bands with the upright spear,
> 'Twixt palace and church,—Riccardi where they lived,
> His race, and San Lorenzo where they lie.
> This book,—precisely on that palace-step
> Which, meant for lounging knaves o' the Medici,
> Now serves re-venders to display their ware. . . .

The "Square" in Florence where Browning discovers the Old Yellow Book is the Piazza "San Lorenzo" (Map F:7H). In the piazza stands "Baccio's marble," the statue of "John of the Black Bands," by Baccio Bandinelli (1497-1559). John, as Figs. 140 and 141 show, is mounted on a "pedestal" as he holds an "upright spear." Piazza San Lorenzo is located "Twixt palace and church," between Palazzo Medici-Riccardi and the Church of San Lorenzo (COOK, 8). The members of the Medici family "lie," that is, are

Fig. 140
Baccio Bandinelli
John of the Black Bands
Piazza San Lorenzo
Florence

Fig. 141

Background,
center dome: Cappella de' Principi
side dome: New Sacristy
                 Church of San Lorenzo
                 Florence

Foreground,
statue: Bandinelli
                 John of the Black Bands

buried in the crypt and are commemorated with tomb monuments in the Old and New Sacristies and the Cappella de' Principi of the Church of San Lorenzo. Browning errs where he says that he found the Old Yellow Book "on that Palace-step," for the steps of Palazzo Medici-Riccardi do not front the "Marketplace" or the statue by Bandinelli. What he means are the steps of the Church of San Lorenzo which lead directly down to the statue and marketplace. (Cf. below under I.91-95.) For other

references to the Palazzo Medici-Riccardi, see above under "Fra
Lippo Lippi," 14-18, 61-67, 226-30, and below under "The Statue
and the Bust," 94-96. For other references to the Church of San
Lorenzo, see "Fra Lippo Lippi," 61-67, and "The Statue and the
Bust," 214-16.

I.66-75

> A pile of brown-etched prints, two *crazie* each,
> Stopped by a conch a-top from fluttering forth
> —Sowing the Square with works of one and the same
> Master, the imaginative Sienese
> Great in the scenic backgrounds—(name and fame
> None of you know, nor does he fare the worse:)
> From these . . . Oh, with a Lionard going cheap
> If it should prove, as promised, that Joconde
> Whereof a copy contents the Louvre!—these
> I picked this book from.

The "imaginative Sienese" is identified by Porter and Clarke as
Ademollo, who is mentioned below under I.369-72 (POR, VII,
322). This is probably Luigi Ademollo (1764-1849), who rendered
a fresco of St. Michael in the church of San Donato, in Siena.

The "Lionard going cheap" is a reference to Leonardo da
Vinci's *Mona Lisa*—"that Joconde" (*La Gioconda*), in the Louvre
(COOK, 8, KING, VII, 265; Fig. 142).

I.91-95, 110-16

> That memorable day,
> (June was the month, Lorenzo named the Square),
> I leaned a little and overlooked my prize
> By the low railing round the fountain-source
> Close to the statue, where a step descends:
> . . .
> Still read I on, from written title-page
> To written index, on, through street and street,
> At the Strozzi, at the Pillar, at the Bridge;
> Till, by the time I stood at home again
> In Casa Guidi by Felice Church,
> Under the doorway where the black begins
> With the first stone-slab of the staircase cold. . . .

Browning accurately describes details here concerning the
"statue" of John of the Black Bands, the father of Cosimo I, in
Piazza San Lorenzo (Fig. 140; Map F:7H). A "low railing" goes
"round the fountain-source," which is "Close to the statue," that
is, the fountain which is in the pedestal of the statue, and a "step

Fig. 142
Leonardo da Vinci
Mona Lisa (detail)
Louvre
Paris

descends" from the adjacent stairs of the Church of San Lorenzo. For another reference to the statue and Piazza San Lorenzo, see above under I.38-52, and see that reference and the present reference in the Supplement to Citations and Notes.

After discovering the Old Yellow Book, Browning reads it while walking from Piazza San Lorenzo back to his home, "Casa Guidi by Felice Church" (Fig. 197; Map F:9G). On the way he passes "the Strozzi, at the Pillar, at the Bridge." The Palazzo Strozzi was designed by Maiano in 1489 and continued by Cronaca in 1507 (Fig. 143; Map F:8G,8H). The Pillar of Cosimo I, in the Piazza di Trinita, was made from a column from the Baths of Caracalla and is surmounted by a statue of Minerva sculptured by Tadda in 1581 (Fig. 144; Map F:8G). And the Trinity Bridge was designed by Ammanati in 1558 for Cosimo I (Fig. 145; Map F:8G). We know that Browning crossed the Trinity Bridge because it makes a direct line from Piazza San Lorenzo to Casa Guidi (cf. COOK, 8-9).

I.350-60

> —Not at the proper head-and-hanging place
> On bridge-foot close by Castle Angelo,
> Where custom somewhat staled the spectacle,
> ('T was not so well i' the way of Rome, beside,
> The noble Rome, the Rome of Guido's rank)
> But at the city's newer gayer end,—
> The cavalcading promenading place
> Beside the gate and opposite the church
> Under the Pincian gardens green with Spring,
> 'Neath the obelisk 'twixt the fountains in the Square,
> Did Guido and his fellows find their fate. . . .

"Castle Angelo," or Castel Sant' Angelo, is the Mausoleum of Hadrian, the famous fortress dating from A.D. 130, on the west bank of the Tiber (Fig. 146; Map R:6F,7F). The "bridge-foot" by the castle, where executions were traditionally conducted, is Ponte Sant' Angelo. Guido was executed in Piazza del Popolo (the "Square") below the "Pincian gardens" (the "cavalcading promenading place"). In the Piazza are the Porta del Popolo (the "gate"), Santa Maria del Popolo (the "church"), and the Egyptian "obelisk" surrounded by lion "fountains" (COOK, 13-14; Figs. 147 and 148; Map R:5H,6H). For related references, see below under X.2106-11; XII.138-46, 159-65; and above under "Cenciaja," 228-30.

Fig. 143
Palazzo Strozzi
Florence

I.369-72

> ... Ademollo's name,
> The etcher of those prints, two *crazie* each,
> Saved by a stone from snowing broad the Square
> With scenic backgrounds?

Fig. 144
Pillar of Cosimo I
Piazza di Santa Trinita
Florence

Fig. 145
Trinity Bridge
Florence

Fig. 146
Castel and Ponte Sant' Angelo
Rome

Fig. 147
Piazza del Popolo
Rome

Fig. 148
Church of Santa Maria del Popolo
Piazza del Popolo
Rome

For another reference to "Ademollo's . . . prints" and the "Square of San Lorenzo," see above under I.66-75.

I.472-83, 497-501

> The book was shut and done with and laid by
> On the cream-colored massive agate, broad
> 'Neath the twin cherubs in the tarnished frame
> O' the mirror, tall thence to the ceiling-top.
> And from the reading, and that slab I leant
> My elbow on, the while I read and read,
> I turned, to free myself and find the world,
> And stepped out on the narrow terrace, built
> Over the street and opposite the church,
> And paced its lozenge-brickwork sprinkled cool;
> Because Felice-church-side stretched, aglow
> Through each square window fringed for festival. . . .
> . . .
> Over the roof o' the lighted church I looked
> A bowshot to the street's end, north away
> Out of the Roman gate to the Roman road
> By the river, till I felt the Apennine.
> And there would lie Arezzo. . . .

DeVane dates the genesis of *The Ring and the Book* to August, 1864, when Browning had permanently left Florence and was traveling in France (DEVA, 323). This probably explains why Browning, in the present passage, is inconsistently recalling from memory details about the interior and exterior of Casa Guidi, in Florence (Map F:9G). As regards the interior, the "cream-colored massive agate . . . slab" of the fireplace appears as Browning depicts it. I have observed that the slab is the lintel of the fireplace in the Drawing Room and is indeed a wavy, cream-colored agate. In George Mignaty's 1861 painting the *Drawing Room at Casa Guidi* (Fig. 149), the lintel is "'Neath the twin cherubs in the tarnished frame / O' the mirror," but the mirror is not "tall thence to the ceiling-top," since paintings hang on the wall between the mirror and the ceiling (KING, VII, 275). Perhaps, as Philip Kelley has suggested in conversation, this discrepency is explained by Browning's viewpoint while standing at the fireplace. The mirror is 18 inches thick, and when viewed from beneath the mirror would appear to touch the ceiling. Finally, no "twin cherubs" may be seen in Mignaty's representation of the mirror, yet we may be sure that Browning is correct in locating them there, for they are specifically described in Sotheby (KEL, 503, item H401) and as follows in Sotheran's 1913 catalogue (SOTH):

Fig. 149
George Mignaty
Drawing Room at Casa Guidi
Mills College Library
Oakland

Fig. 150
Fireplace in the Dining Room of Casa Guidi
Florence

> A large and beautifully carved wood gilt mirror, the frame of scroll design, with two amorini at the sides, each supporting two candle branches, 4 ft. 8 in. high by 4 ft. 2 in, wide.

Today the mirror is in the possession of Murial and Betty Edwards, of Chislehurst, England.

As regards the exterior of Casa Guidi, the "narrow terrace" is opposite San "Felice-church-side stretched" (Fig. 197), but the "Lozenge brickwork" of the terrace, though made of bricks that are placed in a zig-zag pattern, is not quite in a lozenge design because the bricks are in the shape of rectangles rather than lozenges; and first-hand observation reveals that the design of the bricks has probably not been changed since Browning's time. The wall of the Church of San Felice "side stretched" opposite Casa Guidi has no "square windows" or, for that matter, square window panes; rather, it has five trefoil Gothic and three upright rectangular windows. But the position of the "Roman gate" (Fig. 184) in relation to the Arno River and Arezzo is in accord with Roma King's explanation (KING, VII, 275-76):

> At first glance the lines seem to mean that the poet looked N toward Rome, which is an impossibility. But a map shows that outside the Porta Romana, which was at the end of the Via Romana, about a quarter of a mile (a bowshot) from the Casa Guidi, the old Roman Road did turn N for a short distance (*away* may be taken in the sense of "a way") to cross the Arno and follow the river's course toward Arezzo.

For other references to Casa Guidi, see above under I.110-116, 472-83, 497-501, below under XII.870-74, "Up at a Villa—Down in the City," 51-52, and in the Supplement to Citations and Notes, *The Ring and the Book*, I.1-4, 15-17, 1391-1401. For another reference to the Roman Gate—the Porta Romana—see below under XI.3-14.

I.507-09

>   . . . the wayside inn
> By Castelnuovo's few mean hut-like homes
> Huddled together on the hill-foot bleak. . . .

The "wayside inn" of Castelnuovo is where Pompilia and Caponsacchi were lodged when Guido caught up with them (Fig. 151). Also see below under II.1003-06 and VI.1397-400.

Fig. 151
Inn at Castelnuovo
Rome (environs)

I.780-84

Count Guido Franceschini the Aretine,
Descended of an ancient house, though poor,
A beak-nosed bushy-bearded black-haired lord,
Lean, pallid, low of stature yet robust,
Fifty years old....

For the pencil sketch of Guido Franceschini, see below under IV.717-19 and VII.394-96. Guido was forty at the time of his execution, not fifty (COOK, 20).

I.874-76

                                                      . . .
By the church Lorenzo opposite. So, they lounge
Midway the mouth o' the street, on Corso side,
'Twixt palace Fiano and palace Ruspoli....

Palazzo "Fiano" and Palazzo "Ruspoli" flank the street that leads west from the Corso into nearby Piazza San Lorenzo in Lucina, where the church of the same name is located (Fig. 152; COOK, 21; Map R:6H). For other references to the Church of San Lorenzo in Lucina, see below under II.83-96, and VII.21-27, 425-30.

I.896-903

                                    ... i' the market-place
O' the Barberini by the Capucins;
Where the old Triton, at his fountain-sport,
Bernini's creature plated to the paps,
Puffs up steel sleet which breaks to diamond dust,
A spray of sparkles snorted from his conch,
High over the caritellas, out o' the way
O' the motley merchandising multitude.

The "Triton" Fountain by Bernini is in the Piazza "Barberini," near the Church of the "Capucins" in the adjoining Via Veneto, in Rome (Map R:7I). Compare Chapter 21 of Hawthorne's earlier *The Marble Faun*, where the elaborate burial grounds in the Church of the Capuchins are described at length. As Fig. 153 shows, the bones and garments of the monks are used to decorate the walls of the burial grounds (Map R:6I). For another reference to *The Marble Faun*, see above under "James Lee's Wife," VIII.27-32.

Fig. 152
Church of San Lorenzo in Lucina
Rome

Fig. 153
Church of the Capuchins (crypt)
Rome

The word "caritellas," in reference to the *Triton Fountain*, has posed a problem for scholars. Cook first interprets it as a misprint for *Cariti*, small figures of the Graces. Then, since there are no such figures adorning the *Triton Fountain*, he suggests another meaning, "carretellas," the vehicles used by the "motley merchandising multitude" (COOK, 21). But this is not possible under normal conditions, for it would mean that the "spray" from the "conch" of the Triton goes, as Browning puts it, "High over the caritellas" and, at the same time, "out o' the way" / O' the . . . multitude" that is presumably using the carretellas. A more probable explanation is espoused by Porter and Clarke, who interpret the word "caritellas" as follows (POR, VII, 324, note 894; KING, VII, 281; Figs. 154 and 155):

> Perhaps a misprint for *cartellas*, which, according to Milizia's "Dizionario delle Belle Arti del Disegno," are the ornamental sculptured tablets of various shapes placed in a structure to bear an inscription, its name, that of its designer or erecter, his arms or monogram, or the like. In this case it refers to the scutcheon-shaped scrolls sculptured on the fountain, which bear the three bees, the insignia of Maffeo Barberini, Pope Urban XII, surmounted by the Papal tiara.

For a description of the dome of St. Peter's Church, in the Vatican, as an image of a Papal tiara, see above under *Prince Honenstiel-Schwangau, Saviour of Society*, 861-65.

I.1207-08

> Since to the four walls, Forum and Mars' Hill,
> [Bottini] Speaks out the poesy....

Bottini's studio is being compared to a kind of "Forum" (Fig. 68; Map R:8I) and Areopagus (COOK, 25). Compare the reference to the Temple of Mars Ultor in the Forum of Augustus, above under "Imperante Augusto Natus Est—," 31-40.

I.1284-85

> In that New Prison by Castle Angelo
> At the bridge-foot . . .

Browning confuses the New Prisons on Via Giulia with the Tordinona at Ponte Sant' Angelo. See above under I.350-60 and below under V.324-25; XII.138-46.

Fig. 154
Gian Lorenzo Bernini
Triton Fountain
Piazza Barberini
Rome

Fig. 155
Gian Lorenzo Bernini
Triton Fountain (detail)
Piazza Barberini
Rome

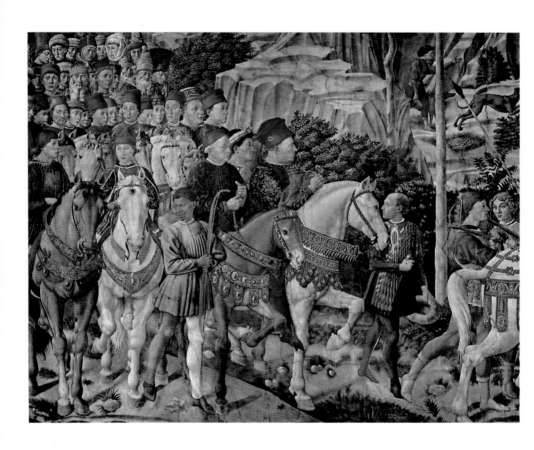

Fig. 156
Benozzo Gozzoli
Procession of the Kings
Cappella de' Medici
Palazzo Medici-Riccardi
Florence

I.1391-92

O lyric Love, half angel and half bird,
And all a wonder and a wild desire....

As a source for Browning's "lyric Love, half angel and half bird,"
Griffin and Minchen nominate *Jacob's Dream*, a painting in the
Dulwich Picture Gallery that Browning undoubtedly saw in his
youth (GRI, 13n, 207; Fig. 157). Formerly attributed to Rem-
brandt, the painting is now identified with Aert de Gelderin
(Dutch, 1645-1727; DULW, 20, item no. 126). For other references
to Browning's "Lyric Love," see below under XII.870-74 and
under the present reference in the Supplement to Citations and
Notes.

II.83-96

Just at this altar where, beneath the piece
Of Master Guido Reni, Christ on cross,
Second to naught observable in Rome,
That couple lie now, murdered yestereve.
Even the blind can see a providence here.

From dawn till now that it is growing dusk,
A multitude has flocked and filled the church,
Coming and going, coming back again,
Till to count crazed one. Rome was at the show.
People climbed up the columns, fought for spikes
O' the chapel-rail to perch themselves upon,
Jumped over and so broke the wooden work
Painted like porphyry to deceive the eye;
Serve the priests right! The organ-loft was crammed....

The description here of the interior of the Church of San
Lorenzo in Lucina, in Rome, evidently derives from an inquiry
in a letter that Browning wrote to his friend Lord Leighton on
October 17, 1864 (see DEVA, 323, for quotations from the letter;
for a fuller account, see ORMO, p. 79). As a probable result of
this second-hand knowledge, Browning's depiction of the
architectural features in the interior of the church is vague and
needs proper placing. The two "columns" in the rear of the
church supporting the "organ-loft" and the "wooden work"
railing of the organ-loft are indeed "Painted like porphyry to
deceive the eye," and conceivably the "people climbed up the
columns . . . and so broke the wooden work" so that the "organ-
loft was crammed." There are iron "spikes / O' the chapel-rail to

Fig. 157
Aert de Gelderin
Jacob's Dream
Dulwich Picture Gallery
London

perch themselves upon," but these are below the organ-loft and are on top of the rail of the first chapel to the left of the church entrance.   For details of another inaccuracy, see below under VII.21-27 for the description of the lion statues attached to the outer wall of the church.   Guido Reni's painting of "Christ on cross," that is, his *Crucifixion*, may still be seen over the high altar of the church (Fig. 158).   After Pietro and Violante Comparini were murdered, their bodies were displayed on this altar (COOK, 36, note 6).

II.200-07

> . . . wealthy is the word,
> Since Pietro was possessed of house and land—
> And specially one house, when good days smiled
> In Via Vittoria, the aspectable street
> Where he lived mainly; but another house
> Of less pretension did he buy betimes,
> The villa, meant for jaunts and jollity,
> I' the Pauline district, to be private there. . . .

Treves, as confirmed by Cook, maintains that there was only one Comparini home, the one that was situated at the corner of Via Vittoria and Via del Babuino but that is now no longer in existence (TRE, 101-03; COOK, 279-82; Map R:6H).   Treves bases his argument on the fact that Via Paulina, "I' the Pauline district," was formerly Via del Babuino.   The villa, which Browning erroneously places near the Pyramid of Cestius just inside the Porta San Paolo, is also mentioned in the poem under I.604-05; III.1596; IV.1369, 1394; V.1335-37; and VII.233-38.

II.471-72

> . . . this black stone heap, the street's disgrace,
> Grimmest as that is of the gruesome town. . . .

The palace of the Franceschini family no longer exists in Arezzo, where it used to be on Via de' Cenci (HOD, 298, note 38; COOK, 39).   There is still in the city, however, a street named Via de' Cenci.

Fig. 158
Guido Reni
Crucifixion
Church of San Lorenzo in Lucina
Rome

II.1003-06

> Pompilia, soon looked Helen to the life,
> Recumbent upstairs in her pink and white,
> So, in the inn-yard, bold as 't were Troy-town,
> There strutted Paris in correct costume. . . .

During their escape from Arezzo to Rome, Pompilia ("Helen") and Caponsacchi ("Paris") stopped at the Inn of Castelnuovo ("Troy-town"), about twenty miles to the north of Rome (Fig. 151). Also see above under I.507-09 and below under VI.1397-400.

II.1229-31

> Pompilia, as enjoined, betook herself
> To the aforesaid Convertites, soft sisterhood
> In Via Lungara, where the light ones live. . . .

Browning confuses the Scalette, the Conservatorio di Santa Croce della Penitenza, which is in the Via Lungara (Fig. 159; Map R:8F), with the convent of the "Convertite," which no longer exists (HOD, 316, no. 278, 321-22, no. 351, 323, no. 364; COOK, 48-49; TRE, 104). The street Via delle Convertite, however, where the order was located, may still be seen off the Corso connecting with Piazza San Silvestro (Map R:7H). The "light ones" are the nuns on Via Lungara, the Scalette, who wear a white habit. For similar references, see I.1085, II.1197-1202, X.1498-1519, and XII. 761-63.

III.35-37

> There she lies in the long white lazar-house.
> Rome has besieged, these two days, never doubt,
> Saint Anna's where she waits her death. . . .

No house or hospital by the name of "Saint Anna" existed in Rome in connection with the death of Pompilia. Browning probably connected this name with Fra Celestino Angelo, who was of the Church of Santa Anna, in Via Morulana, and took Pompilia's confession on her death-bed. Fra Celestino Angelo was also associated with the Church of Jesus and Maria, on the Corso near the Piazza del Popolo (TRE, 76; COOK, 281; Map R:6H).

Fig. 159
Convent of the Scalette
Rome

III.58-62

> Cavalier Carlo—well there's some excuse
> For him—Maratta who paints Virgins so—
> He too must fee the porter and slip by
> With pencil cut and paper squared, and straight
> There was he figuring away at face. . . .

Carlo Maratta (1625-1713), who is known for painting the Holy Virgin, is depicted here "figuring" an imaginary sketch of Pompilia's face as she lies mortally wounded in the hospital. See below under VIII.634-39.

III.103-04

> ". . . the wind
> That waits outside a certain church, you know!"

Cook identifies the "certain church" as the Church of the Gesù, near the Piazza Venezia (Fig. 160; Map R:8H). In explaining the "wind" outside the church, Cook quotes from Augustus Hare (COOK, 56; HARE, I, 68):

> The piazza before the Gesu Church is considered to be the most draughty place in Rome. The legend runs that the devil and the wind were one day taking a walk together. When they came to this square, the devil, who seemed to be very devout, said to the wind, "Just wait a minute, mio caro, while I go into this church." So the wind promised, and the devil went into the Gesu, and has never come out again—and the wind is blowing about the Piazza del Gesu to this day.

From this reference to the anecdote of the wind and the devil, it is clear that Browning is criticizing the Catholic Church. Also see above under *Prince Hohenstiel-Schwangau, Saviour of Society*, 861-65.

III.388-93

> Wheron did Pietro . . .
> Sally forth dignifiedly into the Square
> Of Spain across Babbuino the six steps,
> Toward the Boat-fountain where our idlers lounge. . . .

In the Piazza di Spagna, or "Square / Of Spain," in Rome (Map R:6H,6I), is the "Boat-fountain" of Pietro Bernini, the father of the famous Gian Lorenzo Bernini. The fountain, as Fig. 161

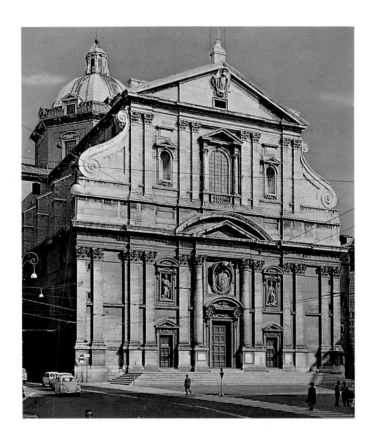

Fig. 160
Church of the Gesù
Rome

shows, is in the shape of a ship of war with water pouring out of
its cannons. Called *"Barcaccia"* (wrecked boat) by the Italians, the
name, according to Cesare D'Onofrio, is "a symbol of danger,
almost of ruin"—*"un simbolo di pericolo, quasi di rovina"* (ON,
175). Thus the ruination of "Pietro" Comparini and his family is
foreshadowed by the *Boat-fountain* in the Piazza di Spagna.
Also see below under VII.21-27 for another family portent.

Fig. 161
Pietro Bernini
Boat Fountain
Rome

III.566-72

So, with the crowd she mixed, made for the dome,
Through the great door new-broken for the nonce
Marched, muffled more than ever matron-wise,
Up the left nave to the formidable throne,
Fell into file with this the poisoner
And that the parricide, and reached in turn
The poor repugnant Penitentiary. . . .

The Jubilee year, or the Holy Year, is a time of special indul-
gences occurring every twenty-five years. In the "dome," the
Church of St. Peter, the "great door, new-broken for the nonce,"
is a particular walled-up door—the Porta Aurea, or Golden Door
—which is opened for the Holy Year occasion and sprinkled
with holy water for the Pope to pass through. When the Jubilee
Year is over, the Golden Door is ceremonially walled up again.
The door is part of the portal of the church and is the last, or fifth
door, on the right (Fig. 162). The "formidable throne" was an
elevated seat by the pier of St. Veronica below the statue of St.
Juliana, in the left transept of St. Peter's. It was used by the
Grand "Penitentiary," who dispensed absolution during high
festivals like the Jubilee (COOK, 61), but I can find no evidence
that the seat has been used in recent years. For another reference
to the Jubilee year and the Porta Aurea, see below under XII.61-
62.

III.1575-76

> He rushed to Vittiano, found four sons o' the soil,
> Brutes of his breeding. . . .

Guido was known to have a villa at Vittiano, a hamlet nine
miles on the road from Arezzo to Perugia. It was at this villa
that the plot to murder the Comparini was hatched (HOD, 319,
no. 311; COOK, 44; TRE, 182). The villa and/or locale is
mentioned in the poem under II.815-16; III.314; IV.1360; V.253,
364, 1006, 1142; and VI.519, 591.

III.1582-85

> And so arrived, all five of them, at Rome
> On Christmas-Eve, and forthwith found themselves
> Installed i' the vacancy and solitude
> Left them by Paolo. . . .

For nine days Guido and his henchmen stopped at the villa of
Guido's brother Paolo. The villa was located at the Ponte
Milvio, just outside of Rome on the Via Flaminia (HOD, 320, no.
318). The bridge (Fig. 166) was rebuilt over an ancient Roman
structure. For other references to the same locale, see below
under IV.1364-65 and V.1588-89.

Fig. 162
Holy Door (exterior)
Church of St. Peter
Vatican

III.1633-36

> Accomplished [they] a prodigious twenty miles
> Homeward, and gained Baccano very near,
> Stumbled at last, deaf, dumb, blind through the feat,
> Into a grange. . . .

The inn in Merluzza, near "Baccano," is the "grange" where Guido and the others were arrested (HOD, 321, n. 340; COOK, 70-71; Fig. 163, reproduced from TRE, plate 32). For similar references to this locale, see IV.1397-98 and X.846-49.

IV.168-70

> . . . her ostensible work
> Was washing clothes, out in the open air
> At the cistern by Citorio. . . .

The "Citorio" is the Piazza Montecitorio, in Rome; it is just west of the Corso near the Piazza Colonna (COOK, 77; Map R:7H). The piazza includes the Montecitorio Palace, a majestic building designed by Bernini and now used as the Chamber of Deputies, and a seventh-century B.C. obelisk brought from Heliopolis (Egypt) by Augustus (Fig. 164). An examination of the map in COOK (between pp. 234 and 235) reveals that Piazza Montecitorio lies along the processional route to Guido's execution, although Browning does not include the piazza in his description of the execution route noted below under XII.138-46.

IV. 377-78

> And yonder's the famed Rafael, first in kind,
> The painter painted for his grandfather. . . .

This painting by Raphael that is supposed to hang in the home of Guido Franceschini in Arrezo is imaginary. See below under VI.400-06, 668-73 for references to another imaginary painting by Raphael in Arezzo. For another reference to the Franceschini home in Arezzo, see above under II.471-72.

IV.439-42

> . . . down we go
> To the woman-dealer in perukes, a wench
> I and some others settled in the shop
> At Place Colonna. . . .

Fig. 163
Inn in Merluzza
Baccano (environs)
Italy

Fig. 164
Piazza Montecitorio
Rome

For another reference to the "Place Colonna," see below under XII.138-46.

IV.717-19

> A husband poor, care-bitten, sorrow-sunk,
> Little, long-nosed, bush-bearded, lantern-jawed,
> Forty-six-years old. . . .

Fig. 165 shows a sketch in pencil of Guido Franceschini just before his execution. While Browning was writing *The Ring and the Book,* it was sent to him after being found in a bundle of miscellaneous items in London (COOK, 81-82). The sketch is reproduced in Hodell (HOD) opposite page 274 and in COOK as the Frontispiece. The original sketch is in Balliol College, Oxford. Also see under VII.394-96.

IV.888-89

> And curtaining Correggio carefully
> Lest I be taught that Leda had two legs. . . .

This is the same *Leda and the Swan* by Correggio discussed above under *The Inn Album,* I.392-93 (see Fig. 78; cf. COOK, 83). Today the painting is in the Gemäldegalerie of the Staatliche Museen in Berlin-Dahlem. For other references to Correggio, see "Bishop Blougram's Apology," 113-17; "A Face," 14; "Parleying with Francis Furini," 173,175; and *Pippa Passes,* IV.58-59.

IV.1282-83

> You've seen the puppets, of Place Navona, play,—
> Punch and his mate. . . .

For another reference to "Place Navona," see below under XII.138-46.

IV.1364-65

> . . . the Abate's dried-up font,
> The lodge where Paolo ceased to work the pipes.

The "lodge" of Paolo was near Ponte Milvio (HOD, 320, no. 318; Fig. 166; COOK, on pp. 87 and 109, uses the popular form "Ponte Molle"; elsewhere, on p. 71, he uses "Ponte Milvio," the form of the name used by Hodell). Also see below under V.1588-89.

Fig. 165
Count Guido Franceschini
Anonymous pencil sketch
Balliol College Library
Oxford

Fig. 166
Ponte Milvio
Rome

IV.1397-98

So, that same night was he, with the other four,
Overtaken near Baccano. . . .

See above under III.1633-36.

IV.1516-17

The Stinche, House of Punishment, for life.—
That's what the wife deserves in Tuscany. . . .

The "Stinche" was a prison in Florence on the Via Ghibellina at the Via Isola delle Stinche. Fig. 167 is a sketch of how it looked in 1839 (TER, I, 43; BEC). It later became part of a theatre (COOK, 89), as it is today, and in no way resembles the original building. Also see below under XI.1667.

Fig. 167
The Stinche (1839)
Florence

V.324-25

> ... the warrant for my transfer late
> To the New Prisons from Tordinona. . . .

The papal prison "Tordinona"—also called Torre di Nona—
could not have been used to retain Guido, for it was destroyed
eight years prior to his arrest. The Torre di Nona was a tower in
the city walls just south of the Ponte Sant' Angelo. Today the
street named after the tower goes by the variant Tor di Nona; it
runs alongside the Tiber River from the Ponte Sant' Angelo
(HOD, 321, no. 345; COOK, 97; HARE, II, 148; Map R:7F,7G). For
another reference to the tower, see above under "Cenciaja," 175-
77. The "New Prisons," where Guido, Pompilia, and Caponsacchi were incarcerated, are located on Via Giulia just south of the
Ponte Sant' Angelo (Fig. 168; Map R:7F,8F). COOK, on page 97,
contradicts himself when he locates the New Prisons at Tor di
Nona and the Carceri Nuove—the same place—in the Via
Giulia. Also, see above under I.1284-85 and below under XII.138-
46, 159-65.

V.487-89

                              ... that piece
          By Pietro of Cortona—probably
          His scholar Ciro Ferri may have retouched....

The "piece" in this passage by Pietro da Cortona is unspecified.
For another reference to this painter and his pupil Ciro Ferri, see
below under IX.110-30.

V.703-05

                              ... a hawk,
          I bought at a hawk's price and carried home
          To do hawk's service—at the Rotunda....

The "Rotunda" is commonly known in Rome as the Pantheon,
in Piazza Santa Maria della Rotonda (COOK, 101; Fig. 169; Map
R:7H). Also see below under XII.138-46.

V.1022-29

          'They climbed the wall—your lady must be lithe—
          At the gap, the broken bit'...—"Torrione, true!
          To escape the questioning guard at the proper gate,
          Clemente, where at the inn, hard by, 'the Horse,'
          Just outside, a calash in readiness
          Took the two principals, all alone at last,
          To gate San Spirito, which o'erlooks the road,
          Leads to Perugia, Rome and liberty."

Fig. 168
New Prisons (Carceri Nuove)
Rome

Fig. 169
The Pantheon
Rome

To the south of the northern "gate" of Arezzo, San "Clemente," is the "Torrione," a bastion in the wall surrounding Arezzo. It was here that Pompilia and Caponsacchi made their escape (HOD, 310, no. 189; COOK, 126-27; Fig. 170). Circling around the wall past the southern gate of Arezzo, "San Spirito" (Fig. 171), the lovers then took the southern route to Rome. Also see below under VI.1080-83.

Fig. 170
The Torrione
Arezzo

Fig. 171
Porta Santo Spirito
Arezzo

V.1588-89

> I bore the hateful house, my brother's once,
> Deserted....

For a connection between the "hateful house" and Ponte Milvio, see above under III.1582-85 and IV.1364-65.

VI.231-34

> When Florence ruined Fiesole, our folk
> Migrated to the victor-city, and there
> Flourished,—our palace and our tower attest,
> In the Old Mercato....

COOK, 119, places the former palace and tower of the Caponsacchi family in the Piazza Vittorio Emanuele, formerly known as the "Old Mercato"—the Mercato Vecchio. Today the Piazza Vittorio Emanuele is renamed the Piazza della Repubblica (BON; Map F:8H).

VI.249-56

> He it was,—when the Granduke Ferdinand
> Swore he would raze our city, plough the place
> And sow it with salt, because we Aretines
> Had tied a rope about the neck, to hale
> The statue of his father from its base
> For hate's sake,—he availed by prayers and tears
> To pacify the Duke and save the town.
> This was my father's father's brother.

The "statue of his father," the grandfather of the "Granduke Ferdinand" II, is the marble statue of Grand Duke Ferdinand I, rendered by Giovanni da Bologna in 1595. The statue stands next to the Duomo of Arezzo (COOK, 119; Fig. 172). Compare the bronze equestrian statue of Grand Duke Ferdinand I, also by Giovanni da Bologna, which is described below under "The Statue and the Bust," 202-05; and compare the imaginary statue described above under "Cleon," 174-80, and below under the same reference in the Supplement to Citations and Notes.

VI.345-48

> ... [I] was punctual to my place
> I' the Pieve, and as diligent at my post
> Where beauty and fashion rule. I throve apace,
> Sub-deacon, Canon. ...

Caponsacchi was a canon in the Church of Santa Maria della Pieve, in Arezzo. Also see below under VI.702-07, 974-76.

VI.400-406

> It was as when, in our cathedral once,
> As I got yawningly through matin-song,
> I saw *facchini* bear a burden up,
> Base it on the high-altar, break away
> A board or two, and leave the thing inside
> Lofty and lone: and lo, when next I looked,
> There was the Rafael!

Fig. 172
Giovanni da Bologna
Ferdinand I
Cathedral (Duomo)
Bishop's Palace (left bottom)
Arezzo

As Cook points out, there is no painting by "Rafael" in Arezzo
(COOK, 122). But as the text here and below under 668-73 combine to specify, there is, as I have observed, a "Madonna" over
the "high-altar" in the "cathedral" of Arezzo. It is the bas-relief

of the Madonna and Child in the center foreground of the sculptured tomb of St. Donatus, and it was rendered in the fourteenth
century by Betto di Francesco and Giovanni di Francesco (THI,
III, 546-47; VAS, I, 39n; Fig. 224). The long hiatus between Browning's visit to Arezzo in 1848 (KELL, 493) and the beginning of his
work in London on *The Ring and the Book* in 1864 (DEVA, 321)
possibly account for Browning confusing a painting by Raphael
with the *Madonna and Child* on the tomb of St. Donatus.

Furthermore, as a joint source for the infant Christ,
Eisenberg advances Raphael's *Small Cowper Madonna* (Fig. 228),
which corresponds in its depiction of what art historians call the
"lively child." And I have noticed that the *Small Cowper
Madonna* is commonly grouped with the *Madonna del
Granduca* (Fig. 111) because of the affinity between the visages of
the Madonnas. Eisenberg concurs and points out that both
Madonnas are dated to around 1505. In addition, Eisenberg notes
that there is a correspondence between the *Madonna del
Granduca* and the Madonna on the tomb of St. Donatus,
inasmuch as both are posed between frontal and three-quarter
views and both show strongly accentuated falls of drapery on the
Virgin's right side (EISE; cf. Figs. 111, 224, and 228).

VI.460-62

> I' the Duomo,—watch the day's last gleam outside
> Turn, as into a skirt of God's own robe,
> Those lancet-windows' jewelled miracle. . . .

The "lancet-windows" of the walls of the Duomo of Arezzo are
those of Guillaume de Marcillat (1467-1529). They depict the Life
of Christ (COOK, 122; see Fig. 172 for the façade of the Duomo).
Also see above under VI.400-06 and below under VI.668-73.

VI.668-73

> Learned Sir,
> I told you there's a picture in our church.
> Well, if a low-browed verger sidled up
> Bringing me, like a blotch, on his prod's point,
> A transfixed scorpion, let the reptile writhe,
> And then said, "See a thing that Rafael made—
> This venom issued from Madonna's mouth!"

COOK, p. 123, correctly identifies "our church" as the Cathedral
or Duomo of Arezzo, which is mentioned above under 400-06.
For sources for the imaginery "Madonna" in the Duomo by
"Rafael," also see above under 400-06.

VI. 702-07

> ... and there at the window stood,
> Framed in its black square length, with lamp in hand,
> Pompilia; the same great, grave, griefful air
> As stands i' the dusk, on altar that I know,
> Left alone with one moonbeam in her cell,
> Our Lady of all the Sorrows.

"Our Lady of all the Sorrows" has been identified by Griffin and Korg as a statue by Raynaldo Bartolini in the crypt of the Church of the Pieve, in Arezzo (KO, 179; Fig. 227). For another reference to the Madonna of Sorrows, see below under "Up at a Villa— Down in the City," 51-52, Fig. 220. For other references to the Church of the Pieve, see above under VI.345-48 and below under 974-76.

Fig. 173
Church of Santa Maria della Pieve
Arezzo

VI.974-76, 1000-02

> I' the gray of dawn it was I found myself
> Facing the pillared front o' the Pieve—mine,
> My church. . . .
> . . .
> Now, from the stone lungs sighed the scrannel voice,
> "Leave that live passion, come be dead with me!"

Fig. 173 shows the "pillared front" on the façade of the thirteenth-century Church of the Pieve, in Arezzo. The pillars or columns, from Caponsacchi's point of view, evidently appear as teeth in the mouth of the face—or façade—of the church through which "sighed the scrannel voice" from the "stone lungs" of the body of the church in an effort to induce Caponsacchi to "come be dead with me," that is, be dead with the Church. Compare above under *Prince Hohenstiel-Schwangau, Saviour of Society*, 861-65, for another negative physical image of a Catholic Church, specifically the Church of St. Peter in the Vatican, which is likened to a scorpian body. Also see the present poem, III.103-04, for a characterization of the Gesù Church as a host of the devil and above under "Abt Vogler," 2-4, 13-24, where St. Peter's Church in the Vatican is likened to Pandemonium in Milton's *Paradise Lost*.

VI.1080-83

> Descend, proceed to the Torrione, step
> Over the low dilapidated wall,
> Take San Clemente, there's no other gate
> Unguarded at the hour. . . .

As Cook points out, this passage contradicts itself. The lovers could not "Take San Clemente" if they went over the wall at the Torrione (COOK, 126-27). See above under V.1022-29 for the correct description of the escape.

VI.1249-51, 54

> Once she asked, "What is it that made you smile,
> At the great gate with the eagles and the snakes,
> Where the company entered . . ."
> . . . a certain bishop's villa-gate. . . .

For possible composite sources in this context, see under this reference in the Supplement to Citations and Notes.

VI.1397-400

Suddenly I saw
The old tower, and the little white-walled clump
Of buildings and the cypress-tree or two,—
"Already Castelnuovo—Rome!" I cried. . . .

The "old tower" in Castelnuovo is the Palazzo Governo (TRE, 217; Fig. 174).   It served as the prison where Pompilia and Caponsacchi were incarcerated.   Also see above under I.507-09 and II.1003-06.

VI.1658-59

"The bestiality that posts through Rome,
Put in his mouth by Pasquin."

In the Piazza Pasquino, near Piazza Navona, is an ancient statue that was dug up in the area (Fig. 175; Map R:8G).   The statue was

Fig. 174
Palazzo Governo
Castelnuovo

named after Pasquino, a tailor whose shop at the time was in the square. On the pedestal of the statue were attached pasquinades, that is, satirical remarks upon current topics (HOD, 328, no. 440; BER, 452; COOK, 264-65). For another reference to the Piazza Pasquino, see below under XII.138-46.

Fig. 175
Pasquin's Statue
Piazza Pasquino
Rome

VII.21-27

> I used to wonder, when I stood scarce high
> As the bed here, what the marble lion meant,
> With half his body rushing from the wall,
> Eating the figure of a prostrate man—
> (To the right, it is, of entry by the door)
> An ominous sign to one baptized like me,
> Married, and to be buried there, I hope.

Jutting out from the façade of the Church of San Lorenzo in Lucina, on each side of the door, so that it appears that their heads and shoulders are "rushing from the wall," are two thirteenth-century marble statues of lions. The lion on the right has a benign look as it cradles the figure of a person whose hand is apparently stroking its mane (Fig. 176). The one on the left has a ferocious look as it holds a headless figure—possibly a dog—in its paws (Fig. 177). Browning, probably acting on information he obtained in a letter from Leighton (DEVA, 323), identifies the wrong statue when he has Pompilia speak of the lion "Eating the figure of a prostrate man . . . To the right . . . of entry by the door" (COOK, 146; TRE, 120). Augustus Hare explains why the tame lion is paired with the menacing one (HAR, I, 45):

> . . . the lions symbolize respectively the benignity of the Church towards the neophyte and the docile and her severity towards the impenitent and heretical.

Pompilia, who was misfortunately "Married" and "baptized" in the Church of San Lorenzo in Lucina, was also "buried there" (COOK, 36, 282n). The "ominous sign" of the Malignant Lion statue as related to Pompilia associates with the portent of the *Boat Fountain* (above under III.388-92) as related to Pompilia's father, Pietro Comparini. Also see below under VII.425-30 for a reference to Pompilia and the Mouth-of-Lion Street.

For other references to the Church of San Lorenzo in Lucina, see above under I.874-76 and II.83-96, and below under VII.425-30.

VII.77-81

> . . . the poor Virgin that I used to know
> At our street-corner in a lonely niche,—
> The babe, that sat upon her knees, broke off,—
> Thin white glazed clay, you pitied her the more:
> She, not the gay ones, always got my rose.

Fig. 176
Benign Lion
Church of San Lorenzo in Lucina
Rome

Fig. 177
Malignant Lion
Church of San Lorenzo in Lucina
Rome

According to William M. Jensen, of the Art Department of Baylor University, this street shrine could be one of many which came from the late workshop of Luca della Robbia or someone imitating his style. If this particular shrine existed as Pompilia says, "At our street-corner," then it was at the corner of Via Vittoria and the Via del Babuino, in Rome, where, as Cook demonstrates (COOK, 279-82), the Comparini family lived. But their house is no longer standing, and there is no street shrine at this corner. Consequently, which of the numerous street shrines in Rome that might have inspired Browning in this passage is an open question.

VII.186-96

And, since there hung a tapestry on the wall,
We two agreed to find each other out
Among the figures. "Tisbe, that is you,
With half-moon on your hair-knot, spear in hand,
Flying, but no wings, only the great scarf
Blown to a bluish rainbow at your back :
Call off your hound and leave the stag alone!"
"—And there are you, Pompilia, such green leaves
Flourishing out of your five finger-ends,
And all the rest of you so brown and rough:
Why is it you are turned a sort of tree?"

A possible source for the figure in this imaginary tapestry with "green leaves / Flourishing out of . . . five finger-ends" is, I believe, the painting *Apollo and Daphne*, by Gerard Hoet, in the Dulwich Picture Gallery (DULW, no. 176; Fig. 237). *Pan and Syrinx*, Hoet's companion piece to his *Apollo and Daphne*, is entered as a source above under "The Bishop Orders his Tomb at St. Praxed's Church," 56-61.

For a description of the numerous tapestries owned by Browning—none of which bears any resemblance here—see above under "Childe Roland to the Dark Tower Came," 13:76-78. For more on the "half-moon" symbol of Diana, goddess of the moon and hunt, see above under "Cristina and Monaldeschi," 5-14ff. Also see below under VII.390-93. (Continued under this reference in the Supplement to Citations and Notes.)

VII.262-63

. . . [Pietro had]
Gone sight-see through the seven,
and found no church
To his mind like San Giovanni. . . .

Porter and Clarke correctly identify this "church" as "San Giovanni" in Laterano—St. John Lateran—one of the "seven" basilicas in Rome (POR, VII.339; Fig. 178). Cook, for no apparant reason, confuses the reference with the Church of Santa Maria d'Aracoeli (COOK, 147).

Fig. 178
Church of San Giovanni in Laterano
Rome

VII.390-93

(Tisbe had told me that the slim young man
With wings at head, and wings at feet, and sword
Threatening a monster, in our tapestry,
Would eat a girl else,—was a cavalier). . . .

The tapestries owned by the Brownings naturally come to mind in the present context, but none of them, as catalogued in the Sotheby sale, applies (for details, see above under "Childe Roland to the Dark Tower Came," 13:76-78). Porter and Clarke identify the "cavalier" in the tapestry as Perseus rescuing Andromeda, which recalls the fresco by Polidoro da Caravaggio and the etching of the same subject by Volpato, as described above under *Pauline*, 656-67 (POR, VII, 339). For composite sources including the *Perseus and Andromeda*, see below under this poem, VII.186-92, in the Supplement to Citations and Notes.

VII.425-30

> ... I was hurried through a storm,
> Next dark eve of December's deadest day—
> How it rained!—through our street and the Lion's-mouth
> And the bit of Corso,—cloaked round, covered close,
> I was like something strange or contraband,—
> Into blank San Lorenzo, up the aisle....

The hurrying of Pompilia from her home to the Church of San Lorenzo in Lucina, where she was secretly married, began at the corner of Via del Babuino and Via Vittoria—"our street"—the corner where the Comparini lived in Rome (Map R:6H). From Via Vittoria heading west the wedding party could have turned left at Via Bocca di Leone—the "Lion's-mouth"—right at Via Condotti, left at the "Corso," and right again into the Piazza San Lorenzo in Lucina (Map R:6H). The Brownings, it should be noted, lived at 43 Via Bocca di Leone in the late 1850's. Today a plaque on the side of the residence commemorates their residency there. Also, in association with the name "Lion's-mouth," mention should be made that Pompilia, under VII.21-27 above, makes much of the portentous marble lion statue jutting out from the façade of the Church of San Lorenzo in Lucina. For another reference to Via Vittoria and the home of the Comparini, see above under II.200-07.

VII.1215-19

> "And Michael's pair of wings will arrive first
> At Rome, to introduce the company,

And bear him from our picture where he fights
Satan,—expect to have that dragon loose
And never a defender!"

Pompilia, while in Arezzo, refers to "our picture," the fresco
entitled *Triumph of St. Michael*, by Spinello Aretino (1346?-
1410), in the Church of San Francesco, in Arezzo (HOD, 337, no.
531; COOK, 153; Fig. 179). The fresco is in the Cappella Guasconi,
the chapel to the right of the chancel. For another reference to
St. Michael as a subject for an art object, see below under X.1010-
12, and under "Bishop Blougram's Apology," 666-68, in the Supplement to Citations and Notes.

Fig. 179
Spinello Aretino
Triumph of St. Michael
Church of San Francesco
Arezzo

VII.1323-28

> Our Caponsacchi, he's your true Saint George
> To slay the monster, set the Princess free,
> And have the whole High-Altar to himself:
> I always think so when I see that piece
> I' the Pieve, that's his church and mine, you know:
> Though you drop eyes at mention of his name!"

The "piece / I' the Pieve" on the "High-Altar" is the painting *St. George and the Dragon*, by Vasari (HOD, 297, no. 8; COOK, 154; Fig. 180). Browning no doubt saw the painting during his trip to Arezzo in 1848. In 1865 the painting was transferred to the Church of the Abbey of Santa Flora and Lucina, in Arezzo. It hangs behind the high altar in the chancel (PAS, 108, 133-34). For other references to the Church of the Pieve, see above under VI.345-48 and 974-76.

Fig. 180
Giorgio Vasari
St. George and the Dragon
Church of the Abbey of Santa Flora and Lucina
Arezzo

VIII.634-39

> ... why, trait for trait,
> Was ever portrait limned so like the life?
> (By Cavalier Maratta, shall I say?
> I hear he's first in reputation now.)
> Yes, that of Samson in the Sacred Text:
> That's not so much the portrait as the man!

For a discussion of possible sources here and above under III.58-62, see under this reference in the Supplement to Citations and Notes.

VIII.985-87

> ... then did the tongue
> O' the Brazen Head give license, 'Time is now!'
> Wait to make mind up? 'Time is past' it peals.

Of this passage COOK, 172, says,

> Roger Bacon (1214-94) was believed to have made a head capable of speech. There were different versions of the legend; according to that followed by Browning here and by Byron in *Don Juan*, I., stanza 217—
>
> > Now, like Friar Bacon's brazen head, I've spoken,
> > 'Time is, Time was, Time's past'—.
>
> the head, after uttering the words quoted, the time for consulting it having been neglected, tumbled from its stand and was shattered.

VIII.1080-81

> We hurried to the song matutinal
> I' the Sistine, and pressed forward for the Mass....

Michelangelo, of course, painted his famous frescoes "I' the Sistine" Chapel, in the Vatican. Other painters represented in the chapel are Rosselli, Botticelli, Pinturicchio, Perugino, Signorelli, and Ghirlandaio. The subjects of the paintings are drawn from the Old and New Testaments (COOK, 173).

IX.110-30

> ... its Governor,
> Whose new wing to the villa he hath bought

(God give him joy of it) by Capena, soon
('Tis bruited) shall be glowing with the brush
Of who hath long surpassed the Florentine,
The Urbinate and ... what if I dared add,
Even his master, yea the Cortonese,—
I mean the accomplished Ciro Ferri, Sirs!
(—Did not he die? I'll see before I print.)
...
Thus then, just so and no whit otherwise,
Have I,—engaged as I were Ciro's self,
To paint a parallel, a Family,
The patriarch Pietro with his wise old wife
To boot (as if one introduced Saint Anne
By bold conjecture to complete the group)
And juvenile Pompilia with her babe,
Who, seeking safety in the wilderness,
Were all surprised by Herod, while outstretched
In sleep beneath a palm-tree by a spring,
And killed—the very circumstance I paint. . . .

COOK, 183, identifies "Capena" as the Porta Capena, in Rome, but he misplaces it at the entrance to the city where the Porta San Sebastiano is located.   Actually, the Porta Capena is a square adjoining the Piazza Circo Massimo in the interior of the city.

The "Florentine" is Michelangelo; the "Urbinate," Raphael; the "Cortonese," Pietro (Berrettini) da Cortona (1597-1669); and "Ciro Ferri" (1634-89), the pupil of Pietro da Cortona (COOK, 183).   Ciro Ferri's painting here of a Holy "Family" with a "Saint Anne" being slaughtered by "Herod" is imaginary but possibly a conflation of sources.   (Continued under this reference in the Supplement to Citations and Notes.)

IX.169-71

Never was knock-knee known nor splay-foot found
In Phryne? (I must let the portrait go,
Content me with the model, I believe). . . .

The famous Greek courtesan "Phryne" is said to be embodied in the *Venus Anadyomene* of Apelles and the *Cnidian Venus* of Praxiteles (COOK, 184).   Copies of the *Cnidian Venus* are in the Louvre and the Vatican.   The famous *Medici Venus* in the Uffizi is based on the *Cnidian Venus* of Praxiteles (Map F:8H).

IX.965-70

Methinks I view some ancient bas-relief.
There stands Hesione thrust out by Troy,

> Her father's hand has chained her to a crag,
> Her mother's from the virgin plucked the vest,
> At a safe distance both distressful watch,
> While near and nearer comes the snorting orc.

This "ancient bas-relief" of "Hesione thrust out by Troy," though unspecified, has features in common with the *Perseus and Andromeda* of Polidoro da Caravaggio, discussed above under *Pauline*, 656-67. Also compare with the entries above under VII.186-96, 390-93.

X.42-44

> They set it, that dead body of a Pope,
> Clothed in pontific vesture now again,
> Upright on Peter's chair as if alive.

St. "Peter's chair" is located behind the main altar in the Church of St. Peter, in Rome (Fig. 134).

X.1010-12

> Armed and crowned,
> Would Michael, yonder, be, nor crowned nor armed,
> The less pre-eminent angel?

The Pope, speaking from the Vatican, views St. "Michael, yonder," that is, the statue of St. Michael surmounted on nearby Castel Sant' Angelo. The statue, originally in marble, was rendered in 1535 by Raffaelle da Montelupo (Fig. 181), but in 1752 it was replaced by a bronze version executed by Verschaffelt (Figs. 146 and 182). The original statue by Raffaelle da Montelupo is standing today in a courtyard of Castel Sant' Angelo (COOK, 215).

X.2106-11

> Set with all diligence a scaffold up,
> Not in the customary place, by Bridge
> Saint Angelo, where die the common sort;
> But since the man is noble, and his peers
> By predilection haunt the People's Square,
> There let him be beheaded in the midst....

"Bridge / Saint Angelo" spans the Tiber and leads to Castel Sant' Angelo, Hadrian's Mausoleum. The three central spans of the bridge that remain today were built by Hadrian in 134 A.D. (Fig.

Fig. 181
Raffaelle da Montelupo
St. Michael
Castel Sant' Angelo
Rome

Fig. 182
Verschaffelt
St. Michael
Castel Sant' Angelo
Rome

146; Map R:6F,7F). The "People's Square" is Piazza del Popolo, at the end of the Corso (Figs. 147, 148, 196; Map R:5H,6H). See above under I.350-60 and below under XII.138-46, 159-65.

XI.3-14

. . .

> Acciaiuoli—ah, your ancestor it was,
> Built the huge battlemented convent-block
> Over the little forky flashing Greve
> That takes the quick turn at the foot o' the hill
> Just as one first sees Florence: oh those days!
> 'T is Ema, though, the other rivulet,
> The one-arched brown brick bridge yawns over,—yes,
> Gallop and go five minutes, and you gain
> The Roman Gate from where the Ema's bridged:
> Kingfishers fly there: how I see the bend
> O'erturreted by Certosa which he built,
> That Senescal (we styled him) of your House!

The "huge battlemented convent-block" is the Monastery of the Certosa (Fig. 183), two and one-half miles south of the "Roman Gate," the Porta Romana of Florence (Fig. 184). The monastery

Fig. 183
Monastery of the Certosa
Florence (environs)

Fig. 184
Porta Romana
Florence

was founded by the "Acciaiuoli" family, which was notable in
Naples and Greece before settling in Florence (COOK, 238). For
another reference to the Porta Romana, see above under I.472-
501.

XI.187-88

> Out of the way, in a by-part o' the town,
> At the Mouth-of-Truth o' the river-side, you know. . . .

The "Mouth-of-Truth" is the Piazza Bocca della Verità, which is on the Corso near the "river-side" of the Tiber (Fig. 185; Map R:9H). The piazza derives its name from a large marble disc—or mascaron—in the vestibule of the Church of Santa Maria in Cosmedin, on the east side of the square. The mascaron is a bas-relief in the form of a Triton with an open mouth (Figs. 185, 186). Hare explains the legend connected with the mouth of the mascaron (HARE, I, 159; COOK, 239):

> It was believed that if a witness, whose truthfulness was doubted, were desired to place his hand in the mouth of this mask, it would bite him if he were guilty of perjury.

XI.272-74

> Florid old rogue Albano's masterpiece,
> As—better than virginity in rags—
> Bouncing Europa on the back o' the bull....

Francesco "Albano's masterpiece" is the *Rape of Europa*, the original of which is in the Hermitage, in Leningrad (Fig. 187). Browning could have seen the painting during his 1834 trip to Russia, or he could have seen a copy of the painting in Florence, where it is now housed in the Vasari Corridor of the Uffizi Gallery (Map F:8H). COOK, 240, points out that historically the picture could have been seen by Guido, inasmuch as Albano died in 1660, thirty-three years prior to Guido's marriage in 1693.

XI.902-09

> The wife kissed both eyes blind,
> Explained away ambiguous circumstance,
> And while she held him captive by the hand,
> Crowned his head,—you know what's the mockery,—
> By half her body behind the curtain. That's
> Nature now! That's the subject of a piece
> I saw in Vallombrosa Convent, made
> Expressly to teach men what marriage was!

There is no "piece" in the "Vallombrosa Convent" showing a cuckold whose wife has "Crowned his head" (SPO). A stay of five days by the Brownings at the Monastery of Vallombrosa is recounted by Elizabeth Barrett Browning in her letters of August and September, 1847 (KEN, I, 343).

Fig. 185
Left: Church of Santa Maria in Cosmedin
Right: Atrium and Mascaron
          Church of Santa Maria in Cosmedin
          Rome

Fig. 186
Mascaron
Church of Santa Maria in Cosmedin
Rome

Fig. 187
Albano
Europa and the Bull
Hermitage
Leningrad

XI.1115-25

                            ... think you see
The dreadful bronze our boast, we Aretines,
The Etruscan monster, the three-headed thing,
Bellerophon's foe! How name you the whole beast?
You choose to name the body from one head,
That of the simple kid which droops the eye,
Hangs the neck and dies tenderly enough:

I rather see the griesly lion belch
Flame out i' the midst, the serpent writhe her rings,
Grafted into the common stock for tail,
And name the brute, Chimaera, which I slew!

The "Etruscan monster" is a bronze statue of the "Chimaera," which has the head of a lion in front, the head of a kid in the middle, and the head of a serpent for a tail. The statue was discovered at Arezzo in 1554 and is believed to be of Etruscan origin. Today it is housed in the Archeological Museum of Florence (COOK, 246-47; Fig. 188). Two bronze copies of the statue are mounted in the park in front of the railway station in Arezzo. Compare the reference to the portentious lion statue in the Church of San Lorenzo in Lucina, above under VII.21-27.

Fig. 188
Chimera of Arezzo
Archeological Museum
Florence

XI.1241-49

> Panciatichi!
> There's a report at Florence,—is it true?—
> That when your relative the Cardinal
> Built, only the other day, that barrack-bulk,
> The palace in Via Larga, some one picked
> From out the street a saucy quip enough
> That fell there from its day's flight through the town,
> About the flat front and the windows wide
> And bulging heap of cornice. . . .

That "barrack-bulk, / The palace in Via Larga," is the Palazzo Panciatichi, which is directly across Via Larga—Via Cavour today—facing the Palazzo Medici-Riccardi (see above under I.38-52). Fig. 42 shows Palazzo Medici-Riccardi on the left and Palazzo Panciatichi on the right as they looked in the nineteenth century (the illustration is reproduced from TER, 43).

XI.1667

> Seclusion at the Stinche for her life.

Concerning the "Stinche" prison in Florence, see above under IV.1516-17.

XI.2159-64

> Those are my arms: we turned the furze a tree
> To show more, and the greyhound tied thereto,
> Straining to start, means swift and greedy both;
> He stands upon a triple mount of gold—
> By Jove, then, he's escaping from true gold
> And trying to arrive at empty air!

This description of the Franceschini coat of arms is taken from a water-color drawing by Seymour Kirkup, Browning's friend. The drawing (Fig. 189) was given by Kirkup to Browning, who pasted it inside the cover of The Old Yellow Book. Today this manuscript is housed in the library of Balliol College, Oxford (HOD, frontispiece; COOK, xx-xxi). Besides "gold," the colors green, buff, and blue are employed in the picture (KO, 171). For another reference to the coat of arms, see below under XII.818-20. For other references to Kirkup, see above under "Old Pictures in Florence," 24:185-92; "Of Pacchiarotto, and How He Worked in Distemper," 2:5-19; and below under A Soul's Tragedy.

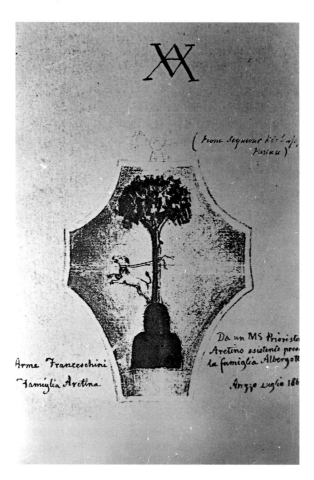

Fig. 189
Seymour Kirkup
Franceschini Coat of Arms
Balliol College Library
Oxford

XII.51-52

Along the river-side; he loves to see
That Custom-house he built upon the bank . . . .

As Cook points out, Pope Innocent XII did not build a "Custom-house . . . upon the bank" but rather far away from the Tiber, in the Piazza di Pietra (Map R:7H). Today the building serves as the Roman Exchange (COOK, 263). Fig. 190 shows three of the columns of the original structure. Also see below under XII.89-90.

Fig. 190
The Exchange (detail)
Rome

XII.61-62

> He may hold Jubilee a second time,
> And, twice in one reign, ope the Holy Doors.

For another reference to the "Jubilee" year in the Church of St. Peter, in Rome, and the "Holy Doors" of the church, that is, the Porta Aurea in particular, see above under III.566-72. Pope Innocent XII commemorated only one Jubilee, that of 1694 (COOK, 263).

XII.89-90

> To that Dogana-by-the-Bank he built,
> The crowd,—he suffers question, unrebuked. . . .

For another reference to the "Dogana-by-the-Bank," that is, the Custom-house built by Innocent XII, see above under XII.51-52.

XII.110-11

> But the French Embassy might unfurl flag,—
> Still the good luck of France to fling a foe!

The "French Embassy" has existed in Palazzo Farnese, in Rome, since 1552 (Fig. 191; Map R:8G). Today the embassy operates there on a 99-year lease. The cornice of the palace was designed by Michelangelo.

XII.138-46

> Then the procession started, took the way
> From the New Prisons by the Pilgrim's Street,
> The street of the Governo, Pasquin's Street,
> (Where was stuck up, 'mid other epigrams,
> A quatrain . . . but of all that, presently!)
> The Place Navona, the Pantheon's Place,
> Place of the Column, last the Corso's length,
> And so debouched thence at Mannaia's foot
> I' the Place o' the People.

Various landmarks in Rome trace the processional route taken by Guido on the day of his execution (HOD, 328, note 440; COOK, 264). These are the "New Prison" (Fig. 168; Map R:8F), which is

Fig. 191
Palazzo Farnese
Rome

situated in Via Giulia and was built by Pope Innocent X in 1604;
"Pasquin's Street," which leads to the Piazza Pasquino (Fig. 192;
Map R:8G); the "Place Navona," which is the largest square in
Rome (Fig. 194; Map R:7G); the "Pantheon's Place," which is the
square of the ancient Roman Pantheon, or Rotunda, the
structure that now serves as a church and houses the tomb of
Raphael (Fig. 169; Map R:7H); the "Place of the Column," or
Piazza Colonna, on Via "Corso," where the Roman column of
Marcus Aurelius stands (Fig. 193; Map R:7H); and the "Place o'"

the People"—Piazza del Popolo—at the end of the Corso, which includes an Egyptian obelisk, two fountains, two Baroque churches, and the Renaissance church, Santa Maria del Popolo (Figs. 147, 148, and 196; Map R:5H,6H). For other references to these landmarks along the execution route, see above under VI.1658-59 for Pasquin's Street, where "epigrams" were "stuck up"; above under IV.1282-83 and below under XII.159-65 for Piazza Navona; above under V.703-05 for the Pantheon's Place; above under IV. 439-42 for Piazza Colonna; and above under I.350-60 for the Church of St. Mary, in Piazza del Popolo (also, see XI.182).

Fig. 192
Piazza Pasquino
Rome

Fig. 193
Piazza Colonna
Rome

Fig. 194
Piazza Navona
Rome

XII.159-65

> Now did a beggar by Saint Agnes, lame
> From his youth up, recover use of leg,
> Through prayer of Guido as he glanced that way:
> So that the crowd near crammed his hat with coin.
> Thus was kept up excitement to the last,
> —Not an abrupt out-bolting, as of yore,
> From Castle, over Bridge and on to block....

Along the execution route, Guido passed by "Saint Agnes," which I believe is meant to be the Church of Sant' Agnese in Agone, in Piazza Navona. The Church is a seventeenth-century structure with two bell-towers on each side of the façade (Figs. 194 and 195; Map R:7G). The "Castle" and "Bridge" are Castel Sant' Angelo and Ponte Sant' Angelo, where the execution route began. For other references to Piazza Navona, see above under IV.1282-83 and XII.138-46. For other references to Castel and Ponte Sant' Angelo, see above under I.350-60, X.2106-11, and XII.138-46.

XII.818-20

> Shield, Azure, on a Triple Mountain, Or,
> A Palm-tree, Proper, whereunto is tied
> A Greyhound, Rampant, striving in the slips?

For details about the Franceschini coat of arms as drawn by Seymour Kirkup, see above under XI.2159-64.

XII.870-74

> Render all duty which good ring should do,
> And, failing grace, succeed in guardianship,—
> Might mine but lie outside thine, Lyric Love,
> Thy rare gold ring of verse (the poet praised)
> Linking our England to his Italy!

The home of the Brownings in Florence was Casa Guidi, across from the Palazzo Pitti at the junction of Via Romana, Via Maggio, and Via Mazzetta (Fig. 197; Map F:9G). Over the portal on Via Maggio is a tablet with an inscription that was written by the poet Tommaseo and which was placed there by the municipality of Florence after the death of Mrs. Browning. As Cook points out, the last two lines of this passage—the very end of the poem—refer to the tablet (COOK, 273). In translation the inscription on the tablet reads:

Fig. 195
Church of Sant' Agnese in Agone
Piazza Navona
Rome

> Here wrote and died Elizabeth Barrett Browning, who with
> the heart of a woman reconciled the knowledge of learning and
> the spirit of poetry and made of her verse a golden ring between
> Italy and England. Put here in grateful memory, Florence, 1861.

For other references to Casa Guidi, see above under I.110-16, 472-83. For other references to "Lyric Love," see above under I.1391-92 and under I.1391-1401 in the Supplement to Citations and Notes. For a discussion of the rings in *The Ring and the Book*, see above under I.1-4, 15-17, and under this reference in the Supplement to Citations and Notes.

Fig. 196
Piazza del Popolo at the Corso
Rome

Fig. 197

Center:	Church of San Felice
Right:	Casa Guidi
	Florence

A SCENE IN THE BUILDING OF THE INQUISITORS AT ANTWERP

1-5

Therefore the hand of God
Thy sentence with His finger
Hath written, and this tribunal
Consigneth it now straightway
Unto the secular arm.

DeVane tells us that these five unrhymed lines were probably meant to accompany Pen Browning's picture of the same subject. Pen studied in Antwerp for some time after 1874 under Jean-Arnold Heyermans, but DeVane gives neither a date of composition for the painting nor one for the poem (DEVA, 573). The lines are reproduced from a collection entitled *New Poems* (NE, 69). The painting has been identified as *The Delivery to the Secular Arm* and is a very large work showing a girl being delivered to secular agents by the Inquisition. The painting was exhibited in the Hanover Gallery in 1880 and is now housed in the Armstrong Browning Library (Fig. 197.5). For another reference to a painting by Pen Browning, see above under "Parleyings with Francis Furini," 11:601-07.

Fig. 197.5
Robert Wiedemann Barrett Browning
The Delivery to the Secular Arm
Armstrong Browning Library
Baylor University
Waco, Texas

SIBRANDUS SCHAFNABURGENSIS

13-14

> Chapter on chapter did I count,
>   As a curious traveller counts Stonehenge. . . .

Counting the chapters in a laborious tome like the imaginary "Sibrandus Schafnaburgensis" is like counting the numerous stones of Stonehenge, the famous ruins near Salisbury (Fig. 198). Tradition has it that a person can never arrive at the same number when counting the stones.

Fig. 198
Stonehenge
Salisbury

SORDELLO

I.138-39

> ... Ecelin, they say,
> Dozes now at Oliero. . . .

Oliero is a small village five miles north of Bassano. Ecelin II is presumably buried at Solagna, near Campese, which is between Oliero and Bassano. See below under VI.687-90 for the effigy of Ecelin.

I.381-82

> Goito; just a castle built amid
> A few low mountains. . . .

The castle of Goito, which lay ten miles from Mantua on the road to Brescia, no longer exists. The extended description following this quotation details the architectural and sculptural adornments that were presumably in and around the castle. Today there are the remains of a very old red brick wall that surrounded the castle and a red brick tower called the "Torre Sordello" (KING, II, 383). A succession of wars, earthquakes, and neglect explains the destruction of the castle (MES).

I.567-83

> Fool, who spied the mark
> Of leprosy upon him, violet-dark
> Already as he loiters? Born just now,
> With the new century, beside the glow
> And efflorescence out of barbarism;
> Witness a Greek or two from the abysm
> That stray through Florence-town with studious air,
> Calming the chisel of that Pisan pair:
> If Nicolo should carve a Christus yet!
> While at Siena is Guidone set,
> Forehead on hand; a painful birth must be
> Matured ere Saint Eufemia's sacristy
> Or transept gather fruits of one great gaze
> At the moon: look you! The same orange haze,—
> The same blue stripe round that—and, in the midst,
> Thy spectral whiteness, Mother-maid, who didst
> Pursue the dizzy painter!

The "Pisan pair" is Nicola Pisano and his son Giovanni Pisano, the famous thirteenth-century sculptors and architects of Pisa (BER, 498; COOKE, 391; KING, II, 384). Vasari mentions three pieces by "Nicolo" representing a "Christus": a bas-relief marble lunette of the Descent from the Cross, on the façade of the Church of San Martino, in Lucca, and the pulpits in the Baptistery at Pisa and the Duomo of Siena, both of which feature marble panels in bas-relief illustrating the life of Christ (VAS, I, 29, 32, 33). Of these three possibilities, Korg relates the present text only to the pulpit in the Baptistery at Pisa. The scene from the pulpit that Korg illustrates is the *Crucifixion* (KO, 33, 34), and this I think is appropriate because it ties in with the *Descent from the Cross* in Lucca. In this study, Fig. 208 illustrates the *Descent from the Cross*, and Fig. 199 shows the *Crucifixion* from the pulpit in the Duomo of Siena.

The line "While at Siena is Guidone set" refers to the thirteenth-century painter Guido da Siena and his famous *Madonna Enthroned* in the Palazzo Pubblico, in Siena (BER, 498; POR, II, 358; COOKE, 391; KING, II, 384; Fig. 200). Browning approximately specifies the colors of the painting when he describes the "orange haze"—actually more red than orange—of the background, the "blue stripe" of the Madonna's gown, and the "spectral whiteness" of the Madonna's cowl "in the midst" of the picture. The misinformation about the "orange haze" is possibly owing to the fact that Browning had not been to Siena when he wrote *Sordello* in the 1830's. At that time the painting was in the Church of San Domenico, in Siena, where Crowe and Cavalcaselle record it having been housed during the nineteenth century (CROWE, I, 150).

"Saint Eufemia's sacristy" has been identified with the church of that name in Verona because Browning probably visited the church during his 1838 trip through northern Italy, including Verona (BER, 498-99; KELL, 492; KING, II, 384). Although the "transept" of the church is too narrow for a fresco, I have observed that the sacristy, being vast, bare, and vaulted, would indeed require a supreme effort—"a painful birth"—for the painter Guido da Siena to cover with frescoes.

I.820-21

Saint Mark's a spectacle, the sleight o' the sword
Baffling the treason in a moment....

Fig. 199
Nicola Pisano
Pulpit (detail)
Duomo
Siena

Ecelin II was unsuccessfully attacked by assassins in the Square of
St. Mark, in Venice (KING, II, 385). Also see below under III.136-
37, and 876-77. For references in other poems to the Church of

St. Mark, see above under *Fifine at the Fair*, 107:1846, and below under "A Toccata of Galuppi's," 5-8.

Fig. 200
Guido da Siena
Madonna Enthroned
Palazzo Pubblico
Siena

III.119-21

> The hot torchlit wine-scented island-house
> Where Friedrich holds his wickedest carouse,
> Parading,—to the gay Palermitans. . . .

Reference librarians at the Biblioteca Centrale della Regione Siciliana, in Palermo, assure me in conversation that no "island-house"—house on the island of Sicily—existed in Palermo—among the "Palermitans"—that was used by Frederick II to entertain his court.   But a source for this house is possibly the Palazzina Cinese, which is a well-known tourist attraction of Palermo.   Berdoe and Peckham advance this source in the present context but erroneously label the house La Favora (BER, 504; KING, II, 394; Fig. 202), when in fact the Palazzina Cinese has always been called La Favorita, the name of the park in which

Fig. 201
Left: Square of St. Mark (with Ducal Palace)
Right: Sansovino, *Neptune*
            Giant Staircase, Ducal Palace
            Venice

the Palazzina Cinese is located. The park was the favorite—La Favorita—of the Bourbon King Ferdinand III and was used as a hunting ground for the court. Palazzina Cinese was completed in 1799 and was thus possibly known to Browning while writing his poem. The anachronism of associating the medieval Frederick II with the Palazzina Cinese is not explained by Berdoe and Peckham, but I think it might be accounted for by Browning's confusion in mentally connecting the names and titles of Ferdinand III and Frederick II. In their official capacity as rulers of Sicily, the kings were respectively known in Italian as Ferdinando I di Sicilia and Federico I di Sicilia.

Another well-known palace of Palermo that Browning could be referring to in the present passage is the Palazzo della Zisa, a pleasure palace in the Arab-Norman style built from 1160 onwards by William I.

Fig. 202
Palazzina Cinese
Palermo (environs)

III.136-37

What pillar, marble massive, sardius slim,
'T were fittest he transport to Venice' Square. . . .

In St. Mark's Square there are two granite columns that were brought from Constantinople. One is surmounted by the Lion of St. Mark, and the other by a statue of St. Theodore (Fig. 201).

III.422-23

> ... passing out by Gate Saint Blaise,
> He stopped short in Vicenza. . . .

A "Gate Saint Blaise" in or outside of Vicenza has not yet been identified (cf. KING, II, 396).

III.586-87

> ... that golden Palma,—thank
> Verona's Lady in her citadel. . . .

"Verona's Lady"—or the *Madonna of Verona*—is an ancient statue on a fountain in the Piazza delle Erbe, in Verona. The steel crown that the Lady wears signifies that Verona is an imperial residence. The statue, which is being associated here with "Palma," reportedly was found on the site of the old capitol, where the castle of St. Peter now stands (BER, 507; KING, II, 398; Fig. 203).

III.876-77

> Thus, prisoned in the Piombi, I repeat
> Events one rove occasioned, o'er and o'er. . . .

The "Piombi" are the prisons adjoining the Palace of the Doges, in Venice (KING, II, 401; Fig. 204). The famous Bridge of Sighs connecting the prison with the palace was added in about 1600.

IV.157-71

>   ... the Fighter stood
> For his last fight, and, wiping treacherous blood
> Out of the eyelids just held ope beneath
> Those shading fingers in their iron sheath,
> Steadied his strengths amid the buzz and stir
> Of the dusk hideous amphitheatre
> At the announcement of his over-match
> To wind the day's diversion up, dispatch
> The pertinacious Gaul: while, limbs one heap,
> The Slave, no breath in her round mouth,
>   watched leap
> Dart after dart forth, as her hero's car

Clove dizzily the solid of the war
—Let coil about his knees for pride in him.
We reach the farthest terrace, and the grim
San Pietro Palace stops us.

Fig. 203
Madonna of Verona
Piazza delle Erbe
Verona

Fig. 204

Left:　　　Ducal Palace
Center:　　Bridge of Sighs
Right:　　　Piombi (prisons)
　　　　　　Venice

Salinguerra's "San Pietro Palace," in Ferrara, no longer exists. In its place, on Via Carlo Mayr 191, is a tablet identifying the surrounding area as the site of "le torri dei Torelli-Salinguerra" —"the towers of the Torelli-Salinguerra." Browning's description of the statues of the "Fighter" and the "Slave" on the palace grounds is probably imaginary. Roma King points out that Salinguerra's residence was in the San Pietro Quarter, the southeast corner of Ferrara. The quarter included within its grounds the Church of San Pietro, after which the quarter was probably named (KING, II, 405). The church is a Romanesque structure and still stands in Via San Pietro near Via Salinguerra. It is presently being used as a movie house (CAP; Fig. 205).

IV.533-35

> He only waits they end his wondrous girth
> Of trees that link San Pietro with Tomà,
> To visit Mantua.

The Quarter of San Pietro is in the same southeastern part of Ferrara as is the "Tomà," the Bastione di San Tommaso, mentioned below under V.282-83.

IV.607-11

> Come to Bassano, see Saint Francis' church
> And judge of Guido the Bolognian's piece
> Which, lend Taurello credit, rivals Greece—
> Angels, with aureoles like golden quoits
> Pitched home, applauding Ecelin's exploits.

"Saint Francis' church," that is, the Church of San Francesco, in Bassano (Fig. 206), was constructed in 1158. The fresco of Ecelin I by "Guido the Bolognian" was executed in 1177 and destroyed in 1720 by Franciscan fathers, who were first affiliated with the church in 1327. The Franciscan fathers, who of course were part of the Guelph cause, nourished an ancient antipathy for the Ghibelline Ecelins (RIG; cf. KING, II, 408). Berdoe erroneously identifies the medieval Guido the Bolognian as Guido Reni, the Baroque painter from Bologna (BER, 509; POR, II, 377).

IV.1014-22

> Of the Capitol, of Castle Angelo;
> New structures, that inordinately glow,

Fig. 205
Church of San Pietro (formerly)
Ferrara

Fig. 206
Left: Tower of Ecelin
Right: Church of San Francesco
            Bassano

> Subdued, brought back to harmony, made ripe
> By many a relic of the archetype
> Extant for wonder; every upstart church
> That hoped to leave old temples in the lurch,
> Corrected by the Theatre forlorn
> That,—as a mundane shell, its world late born,—
> Lay and o'ershadowed it.

For other references to the "Capitol" of Rome, see above under "Imperante Augusto Natus Est—," 31-40, 92-94, 100-01, and 139-42, 157-60. For the "Castle Angelo," in Rome, see "Cenciaja," 219-21, and *The Ring and the Book*, I.350-60. For the "Theatre" of Marcellus, in Rome, see "Imperante Augusto Natus Est—," 31-40.

V.282-83

>   ... the southern wall,
> Tomà, where Richard's kept. ...

King identifies "Tomà" as the Bastione di San Tommaso, in Ferrara, the place of Count Richard's imprisonment (KING, II, 407, line 534). The bastion was rebuilt in the fourteenth century by the Este family and today forms a triangular projection in the "southern wall" of Ferrara (CAP). See above under IV.533-35.

V.751, 755

> ... that Vicenza night
> ...
> ... through—San Biagio rocks!

King identifies "San Biagio rocks" with a church in Vicenza (KING, II, 417), but all that I can find there is a street named San Biagio.

VI.687-90

> Ecelin at Campese slept; close by,
> Who likes may see him in Solagna lie,
> With cushioned head and gloved hand to denote
> The cavalier he was. ...

At Solagna, a half mile north of Campese and two and a half miles north of Bassano, a tomb is built into the outside wall of the parish church there. According to tradition, this is the tomb of Ecelin II. The effigy on the tomb, as seen in Fig. 207, shows a "cushioned head and gloved hand." Browning no doubt saw the church during his visit to Italy in 1838, which included a stop in Bassano (KELL, 492; KING, II, 419).

Fig. 207
Effigy of Ecelin II
Parish Church
Solagna
Italy

Fig. 208
Nicola Pisano
Descent from the Cross
Church of San Martino
Lucca, Italy

VI.777-81

> By San Zenon where Alberic in turn
> Saw his exasperated captors burn
> Seven children and their mother; then, regaled
> So far, tied on to a wild horse, was trailed
> To death through raunce and bramble-bush.

"San Zenon" is not the basilica of San Zeno, in Verona, as
Berdoe claims (BER, 514), but, according to Korg, the town of San
Zenone degli Ezzelini, which is east of Bassano (KO, 27).

A SOUL'S TRAGEDY

On the verso of the title page of *A Soul's Tragedy*, in the 1846 edition of *Bells and Pomegranates* (London: Edward Moxon; no. 8 of eight pamphlets), Browning specifies two paintings that he associates with the title of the edition:

> Here ends my first series of "Bells and Pomegranates:" and I take the opportunity of explaining, in reply to inquiries, that I only meant by that title to indicate an endeavour towards something like an alternation, or mixture, of music with discoursing, sound with sense, poetry with thought; which looks too ambitious, thus expressed, so the symbol was preferred. It is little to the purpose, that such is actually one of the most familiar of the many Rabbinical (and Patristic) acceptations of the phrase; because I confess that, letting authority alone, I supposed the bare words, in such juxtaposition, would sufficiently convey the desired meaning. "Faith and good works" is another fancy, for instance, and perhaps no easier to arrive at: yet Giotto placed a pomegranate fruit in the hand of Dante, and Raffaelle crowned his Theology (in the *Camera della Segnatura*) with blossoms of the same; as if the Bellari and Vasari would be sure to come after, and explain that it was merely "*simbolo delle buone opere—il qual Pomogranato fu pero usato nelle vesti del Pontefice appresso gli Ebrei.*"

In the Bargello of Florence there is the *Last Judgment*, a fresco attributed to Giotto. Included in the fresco is a portrait of Dante, which Browning probably read about in Vasari (VAS, I, 50; Fig. 209; Map F:8H,8I). The portrait only faintly shows a sprig of pomegranate fruit in the hand of Dante because changes were made when the painting was restored in 1841-42 (cf. "Old Pictures in Florence," 24:185-92). Before the restoration, however, Browning's friend Seymour Kirkup made a sketch of the original portrait showing more clearly the sprig of fruit (Fig. 210). For many years the sketch hung below the restored portrait in the Bargello (VAU, 245); today the sketch is conserved in the library of the Bargello. As for the other painting, the fresco of Raphael's Theology "crowned" with pomegranate blossoms, it is, as Browning places it, in the Stanza—"Camera"—della Segnatura of the Vatican (Fig. 211).

Eleanor Cook identifies the Italian quotation that Browning uses here to represent the pomegranate as "un simbolo delle buone opere"—a symbol of good works. It is taken from Giovanni Pietro Bellori's *Descrizione delle imagini dipinte da Raefaello d'Urbino nelle camere del Palazzo Apostolico Vati-*

Fig. 209
Giotto (attributed to)
Last Judgment (detail)
National Museum (Bargello)
Florence

cano (Rome, 1695), page 5, in the section on Raphael's painting *Theology.*   Browning's misspelling "Bellari" is probably a printer's error (COO, 334-35).

Act II. Stage directions

> *The Market-place.   LUITOLFO in disguise mingling with the* Populace *assembled opposite the* Provost's *Palace.*

Fig. 210
Seymour Kirkup
Portrait of Dante by Giotto
National Museum (Bargello Library)
Florence

Fig. 211
Raphael
Theology
Stanza della Segnatura
Vatican

Fig. 212 shows the "Market-place"—Piazza del Popolo—of Faenza, Italy, the setting for Act II. In the stage directions to Act I the city of Faenza is specified along with the time of the play, "15—." From left to right Fig. 212 shows the fifteenth-century Cathedral, the Bell-tower, and the twelfth-century Provost's Palace (Palazzo Governo). The palace is surrounded by an arcade surmounted by a gallery, which was obviously added at a later time.

Fig. 212
Piazza del Popolo
Faenza

THE STATUE AND THE BUST

1-6

> There's a palace in Florence, the world knows well,
> And a statue watches it from the square,
> And this story of both do our townsmen tell.
>
> Ages ago, a lady there,
> At the farthest window facing the East
> Asked, "Who rides by with the royal air?"

The "palace in Florence" is Palazzo Budini-Gattai, in the Piazza Santissima Annunziata (WIT, 45-46; Fig. 213; Map F:7I).   The

Fig. 213

Right: Giovanni da Bologna
           Duke Ferdinand I
Center: Palazzo Budini-Gattai
           Piazza Santissima Annunziata
           Florence

"statue . . . [in] the square" is that of Duke Ferdinand I (Figs. 2, 213, and 214), who looks at the "farthest window facing the East," that is, to be precise, the lower corner window facing the right hand of the Duke, while the façade of the palace faces northeast. For details concerning the statue in the square and the bust that is presumably placed in the window described here, see below under 166-71 and 199-202.

Fig. 214
Giovanni da Bologna
Duke Ferdinand I
Piazza Santissima Annunziata
Florence

32-34

> A feast was held that selfsame night
> In the pile which the mighty shadow makes.
>
> (For Via Larga is three-parts light. . . .

The "pile" is Palazzo Medici-Riccardi, in Florence. "Via Larga," now called Via Cavour, is the street where the palace is located (Fig. 42; Map F:7H). For other references to the palace, see above under "Fra Lippo Lippi," 14-18, 61-67, 226-30, and *The Ring and the Book*, I.38-52.

94-96

> "What if we break from the Arno bowers,
> And try if Petraja, cool and green,
> Cure last night's fault with this morning's flowers?"

"Arno's bowers" locate the vicinity of the Palazzo Medici-Riccardi, which is less than a mile north of the Arno River in the center of Florence. The Duke proposes to hold a festive occasion in his Villa Medici della Petraia (Fig. 215), a country residence about two miles north of Florence and the Arno River. For the antecedent referring to Palazzo Medici-Riccardi, see above under 32-34.

166-71

> "Let Robbia's craft so apt and strange
> Arrest the remains of young and fair,
> And rivet them while the seasons range."
>
> "Make me a face on the window there,
> Waiting as ever, mute the while,
> My love to pass below in the square!"

The bust that is to represent "a face on the window" of Palazzo Budini-Gattai (see above under 1-6) is an imaginary conception attributed to one of the famous members of the "Robbia" family. Browning when asked by Thomas Hardy about the identity of the bust replied, "I invented it" (HA, 261-62; TUR, 331). The name of the Robbia family, however, might have come to the lady's mind here—as conceived by Browning—because she could have noticed the medallions by Andrea della Robbia from her window in the palace. These medallions depict babies and are placed on the spandrels between the arches which form the arcade of the Foundlings Hospital. The hospital, as Fig. 2 shows, faces to the right of the palace (ALB, 56, 57; Map F:7I). (Continued under this poem, lines 187-93, in the Supplement to Citations and Notes.)

Fig. 215
Villa Medici della Petraia
Castello

199-202

"John of Douay shall effect my plan,
Set me on horseback here aloft,
Alive, as the crafty sculptor can,

"In the very square I have crossed so oft...."

Duke Ferdinand I de' Medici, the Grand Duke of Tuscany (1549-1609), is the subject of a bronze equestrian statue fashioned by "John of Douay" (1524-1608), commonly known as Giovanni da Bologna (Figs. 2, 213, and 214; BER, 521). The "Square" the statue stands in is Piazza Santissima Annunziata, in Florence (Figs. 2 and 213; Map F:7I).   For a reference to the Church of the Santissima Annunziata in the piazza, see above under "Andrea del Sarto," 41-43. Giovanni da Bologna also sculptured a marble statue of Ferdinand I in Arezzo, as described above under *The Ring and the Book*, VI.249-56.

214-16

Still I suppose they sit and ponder
What a gift life was, ages ago,
Six steps out of the chapel yonder.

The "chapel yonder" is no doubt the Cappella de' Principi, adjoining the Church of San Lorenzo, across from Palazzo Medici-Riccardi (Fig. 141; Map F:7H).   This identification may be surmised from the association with line 212, where Duke Ferdinand I speaks of "my tomb," which is in the Cappella de' Principi. Begun in 1604 by Nigetti, the chapel was mainly sponsored by Duke Ferdinand I before his death in 1609. For another reference to this chapel, see above under *The Ring and the Book*, I.38-52.

A TOCCATA OF GALUPPI'S

5-8

What, they lived once thus at Venice where
the merchants were the kings,
Where St. Mark's is, where the Doges used
to wed the sea with rings?

> Ay, because the sea's the street there; and
>   't is arched by . . . what you call
> . . . Shylock's bridge with houses on it, where
>   they kept the carnival. . . .

"Where St. Mark's is," of course, is the Square of St. Mark, in Venice (Fig. 216); and "Shylock's bridge with the houses on it" is the Rialto Bridge over the Grand Canal (BER, 546; Fig. 217). The ceremony in which the Doges "used to wed the sea with rings" occurred every year on Ascension Day between 1173 and 1797. Dressed in gold cloth on board his *Bucentaur*, a gilded state galley, the Doge used to throw a ring into the water as a symbol of his rule over the sea. Today, in the Naval Museum of Venice, a small model of one of the Doge's *Bucentaurs* is on display.

For other references to the Church or Square of St. Mark, see above under *Fifine at the Fair*, 107:1846, and *Sordello*, I.820-21, III.136-37.

Fig. 216
Square of St. Mark
Venice

Fig. 217
Rialto Bridge
Venice

UP AT A VILLA—DOWN IN THE CITY

26-30

Is it ever hot in the square? There's
a fountain to spout and splash!

> In the shade it sings and springs;
>   in the shine such foambows flash
> On the horses with curling fish-tails,
>   that prance and paddle and pash
> Round the lady atop in her conch—fifty gazers
>   do not abash,
> Though all that she wears is some weeds round
>   her waist in a sort of sash.

This imaginary fountain is, I think, a composite of several real fountains and a painting in Italy. For models of the "lady atop her conch," I propose two possibilities. One is the *Fountain of Good Fortune*, in Piazza 20 Settembre, in Fano (Fig. 218). In 1848, seven years before publishing the present poem, Browning was in Fano, where he no doubt saw the fountain along with Guercino's *The Guardian Angel*, described above under the poem of the same name. The fountain displays a protecting goddess perched on a pivoting globe over a sea-shell or conch. The cloak the revolving goddess holds as a weathervane corresponds, in the poem, to "some weeds round her waist," which in her nudity she wears "in a sort of sash." The other possibility is the famous painting *Birth of Venus*, by Botticelli, which in Browning's time was in the Accademia, in Florence, but now is in the Uffizi (Fig. 219; Map F:8H). In the picture, the goddess rides a sea shell with only her hair as a kind of clothing or sash covering her. Models of sea-horses "that prance and paddle and pash" in fountains can be viewed throughout Italy. Most influential, however, are no doubt those seen by Browning prior to publishing his poem in 1855. These possible sources are the *Fountain of Neptune*, by Giongo, in Trent (see above under "My Last Duchess," 54-56; Fig. 92); the *Fountain of Neptune*, by Ammanati, in the Piazza della Signoria, in Florence (see above under *Luria*, I.67-73; Fig. 86; Map F:7H); and the *Fountain of Trevi*, in Rome (Map R:7I; Fig. 251).

51-52

> Noon strikes,—here sweeps the procession!
>   our Lady borne smiling and smart
> With a pink gauze gown all spangles,
>   and seven swords stuck in her heart!

This description of an effigy of the Virgin of Sorrows being

Fig. 218
Fountain of Good Fortune
Piazza 20 Settembre
Fano

Fig. 219
Botticelli
Birth of Venus (detail)
Uffizi
Florence

carried in procession has been identified with the Order of the Servites (NEY, 27), but which effigy or effigies Browning has in mind depends on where the locale of the poem is set. DeVane places the composition of the poem to 1850, when the Brownings lived two miles outside of Siena in a villa in the hills. To support his position, DeVane quotes a letter of Elizabeth, which he thinks harmonizes with the rustic setting and inexpensiveness of the villa in the poem (DEVA, 215). Turner, on the other hand, identifies the house in the city as Casa Guidi, in Florence, where, in the late 1840's, the Brownings lived just across from the Grand Duke's residence in Palazzo Pitti (TUR, 316). From Casa Guidi the Brownings undoubtedly saw the Duke's guard in procession as described at the end of the poem. If Browning had both Siena and Florence in mind while composing the poem, then several effigies of the Virgin of Sorrows become possible sources for the passage here. In Siena, in the Church of the Servites, there is one such effigy; in Florence there are three: one in the Church of the Santissima Annunziata, one in the refectory of the Monastery of the Santissima Annunziata, and one in the Convent of the Suore Montelatte on Via S. Gallo. All of the effigies are made of papier-mâché (*cartapesta*), and, according to state archives, none of them can be dated (CHIA). Eugenio Casaline, however, the curator of the Monastery of the Santissima Annunziata, believes that all of the effigies were probably used during Browning's time. Furthermore, Father Casaline explains that the "pink gauze gown" that covered the effigies while used in procession was made of silk, was commonly of a violet color rather than the pink that Browning recalls, and that the only decorations on the mantles were flowers painted in gold. In addition, Father Casaline believes that Browning confuses these gold flowers with the "spangles" mentioned in the poem, for the gold coloring sparkled like spangles under the sun during a procession. Fig. 220, which shows the effigy of the Virgin of Sorrows in the Church of the Servites, in Siena, displays the effigy without a gown. For a black-and-white illustration of a Virgin of Sorrows complete with a gown of silk covered with presumably gold flowers, see Father Casaline's "Note d'arte e d'archivio," in *La SS. Annunziata di Firenze* (Firenze: Convento della SS. Annunziata, 1978), 2:275, Fig. 67. For another reference to the Virgin of Sorrows, see above under *The Ring and the Book*, VI.702-07.

Fig. 220
Virgin of Sorrows
Church of the Servites
Siena

"YELLOW AND PALE AS RIPENED CORN"

1-4

> Yellow and pale as ripened corn
> Which Autumn's kiss frees,—grain from sheath,—
> Such was her hair, while her eyes beneath
> Showed, Spring's faint violets freshly born.

These four lines were written to accompany a painting by Lord Leighton and are published in *Letters of Robert Browning: Collected by Thomas J. Wise*, ed. by Thurman L. Hood (London: John Murray, 1933), p. 368. The Ormonds report that the picture has no title but is described in the Royal Academy catalogue as "a picture of a little girl with golden hair and pale blue eyes." The Ormonds further tell us that the painting was rendered around 1887, at the time Browning wrote his epigram for it; that the painting was exhibited by the Royal Academy in 1887; and that today it is untraced. The little girl with "faint violets" for eyes, according to Leighton's correspondence with Browning, was known to Browning as Letty Dene, the younger sister of Dorothy Dene, whom Browning befriended (ORMO, 80, 168; DEVA, 573).

For other references to the works of Leighton, see above under *Balaustion's Adventure*, 2672-97, and "Eurydice and Orpheus," 1-8.

Fig. 221
Giovanni Mazzolan da Bergamo
Neptune
Piazza della Borsa
Trieste

Fig. 222
Bronzino
Lucrezia de' Medici
Pitti Palace
Florence

Fig. 223
Masaccio
The Expulsion
Brancacci Chapel
Church of the Carmine
Florence

Fig. 224
Betto di Francesco
Giovanni di Francesco
Madonna and Child (detail)
Tomb of St. Donatus, high altar
Cathedral
Arezzo

Fig. 225
Fra Bartolommeo
Portrait of Savonarola
Monastery of San Marco
Florence

Fig. 226
Jacopo della Quercia
Creation
Church of St. Petronius
Bologna

Fig. 227
Raynaldo Bartolini
Virgin of Sorrows (detail)
Church of the Pieve
Arezzo

Fig. 228
Raphael
Small Cowper Madonna
National Gallery
Washington

Fig. 229
Fra Angelico
Martyrdom of St. Lawrence
Chapel of Nicholas V
Vatican
Rome

Fig. 230
Old Jewish Cemetery
Florence

Fig. 231
Raphael
La Fornarina
Palazzo Barbarini
Rome

Fig. 232
Naples Liquefaction
Treasure Chapel
Duomo
Naples
Left: Crystal with ampules of blood mounted in a shrine
Right: Crystal with ampules of blood removed from the shrine

Fig. 233
Cappella San Carlo Borromeo
Church of Santa Prassade
Rome

Fig. 234
Left: Rocca Guàita
Center: Rocca della Fratta
Right: Rocca Montale
San Marino
Italy

Fig. 235
Oratorio at Rifubbri
(as seen from the one-arched bridge)
Bagni di Lucca (environs)
Italy

Fig. 236
Interior of the Oratorio at Rifubbri
Bagni di Lucca (environs)
Italy

Fig. 237
Gerard Hoet
Apollo and Daphne (detail)
Dulwich Picture Gallery
London

Fig. 238
Michelangelo
Awakening Captive (detail)
Accademia
Florence

Fig. 239
Hiram Powers
Loulie's Hand

Fig. 240
Neptune Chalice
Treasury
Residenz
Munich

Fig. 241
Tiepolo
Venice Receives the Homage of Neptune
Palazzo Ducale
Venice

Fig. 242
Left: Lateral façade
         Duomo
         Foligno
         Italy
Right: Old Bishop's Palace

Fig. 243
Romanesque Portal, lateral façade
Duomo
Foligno
Italy

Fig. 244
Master of the Triumph of Death
Triumph of Death (detail)
Camposanto
Pisa
Italy

Fig. 245
Tiepolo
Diana (detail)
Dulwich Picture Gallery
London

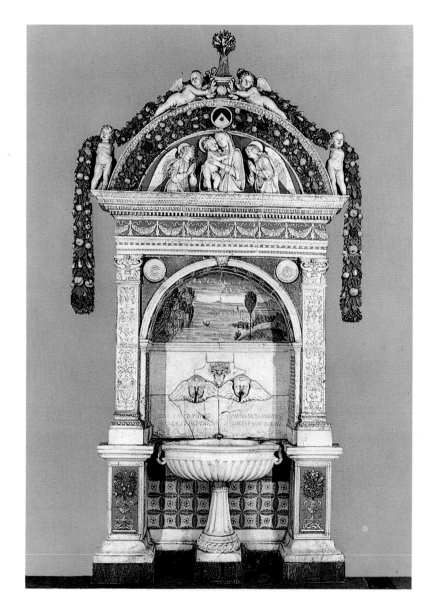

Fig. 246
Giovanni della Robbia
Lavabo
Sacristy
Church of Santa Maria Novella
Florence

Fig. 247
Carlo Maratta
Holy Family (detail)
Dulwich Picture Gallery
London

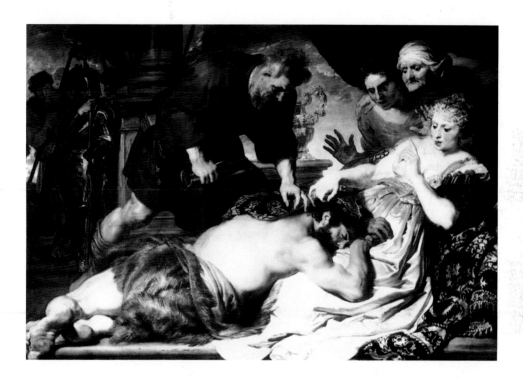

Fig. 248
Van Dyck
Samson and Delilah
Dulwich Picture Gallery
London

Fig. 249
Guido Reni
Death of Lucretia (detail)
Dulwich Picture Gallery
London

Fig. 250
Dante Gabriel Rossetti
First Anniversary of the Death of Beatrice
Birmingham Museum and Art Gallery
Birmingham
England

Fig. 251
Left: Fountain of Trevi
             Rome
Right: Palazzo Castellani

Fig. 252
Diamond Betrothal Ring of the Brownings
The Browning Institute (agent)
New York

Fig. 253
Fleur-de-lis device
Emblem of Florence
Cappella de' Principi
Church of San Lorenzo
Florence

Fig. 254
Spinello Aretino
Portrait of Margheritone
Giorgio Vasari's *Lives*
(Florentine edition, 1846-57)

Fig. 255

Left:	Carrara Mountains, Italy
Center top:	Malaspina Castle, Massa
Right bottom:	Solitary Tower

Fig. 256
Solitary tower below the Malaspina Castle
Massa
Italy

Fig. 257
Bandinelli
John of the Black Bands
(detail from the pedestal of the statue, as seen in Figs. 140 and 141)
Top: Diamond ring of Lorenzo the Magnificent
Bottom: Top part of the Medici coat of arms
with a *fleur-de-lis* design

Fig. 258
Castellani *Fleur-de-lis* Ring
(scale in millimeters)
Villa Giulia National Museum
Rome

Fig. 259
Ceiling of the Master Bedroom
Casa Guidi
Florence

Fig. 260
Leonardo da Vinci
Madonna of the Rocks (with detail)
Louvre
Paris

SUPPLEMENT TO CITATIONS AND NOTES

ANDREA DEL SARTO

148-51 (cont.)

> That Francis, that first time,
> And that long festal year at Fontainebleau!
> I surely then could sometimes leave the ground,
> Put on the glory, Rafael's daily wear....

Allan C. Dooley turns to Vasari for details about Andrea's boast that he "Put on the glory" while residing with the court of Francis I at "Fontainebleau" (DOOL, 43). In Vasari's life of Andrea del Sarto, two paintings are specified as the fruit of Andrea's labor on behalf of Francis I. One is *A Portrait of the Dauphin,* catalogued by Shearman as lost (SH, II, 314); the other is the *Charity,* presently in the Louvre (VAS, III, 264). "Rafael's daily wear," that is, his daily effort at the time Andrea was in France, resulted in two major paintings that Raphael rendered for Francis I: the late *St. Michael,* discussed below under "Bishop Blougram's Apology," 666-68; and the *Holy Family of Francis I,* listed above under "One Word More," 2:5-17. Both of the paintings by Raphael are hanging in the Louvre.

188-92

> "Friend, there's a certain sorry little scrub
> "Goes up and down our Florence, none cares how,
> "Who, were he set to plan and execute
> "As you are, pricked on by your popes and kings,
> "Would bring the sweat into that brow of yours!

These words in praise of Andrea del Sarto, and presumably spoken by Michelangelo to Raphael, are recorded in Vasari's chapter on Andrea as part of a footnote taken from Francesco Bocchi's *Bellezze della Citta' di Firenze* (VA, VIII, 293, note 1; VASA, III, 232, note). In Bocchi's book, this quotation, which is essentially the same in Browning's present text, is in the middle of a five-page discussion of the merits of Andrea's *Madonna del Sacco* (BOC, 227-33). The inference, then, as Alberti maintains, is that the *Madonna del Sacco* would impress Raphael to such a degree that it would "bring the sweat into that brow" of his (AL, 456-60, illus. on 458 and in KO, 121). For a further consideration of this painting as a source, see below under 229-31.

229-31 (cont.)

> How I could paint, were I but back in France,
> One picture, just one more—the Virgin's face,
> Not yours this time!

Andrea del Sarto's *Madonna del Sacco*, a fresco in the Large Cloister of the Church of the Santissima Annunziata, in Florence (Map F:6I,7I), is put forth by Alberti as a source here on six counts: (1) the Bocchi reference, entered above under 188-92, provides a literary source for the painting; (2) the "Virgin's face" in the fresco is "not yours," that is, is not *necessarily* that of Andrea's wife, Lucrezia; (3) the Latin inscription on the fresco, "*QVM. GENVIT. ADORAVIT*," indicates that the painting was inspired; (4) Browning, in the company of Mrs. Jameson, might have seen the six sketches of the *Madonna del Sacco* in the British Museum; (5) Vasari, in addition to Bocchi, praises the work (VAS, III, 283); and (6) Andrea's prophecy, "How I could paint . . . one more . . . Virgin," is fulfilled in that the *Madonna del Sacco* is considered his last great work (AL, 460-63; illus. in KO, 121).

254-55

> Some good son
> Paint my two hundred paintings—let him try!

In Freedberg's book I count well over 200 paintings by Andrea del Sarto (FRE), but Browning could not have known this from a tabulation of paintings entered in Vasari. Vasari, however, stresses the rapidity with which Andrea worked (VAS, III, 265), and Alberti estimates that Andrea turned out ten pictures a year during twenty years of professional activity (AL, 435-36).

259-63 (cont.)

> In Heaven, perhaps, new chances, one more chance—
> Four great walls in the new Jerusalem,
> Meted on each side by the angel's reed,
> For Leonard, Rafael, Agnolo and me
> To cover. . . .

As I have observed, the Uffizi Gallery is the only place where, when Browning's poem was published in 1855, "four great walls" could have been covered with paintings by "Leonardo, Rafael, Agnolo [Michelangelo]," and Andrea (Map F:8H). Eisenberg agrees and has found that four years before the publication of Browning's poem the 1851 catalogue of the Uffizi listed paintings of Michelangelo, Raphael, and Andrea del Sarto all together in the Tribune, while the *Adoration of the Magi* by Leonardo was only two rooms away. The paintings that were all together in the Tribune are the *Madonna of the Harpies*, by Andrea del Sarto; the *Doni Holy Family*, by Michelangelo; and the *Madonna of the Goldfinch* and the *Pope Leo X with Two Cardinals*, by Raphael (EISE; UFF, 145, 162). For reproductions of 18th-century drawings showing three walls of the Tribune covered with paintings, including Michelangelo's *Holy Family* and Raphael's *Madonna of the Goldfinch*, see the opening pages of Sergio Negrini and Luciano Berti's *Uffizi, Firenze*, published in 1974 by the Touring Club Italiano. For another reference to the painting of *Leo X with Two Cardinals*, see above under 103-12.

Alberti, on the other hand, believes that the "four great walls" are in the Sala Grande of Poggio a Caiano, a former Medici villa outside of Florence. According to Vasari, Ottaviano de' Medici commissioned Andrea del Sarto, Pontormo, and Franciabigio to each paint a third of the Sala Grande, Andrea's part being a work entitled *Caesar Presented with Tribute* (VAS, III, 297; AL, 437-38). The frescoes were started in 1521 and completed by Alessandro Allori in 1579.

The placing of the four walls in the "new Jerusalem" could be, I think, a reference to an item in Vasari's chapter on Michelozzo, who designed the Cloister of the Madonna, described above under this reference in the main body of Citations and Notes. Vasari reports that Cosimo de' Medici commissioned Michelozzo to make a design and a model for a hospital in Jerusalem that was to be used by pilgrims who went to see the tomb of Christ (VAS, II, 14-15).

BISHOP BLOUGRAM'S APOLOGY

700

> Here, we've got callous to the Virgin's winks

The famous Santuario della Santa Casa, in Loreto, is a logical place for a faithful pilgrim to claim witness to the "Virgin's winks" or, as it is phrased in line 377, a "winking Virgin." Dedicated to a veneration of the Mother Mary, the Sanctuary contains the Holy House, which presumably flew from Narareth to its present site in Loreto. Among the art objects in the Sanctuary representing the Virgin are the bas-relief marble panels of Andrea Sansovino and others. My proposal for the Santuario della Santa Casa as a source in the present context is based on Robert Schweik's article nominating W. E. Aytoun's review of George Barrow's book *Lavangro* as a source for various elements in Browning's poem. Schweik's article is convincing. To begin with, Aytoun's review is in *Blackwood's Magazine*, which is mentioned in line 945 by Browning's Bishop. Then, in the first paragraph of the review, four other details concerning the poem appear: "Cardinal Wiseman," who is a known model for Bishop Blougram (see above under 3-9); the "liquefaction of the blood of St. Januarious," which is discussed below under 728-29; the "church of St. Peter ad Vincula [sic]," which is referred to as "Peter's chains" in line 423 of the poem; and "winking images," which is, of course, similar to the text at hand (SC, 416). To this I would add that Barrow's book *The Bible in Spain* was part of Browning's library (KEL, 26, item A280), which strengthens the idea that Browning was interested in the work of Barrow. Finally, evidence supporting my claim for the Santuario della Santa Casa derives from the second paragraph of Aytoun's review, where the phrase is given, "Pilgrims may choose to press forward to Loretto [sic]." The Brownings, we know, visited Loreto in 1848 (KELL, 493), and Aytoun's review came out in 1851, which was an appropriate time for Browning to refresh his impression of Loreto before publishing his poem four years later.

666-68

> With me, faith means perpetual unbelief
> Kept quiet like the snake 'neath Michael's foot
> Who stands calm just because he feels it writhe.

Porter and Clark nominate for this passage the paintings of St.

Michael by Raphael, both versions of which are in the Louvre (POR, V, 295). But these pictures show Michael's sword poised over his head ready to strike, and so Michael hardly "stands calm" as the text requires. Of the three versions of St. Michael that are entered in this study under *The Ring and the Book* (Figs. 179, 181, and 182), none is appropriate, in that they too all show Michael more or less in the heat of battle.

On the other hand, I would propose two paintings based on Browning's well-known reading in Mrs. Jameson's *Sacred and Legendary Art*. One of the paintings is by Innocenza da Imola, in the Brera Gallery, in Milan. It shows Michael in a devotional pose trampling on the demon *after* having striven with him. Browning visited Milan in 1851 (KELL, 493), four years before publishing "Bishop Blougram's Apology." That he missed the Brera Gallery at that time cannot be imagined. The other painting has been given to both Mabuse (Jan Gossaert) and Bernaert van Orley and is presently in the Pinakothek, in Munich. In this version, Michael is poised calmly with one foot on top of the demon, and he is also assuming a devotional stance (JAME, I, 108, with an illustration of the Mabuse on 109; EISE).

728-29

> ... [I] would die rather than avow my fear
> The Naples' liquefaction may be false....

As a miracle, the "Naples' liquefaction" is the melting of the solidified blood of St. Januarius when brought into the presence of the head of the saint. Twice a year, on the first Saturday in September and the 19th of May, the Feast of the Miracle is held in the Duomo of Naples. If the blood of St. Januarius does not solidify on these occasions, disaster is expected to fall on the city of Naples (POR, V, 295; TUR, 345; KING, V, 388).

As an art object, the Naples' liquefaction is a reliquary of silver containing a crystal inside of which are two ampules of blood. The bones of the head of St. Januarius are kept in a silver box, and both the silver box and the reliquary of blood are housed in a shrine behind the altar in the Treasure Chapel of the Duomo of Naples. Fig. 232, left, displays the reliquary placed in an ornamental mount of silver while the blood in the ampules is presumably in a solidified state; Fig. 232, right, shows the reliquary removed from the mount while the blood is presumably in a liquefied condition.

THE BISHOP ORDERS HIS TOMB AT ST. PRAXED'S CHURCH: ROME, 15 —

56-60 (cont.)

> The bas-relief in bronze ye promised me,
> ... [with]
> Saint Praxed in a glory....

In the entry on St. Praxed in Mrs. Jameson's *Sacred and Legendary Art*, the following sentence occurs: "Above, in a glory, is the apotheosis of St. Pudentiana" (JAME, II, 624). Considering Browning's close friendship with Mrs. Jameson and his familiarity with her work, I do not think it unreasonable to assume that Browning is indebted to Mrs. Jameson for the phrase "in a glory." For a close explanation of the meaning of this phrase, see above under this citation.

BY THE FIRESIDE

14:66-68 (cont.)

> And yonder, at feet of the fronting ridge
> That takes the turn in the range beyond,
> Is the chapel reached by the one-arched bridge....

The main feature of the interior of the Oratorio at Rifubbri is the image of a Madonna and Child above the altar (Fig. 236). The image is a copy of an original painting, long ago stolen from the chapel, that was rendered by an unknown artist (BAG). Evidently the painting had been stolen when Browning visited the chapel, and the facsimile had not yet been put up, for Browning writes in stanza 35, lines 178-80:

> For fear of plunder,
> The cross is down and the altar bare,
> As if thieves don't fear thunder.

Viewed biographically, even though Browning did not court Elizabeth in Italy, the architectural and pictorial elements connected with the Oratorio at Rifubbri have symbolic significance. The presumed fresco of St. John in the Desert on the façade of the Rifubbri Chapel represents Browning, alone and single; the Madonna and Child over the altar of the chapel stands for Elizabeth and the future birth of Pen Browning; and the chapel itself signifies the marriage of the Brownings, the objectification of the climactic infinite moment of the poem when Robert makes a lifelong commitment to Elizabeth.

"CHILDE ROLAND TO THE DARK TOWER CAME"

31:181-84 (cont.)

> What in the midst lay but the Tower itself?
> The round squat turret, blind as the fool's heart,
> Built of brown stone, without a counterpart
> In the whole world.

In June, 1849, during his trip from Pisa to Carrara (KELL, 493), Browning most likely took the road from Pisa to Pietrasanta to Massa to Carrara. As he approached Massa from Pietrasanta, he would have had a lateral view of the Malaspina Castle, which, as I have observed from up close, presents a striking image of the solitary tower below the castle in the low hills of Massa as the towering mountains of Carrara frame the castle in the background. The tower, which was once part of a connecting belt of towers and walls below the castle, is, as the text requires, a "round squat turret, blind as a fool's heart," that is, it is circular at the front, "squat" in shape, and without a window, if that is what is meant by the word "blind" (Fig. 256). The tower, also according to the text, is built of "stone," although its color is gray instead of "brown." Perhaps this discrepancy is accounted for by Browning's dim recollection of the tower while writing the poem, as DeVane places its composition, three years later in Paris (DEVA, 229). The importance of the stark, bare tops of the Carrara mountains as part of the setting for the poem derives from the description in stanza 30, line 4, which locates the tower among rugged hills, one of which is described as a "tall scalped mountain" (Fig. 255).

CLEON

174-80

> ". . . what survives myself?
> The brazen statue to o'erlook my [Cleon's] grave,
> Set on the promontory which I named.
> And that—some supple courtier of my heir
> Shall use its robed and sceptred arm, perhaps,
> To fix the rope to, which best drags it down.
> I go then: triumph thou, who dost not go!"

A model for the "brazen statue" of the imaginary King Cleon could be Giovanni da Bologna's statue of Duke Ferdinand I, described above under *The Ring and the Book*, VI.249-56, Fig. 172. Physically, Giovanni da Bologna's statue is placed before the Duomo of Arezzo, at the highest point in the city, and it is indeed, as the text specifies, "Set on the promontory." Furthermore, both statues are presumably to be pulled down with a "rope," the statue in "Cleon" by a rope around an arm, the one in *The Ring and the Book* by a rope around the neck. Politically, the correspondence is close, too. Titled a Duke and given almost absolute power over his subjects, Ferdinand I equates with the imaginary King Cleon. Browning, it should be noted, visited Arezzo in 1848 (KELL, 493), seven years before publishing "Cleon," but he wrote *The Ring and the Book* after "Cleon." Thus, if we cannot be sure that Browning, before 1855, conceived or heard about the rope anecdote that he used in *The Ring and the Book*, we can be certain that he was aware of Giovanni da Bologna's statue of Ferdinand I in Arezzo. According to Roma King, the rope anecdote is imaginary but consistant with the manner of riprisals during the rule of the Medici family (KING, VIII, 331).

FRA LIPPO LIPPI

47-49 (cont.)

> And I've been three weeks shut within my mew,
> A-painting for the great man, saints and saints
> And saints again.

Alberti presents *Seven Saints, Sacred Conversation* as a source for Lippi's painting of many "saints" (Fig. 45). To prove her case, she cites a note from the 1846-1857 edition of Vasari's *Lives* that Browning used (KEL, 200). The note is recorded as follows in the 1851 version of the *Lives*, as translated by Foster (VASA, II, 77):

> Two paintings by Fra Filippo, formerly in the Palazzo Medici, are now in possession of the Brothers Metzger of Florence. The one is an Annunciation. In the other are seven Saints seated, St. John is in the center. . . .

Alberti also points out that in the 1867 edition of Murray's *Handbook for Travellers in Central Italy*, page 88, Metzger is

listed under picture-dealers and that the shop's address is given
as Borgo Ognissanti, which would have been convenient for
Browning to visit while living in Casa Guidi (Map F:7F,8G).
"Fra Lippo Lippi" was published in 1855, and *Seven Saints* was
acquired by the National Gallery of London in 1861 (MAR, 207,
item 30); therefore, Browning could not have seen the painting
in England while writing his poem but could have read about it
in Vasari and/or seen it in Metzger's or possibly in Palazzo
Medici while in Florence (AL, 336-38). In further support of
Alberti's claim, I have noticed in Marchini that there is no other
picture by Lippi with so many saints in it as a collective subject
(MAR). For another possible reference to this painting, see
above under 245-46 in the main body of citations and notes.

145-46 (cont.)

> First, every sort of monk, the black and white
> I drew them....

Alberti identifies the colors "black and white" with both the
habits of the Carmelites and the Domenicans (AL, 339-40). This
fact further supports Leisgang's nomination of Lippi's *Innovation of the Rule of the Carmelites*, as described above under this
citation.

183-93 (cont.)

> Your business is to paint the souls of men—
> ...
> It's vapor done up like a new-born babe—
> (In that shape when you die it leaves your mouth)
> ...
> Paint the soul, never mind the legs and arms!

Korg selects two details from paintings to exemplify the Prior's
admonition to Lippi to represent "the soul" rather than "legs
and arms." These details are (1) the departure of the soul from
the "mouth" at death in the form of a "new-born babe," as
depicted in the *Triumph of Death*, by the Master of the Triumph
of Death, in the Camposanto, Pisa (Fig. 244); and (2) the girl
standing up in the middle of the right side of Lippi's *Coronation
of the Virgin* exposing her leg all the way up to the hip (Fig. 58).
Browning, we may be sure, saw the *Triumph of Death* while in
Pisa in 1846, nine years before publishing his poem (KO, 114, 116;
KELL, 493). In Fig. 244, the detail from the *Triumph of Death*,

the "babe," I notice, is represented departing from the mouth of the dead three times, twice as an infant and once as a child.

DeLaura develops the Prior's concern with painting the soul as a representation of Rio's artistic philosophy of asceticism in his *De la poésie chrétienne* . . . (DEL, 378-79).

286-90 (cont.)

> Do you feel thankful, ay or no,
> For this fair town's face, yonder river's line,
> The mountain round it and the sky above,
> Much more the figures of man, woman, child,
> These are the frame to?

Korg points out that backgrounds to many of Lippi's pictures were idealized scenes from nature; whereas the scenes in the paintings of Masaccio were more realistic versions of nature. In particular, Masaccio's *Tribute Money*, in the Brancacci Chapel in the Church of Santa Maria del Carmine, is an accurate depiction of the Arno valley near Florence and its neighboring mountains, of what Lippi refers to as "this fair town's face, yonder river's line, / The mountain round it" (KO, 132, with an illustration on p. 113; Map F:8F).

For literary sources here, DeLaura turns to Charles Kingsley's novels *Alton Locke* (1850) and *Yeast* (1848), both written well before the publication of "Fra Lippo Lippi" in 1855. As reflected in Browning's poem, DeLaura quotes Kingsley's artistic philosophy of naturalism as follows (DEL, 379):

> [Kingsley's] call for artists with a "patient reverent faith in Nature as they see her," who know that the ideal is only to be "found and left where God has put it, and where alone it can be represented, in actual . . . phenomena" (*Yeast*, Ch. xv). Kingsley praising an art that finds "a world of true sublimity" in common "hedgerow and sandbank" as well as "alp peak and the ocean waste" (*Locke*, pp. 104-05) sounds very much like Lippo extolling "The beauty and the wonder and the power" of town, river, mountain, and sky and thanking God for these gifts by painting them with close attention (11. 283-96).

323-32 (cont.)

> I painted a Saint Laurence six months since
> At Prato, splashed the fresco in fine style:
> 'How looks my painting, now the scaffold's down?'
> I ask a brother: 'Hugely,' he returns—

'Already not one phiz of your three slaves
Who turn the Deacon off his toasted side,
But's scratched and prodded to our heart's content,
The pious people have so eased their own
With coming to say prayers there in a rage:
We get on fast to see the bricks beneath.'

Alberti notes that Browning could be attributing Lippi's presumably "scratched and prodded" fresco to Vasari's description of Andrea del Castagno's *Christ on the Column*, a fresco once in the New Cloister of the Church of Santa Croce, in Florence, but now destroyed. In describing the damage done by viewers of the painting, Vasari, in Foster's translation, specifically uses, it should be noted, the word "scratched" (AL, 335-36; VAS, II, 84):

> This picture is, in fine, of such merit, that were it not for the carelessness which has permitted it to be scratched and injured by children and simple folks, who have maltreated the head, arms, and almost the entire persons of the Jews, as though they would thereby avenge the injuries inflicted on the Savior, this work would, without doubt, be the most beautiful of all that Andrea executed.

Moreover, I believe Browning's erroneous use of a fresco "At Prato" for the Balassi-Dolci canvas of St. Lawrence described above could, in addition to his possible use of Andrea del Castagno's fresco, be explained by Browning's recollection of Fra Angelico's fresco the *Martyrdom of St. Lawrence*, in the Chapel of Nicholas V, in the Vatican. After Browning undoubtedly saw the Balassi-Dolci *St. Lawrence* in the chancel of the Duomo of Prato in the summer of 1853, he went to Rome for the first time after 1844 (KELL, 492-93). In the probable viewing of the fresco of St. Lawrence by Fra Angelico he certainly would have noticed that the composition of the fresco is similar to the Balassi-Dolci painting, in that, as the text describes, "three slaves," that is, two workers and a Roman soldier, are tending to the roasting of St. Lawrence (cf. Figs. 57 and 229). Furthermore, just as the Balassi-Dolci *St. Lawrence* was, until 1860, mounted in the Cappella Manassei (THO, 48), which is next to the chancel in the Duomo of Prato, where Lippi rendered frescoes of the life of St. Stephen, so too Fra Angelico painted his *St. Lawrence* near the frescoes representing the life of St. Stephen in the Chapel of Nicholas V. The juxtaposition of the paintings of St. Lawrence with those of St. Stephen and the similarity of composition in the St. Lawrence paintings indicate, then, that Browning probably mixed together in his mind the Chapel of Nicholas V with the Cappella Manassei and the chancel of the Duomo of Prato, that before publishing his poem in 1855 he mentally conflated the versions of St. Lawrence by Fra Angelico and Balassi-Dolci.

344-81 (cont.)

> I shall paint a piece
>
> . . .
> God in the midst, Madonna and her Babe . . .
> . . . [and]
> St. Lucy, I should say.

The absence of a conspicuous Christ Child in the central scene of Lippi's painting the *Coronation of the Virgin* leads Alberti to believe that Browning is conflating it with one of Lippi's many paintings of the Madonna and Child (AL, 357). But since Alberti does not advance any Madonna and Child in particular as part of the conflation, I propose that when Browning saw the *Coronation of the Virgin* in the Accademia in Florence, he associated it with Lippi's painting which was probably hanging near or next to it, the *Madonna and Child with Four Saints*. Both paintings entered the Accademia in Florence between aproximately 1810 and 1813, and both were transferred to the Uffizi in 1919, where they are hanging today (MAR, 201, note 13, and 204, note 21; *Gli Uffizi, Catalogo generale,* Florence, 1979; EISE).

Regarding Browning's erroneous insertion of St. Lucy into the coronation scene, Alberti refers to Browning's reliance on Mrs. Jameson's *Sacred and Legendary Art*, which was first published in 1848, seven years before Browning's poem. The idea of Lippi coming "Out of a corner when you least expect / As one by a dark stair into a great light" (lines 361-62) is enhanced by the legend of St. Lucy, who sheds light, lucidity, as her name suggests (AL, 360-63; JAME, 1850 ed., 363-68).

What DeLaura calls the "boisterous scene" that characterizes Browning's description of Lippi's *Coronation of the Virgin* is perhaps an echo of Rio's anti-humanism in his *De la poésie chrétienne* (DEL, 379; Rio, 247):

> . . . the profanation committed by the monk Lippi was renewed every day, that is to say, portraits of young girls, generally of the most notorious character, were introduced into altar pieces under the form of the Madonnas, the Magdalene, or St. John, and around these a noisy crowd of curious and profane spectators collected, without any regard for the sacrifice of the altar.

A GRAMMARIAN'S FUNERAL: SHORTLY AFTER THE REVIVAL OF LEARNING IN EUROPE

13-20

Leave we the unlettered plain its herd and crop;
    Seek we sepulture
On a tall mountain, citied to the top,
    Crowded with culture!
All the peaks soar, but one the rest excels;
    Clouds overcome it;
No! yonder sparkle is the citadel's
    Circling its summit.

DeVane places the setting for this poem in Italy (DEVA, 220), but he does not specify the "tall mountain, citied to the top" amidst other pinnacles whose "peaks soar." To my mind, San Marino, in the Apennines, 18 miles from Rimini, best fits this physical description. Situated on the top of Mount Titano, San Marino has three summits lined up into what line 8 in the poem describes as a "rock row." The tallest mountain peak—"one the rest excels" with a citadel . . . "circling its summit"—is the Rocca Guàita. The other two summits, which are also crowned with citadels, are the Rocca della Fratte and the Rocca Montale (Fig. 234). Historically, San Marino satisfies the Renaissance time span designated in the poem's subtitle "Shortly after the Revival of Learning in Europe," for during the last 900 years San Marino has been an independent state. Browning visited Rimini in 1848 (KELL, 493), seven years before publishing his poem, and at that time he could have seen San Marino, which is nearby Rimini.

IN A GONDOLA

190-93 (cont.)

Bold Castelfranco's Magdalen
You'd find retreated from the ken
Of that robed counsel-keeping Ser—
As if Tizian thinks of her. . . .

Alberti reports that there is a *Magdalen* attributed to Giorgione—"Castelfranco"—in a private collection in Milan (AL, 79n). Illustrations of the painting are in the works on Giorgione by Terisio Pignatti (plate 136) and Pietro Zampetti (plate 42). Browning, however, did not visit Milan until 1851 (KELL, 493), nine years after publishing his poem in 1842. (Cf. the *Magdalen* by "Tizian" that I propose above.)

JAMES LEE'S WIFE

VIII.43-48

> ... on the finger which outvied
> His art he placed the ring that's there,
> Still by fancy's eye descried,
> In token of a marriage rare:
> For him on earth, his art's despair,
> For him in heaven, his soul's fit bride.

Karen Levi gives the present text in association with the betrothal ring of Robert and Elizabeth Barrett Browning. The ring, along with Levi's above candidate for a literary context, was called to my attention by Rita S. Humphrey, Administrative and Editorial Assistant to the Director of the Armstrong Browning Library. Patterned after an 18th-century design, the ring, as Fig. 252 shows, features a crowned diamond heart. The agent for the ring is given by Levi as The Browning Institute, in New York (LEV, 24, item A).

The biographical association of "James Lee's Wife" with the life of the Brownings derives from Herford as corroborated by Devane, who both point up the theme "how to live when unanswering love is gone" (HER, 154; DEVA, 285). "James Lee's Wife" was published in 1864, when Elizabeth's death three years earlier was still heavily upon Browning, when she was "For him in Heaven, his soul's fit bride."   Further evidence of the biographical significance of the present poem is entered above under VIII.27-32 in connection with the casts of the *Clasped Hands of the Brownings*, by Harriot Hosmer. Also see below under *The Ring and the Book*, I.38, 45-49, and compare the crowned diamond heart of the betrothal ring with the crowned *fleur-de-lis* in the Medici Chapel (see Fig. 253).

OLD PICTURES IN FLORENCE

1:3-8

> As I leaned and looked over the aloed arch
> Of the villa-gate this warm March day,

> No flash snapped, no dumb thunder rolled
> In the valley beneath where, white and wide
> And washed by the morning water-gold,
> Florence lay out on the mountain-side.

A number of facts leads me to believe that Isa Blagden's former Florentine residence Villa Brichieri is the setting in this opening stanza. Griffin and Minchin date Isa Blagden's first residency at the Villa Brichieri to 1851, while she was in joint occupancy of the villa with Miss Frances Power Cobbe (GRI, 164). McAleer assigns the same year to the beginning of the close friendship between the Brownings and Miss Blagden (MCA, xxiii). Five years later "Old Pictures in Florence" was published as part of the *Men and Women* poems. Most pertinently, the actual view from the villa coordinates with the present passage. Located on the southern hill of Florence in Bellosguardo, Villa Brichieri shows, as I have observed, a view of Florence—if not a prospect of the city through the "arch" of the "villa-gate—a view from the inner driveway through the entrance in the outer wall of the villa, a vista of the "valley beneath where Florence . . . [lies] out on the mountain-side" up to Fiesole opposite.

Compare the discussion below under "Up at the Villa— Down in the City," 56-57, for another possible reference to Villa Brichieri.

8:62-64, 9:69-72

> . . . Old and New are fellows:
> A younger succeeds to an elder brother,
> Da Vincis derive in good time from Dellos.
> . . .
> What, not a word for Stefano there,
> Of brow once prominent and starry,
> Called Nature's Ape, and the world's despair
> For his peerless painting? (See Vasari.)

Dello was chosen by Browning as a precursor to "Da Vinci" because, as Alberti sees it, Browning read in Vasari that Dello revealed the muscles in nude bodies (VASAR, II, 110), and Browning obviously knew that Leonardo was very sophisticated in his anatomical studies (AL, 112-13). Stefano is referrred to as "Nature's Ape" because, as Alberti reads Vasari, Stefano was one of the early pioneers in the use of foreshortening (VASAR, I, 109-10; AL, 114).

The idea that a "younger [artist] succeeds / to an elder

brother" in the progress of art is also advanced by Alberti as a result of Browning's reading in Vasari. In his life of Ghirlandaio, Vasari records that the designs of the scenes from the *Lives of the Virgin and St. John the Baptist,* by Orcagna, in the Church of Santa Maria Novella, in Florence, were painted over by Ghirlandaio about one hundred and fifty years later (AL, 153; VAS, II, 175; Map F:7G). For a direct reference to Orcagna, see below under 33:260-63.

24:185-87 (cont.)

> Their ghosts [the artists] still stand, as I said before,
> Watching each fresco flaked and rasped,
> Blocked up, knocked out, or whitewashed over....

Various frescoes in Florence combine to round out Browning's description of neglected Florentine works of art. Filippo Lippi's *Innovation of the Rule of the Carmelites,* described above under "Fra Lippo Lippi," 145-63, was "whitewashed over" in the Church of Santa Maria del Carmine, but Browning might not have known about this (AL, 158-59; VAS, I, 50n; Fig. 50; Map F:8F). Orcagna's paintings, the *Lives of the Virgin and St. John the Baptist,* in the Church of Santa Maria Novella, mentioned above under 8:62-64, were ruined by rain which leaked through the roof (AL, 153, 156; VAS, I, 131). The face of Jesus in Ghirlandaio's *Last Supper,* in the refectory of the Church of Ognissanti, was repainted by restorers (AL, 153, 156; VAS, II, 169n, 175; Map F:8G; notice the reference to the Church of Ognissanti entered above and below under 31:241-44). The frescoes in the refectory of the Church of Santa Croce were "blocked out" by the looms of a carpet factory installed there (KO, 105, 228, note 11; Map F:8I). The *Portrait of Dante,* in the Bargello, presented above under this citation, had one of its eyes "knocked" out (AL, 158, 248n; VAS, I, 30n; Map F:8H,8I). And Andrea del Castagno's *Christ at the Column,* described above under "Fra Lippo Lippi," 323-32, was "rasped" by the congregation of the Church of Santa Croce (AL, 335-36; VAS, II, 84).

26:201-04 (cont.)

> Not that I expect the great Bigordi,
> Nor Sandro to hear me, chivalric, bellicose;
> Nor the wronged Lippino; and not a word I
> Say of a scrap of Frà Angelico's....

A number of sources for references to artists mentioned here are advanced by Alberti. Most of the sources are taken from Vasari's *Lives*. The "great Bigordi," that is, Domenico Ghirlandaio, and "Sandro" Botticelli tie in with the reference to the Church of Ognissanti mentioned above and below under 31:241-44, for both Botticelli and Ghirlandaio, in competition with each other, painted a St. Jerome for the Church of Ognissanti (AL, 156; VAS, II, 173; Map F:7G). For another painting by Ghirlandaio in the same church, see above under 24:185-87.

Botticelli is "chivalric" because there is a possibility that he took Filippino Lippi in apprenticeship without any monetary compensation. When Filippo Lippi died, Fra Diamonte took for himself the money owed to Filippo Lippi and Fra Diamonte for the frescoes done in the Duomo of Spoleto. Filippino Lippi, who was only twelve when his father Filippo died, was then accepted as an apprentice by Botticelli, who was Filippo Lippi's former pupil. If, in gratitude to Filippo Lippi, Botticelli did not collect the customary fee for this task, then Botticelli was indeed "chivalric" as Browning says (AL, 164-65; VAS, II, 76, 276, 276n).

Botticelli was "bellicose" because of an altercation between him and one of his neighbors, a weaver. As Vasari relates it, the weaver disturbed Botticelli with the noise and shaking made from running his eight looms. When Botticelli could not reason with the weaver to lessen the noise and shaking, he poised a large stone on the outside wall of his house above that of the weaver so that the slightest shaking would cause it to fall through the weaver's roof. With this impending disaster, the weaver came to terms with Botticelli (AL, 164; VAS, II, 218-19).

"Lippino," or Filippino Lippi as he is properly called, was "wronged" for two reasons. First, there was a dispute recorded by the editors of the 1846-1857 Italian edition of Vasari's *Lives* as to what credit should be given to Filippino Lippi for his work in the Brancacci Chapel in the Church of the Carmine, in Florence (Map F:8F). Browning no doubt read the long *Commentario* preceding the life of Masaccio in the 1846-1857 edition and agreed with the editors who assigned the *Disputa* to Filippino rather than to Masaccio. And second, Filippino Lippi was wronged by Alexis François Rio in his *De la poésie chrétienne. . . ."* Among other things, Rio accused Filippino of deficient expressive and mechanical execution of the continuation of the frescoes by Masaccio in the Brancacci Chapel (AL, 165-66, 249-50n; RIO, 138-39; VA, III, 188, note 1).

The phrase "not a word I / Say of a scrap of Frà Angelico's" could refer to a letter from Browning written to Elizabeth
Barrett on September 11, 1845. In the letter, Browning com-
plains that Mary Shelley does not give full credit to Fra Angelico
in her book *Rambles in Germany and Italy in 1840, 1842, and
1843*. Mary Shelley assigns only religious subjects to the work of
Fra Angelico and mentions nothing about the common people
that are part of the crowd scenes in his paintings. Thus, having
written this about Fra Angelico in a letter, Browning has nothing left to say about him—"not a word"—in his poem (AL, 166-
67, 249-50n; KIN, I, 189-90; cf. DEL, 370). Furthermore, in the
same letter Browning observes that Mary Shelley relies heavily
on Rio, and Rio, it should be noted, ties in with what is said
above, in a negative sense, about Filippino Lippi.

27:209-16 (cont.)

> Could not the ghost with the close red cap,
>   My Pollajolo the twice craftsman,
> Save me a sample, give me the hap
>   Of a muscular Christ that shows the draughtsman?
> No Virgin by him the somewhat petty,
>   Of finical touch and tempera crumbly—
> Could not Alesso Baldovinetti
>   Contribute so much, I ask him humbly?

Alberti identifies the "ghost with the red cap" as a portrait of
Pollaiuolo by Filippino Lippi in the fresco *St. Peter and St. Paul
before the Proconsul*, in the Brancacci Chapel of the Church of
the Carmine, in Florence. In the 1846-1857 Italian edition of
Vasari's *Lives*, which was used by Browning, a print of the portrait is included in the life of Masaccio. This print would, of
course, have aided Browning in finding the portrait in the
Brancacci Chapel (AL, 179-81, with a reproduction of the portrait
on p. 180; VA, III, 190-91; KEL, 200; Map F:8F). The idea that
Pollaiuolo is a "twice craftsman" refers to Vasari's account in his
life of Pollaiuolo that the artist was not only an important painter but also a skilled craftsman as a goldsmith (AL, 178-79; VAS,
III, 194).

Alberti also turns to Vasari for the source of the description of Baldovinetti as "somewhat petty / Of finical touch and
tempera crumbly." Baldovinetti's attention to minute detail in
delineating nature is a good example of his "finical touch." In
particular, the stalks and knots of straw can be counted in his

Nativity, in the Church of the Santissima Annunziata, in Florence.   As a fresco, the painting also exemplifies Baldovinetti's "tempera crumbly," for Baldovinetti painted over the dry surface of the wall instead of painting into it while the wall was still wet.   As a consequence, the paint eventually peeled or crumbled (AL, 181-82; VASA, III, 68-69; Map F:6I,7I).

28:217-21 (cont.)

> Margheritone of Arezzo,
> > With the grave-clothes garb and swaddling barret,
> (Why purse up mouth and beak in a pet so,
> > You bald old saturnine poll-clawed parrot?)

The *Portrait of Margheritone*, by Spinello Aretino, is nominated by Alberti as a source for this physical description of Margheritone.   The portrait may be found at the beginning of Vasari's life of Margheritone in the 1846-1857 Italian edition that Browning used.   Vasari copied the portrait from Spinello's *Story of the Magi*, a fresco that was in the now defunct Old Duomo outside of Arezzo.   In the portrait Margheritone is wearing a biretta, a headdress resembling a turban.   This Alberti equates with Browning's phrase "swaddling barret."   Furthermore, Alberti interprets Margheritone's facial expression in the portrait as being, according to the text, "in a pet," that is, the lips and eyebrows are twisted, and the close-set eyes are staring straight ahead with an accusatory look (Fig. 254).   As Alberti reads Vasari, Margheritone was upset because Giotto was receiving too much attention for breaking away from the medieval tradition (AL, 184-87, with a reproduction of the portrait on p. 186; VASA, I, 67; VA, the portrait is facing p. 237; KEL, 200).

30:233-40, 31:241-44 (cont.)

> ... Giotto ['s] ...
> ...
> ... certain precious little tablet
> ...
> I, that have haunted the dim San Spirito,
> > (Or was it rather the Ognissanti?)
> Patient on altar-step planting a weary toe!
> > Nay, I shall have it yet!

Marcus notes about Browning's letter to John Kenyon, which is discussed above under "Andrea del Sarto," 1-3, that Browning properly designates Giotto's painting as the *Death of the Virgin*, yet he incorrectly places the theft of the painting from the Church of Santo Spirito (Map F:8G) instead of the Church of Ognissanti (MARCUS, 54-55; Map F:8G). This letter should be compared with the completely erroneous identification in the Corson letter described above under the present reference in the main body of citations and notes.

33:260-63

> ... once Freedom restored to Florence,
> How Art may return that departed with her.
> Go, hated house, go each trace of the Lorraine's,
> And bring us the days of Orgagna hither!

Alberti perceives an association between "Freedom restored" through the Risorgimento just as Florence was relatively free from oppression in "the days of Orcagna." On March 5, 1849, six years before "Old Pictures in Florence" was published, Mazzini delivered a speech in Orcagna's Loggia, in the Piazza della Signoria, in Florence. The purpose of the speech was to persuade the Tuscans to join the Romans in proclaiming Italy a republic, but the time was not quite ripe for this to happen (AL, 204-11; Map F:8H). The Loggia, which houses many important sculptures, was designed by Orcagna in the fourteenth century.

ONE WORD MORE

2:5-8 (cont.)

> Rafael made a century of sonnets,
> Made and wrote them in a certain volume
> Dinted with the silver-pointed pencil
> Else he only used to draw Madonnas....

Scholarship by Vincenzo Golzio, who has written a chapter on the sonnets of Raphael in *The Complete Work of Raphael* (New York: Harrison House, 1969, pp. 603-07), reveals that six sonnets of Raphael are extant, one of which is apocryphal. The sonnets with their variations are published in Italian, and Golzio gives the chronology, locations, and sketches connected with the sonnets as follows:

> As for their chronology, we accept the one proposed by Zazzaretta. Sonnets I and II are written on a folio with

sketches for the *Disputa del Sacramento*, in the Ashmolean
Museum in Oxford; sonnet III in its final version is found on a
folio in the British Museum, London [Fig. 107 above], its first
draft is found on the folio containing sketches for the *Disputa* in
the Albertina Museum, Vienna; sonnet IV is found on a folio
conserved in the Ashmolean Museum, Oxford, and V on a folio
in the Museum Fabre, Montpellier, which according to some
critics includes a drawing for the *Disputa* [illus. on p. 607]. As
for sonnet VI, Marianni said he had a facsimile of it together
with a true portrait of Raphael's beloved from G. Colbacchini
[illus. on p. 606], which he published in a Venetian edition. C.
Mauro published the same sonnet, repeating that he, too, had
it from Colbacchini in Venice, written on a drawing which portrayed the Fornarina.

For translations in English of four of the sonnets, including one
different than that of Richardson given above, see COOKE, 231-
32.

5:32-33 (cont.)

Dante once prepared to paint an angel:
Whom to please? You whisper "Beatrice."

Leonée Ormond mentions that Dante Gabriel Rossetti rendered
in pen and ink *The First Anniversary of the Death of Beatrice*
(ORM, 184n). Fig. 250 shows in the notation on the drawing that
it was given to Millais in 1849, six years before the publication of
Browning's poem. Also written on the drawing is a description
of the occasion to which the painting refers, as translated from
the Italian original in Chapter 35 of Dante's *Vita Nuova* (cf. the
different translation given in DEVA, 277):

On that day on which a whole year was completed since my
lady had been born into the life eternal,—remembering me of
her as I sat alone, I betook myself to draw the resemblance of an
Angel upon certain tablets. And while I did this, chancing to
turn my head, I perceived that some were standing beside me to
whom I should have given courteous welcome, and that they
were observing what I did: also I learned afterwards that they
had been there a while before I perceived them. Perceiving
whom, I arose for salutation, and said: 'Another was with me.'
See Dante's 'Autobiography of his early life.'

That Browning was familiar with the sketch by Rossetti is not
known. But Browning might have been informed of the drawing by either Rossetti or Millais when he visited London in 1852,
three years before "One Word More" was published (KELL, 493;
OG, 55; GRI, 187).

PROSPICE

27-28

> O thou soul of my soul! I shall clasp thee again,
> And with God be the rest!

Compare the word "clasp" in these lines with the word "clasped" in the quotation from Hawthorne's *The Marble Fawn*, which is given as a source above under "James Lee's Wife," VIII.27-32:

> Harriot Hosmer's clasped hands of Browning and his wife . . .
> [symbolize] the individuality and heroic union of two high
> poetic lives.

Hawthorne's description of Hosmer's *Clasped Hands of the Brownings* and Hosmer's *Hands* as an art object (see Fig. 81) are further supported as sources here for several reasons: (1) both "James Lee's Wife" and "Prospice" date to 1861, three years after the death of Elizabeth Barrett Browning and eight years after the Brownings posed for Hosmer with their hands joined; (2) "Prospice" is described by DeVane as a notable memorializing of the death of Elizabeth (DEVA, 316); (3) Hosmer's cast of the clasped hands objectifies the theme in "Prospice" of the immortal union between the Brownings; and (4) the above lines from "Prospice" compare in imagery with the following lines from "James Lee's Wife," IX.18-20:

> You... / Who never lifted the hand in vain—
> Will hold mine yet from over the sea!

THE RING AND THE BOOK

I.1-4, 15-17 (cont.)

> Do you see this Ring?
>   't is Rome-work, made to match
> (By Castellani's imitative craft)
> Etrurian circlets found...
>   ...
> ... hammer needs must widen out the round,
> And file emboss it fine with lily-flowers,
> Ere the stuff grow a ring-thing right to wear.

Additional evidence that the Castellani *fleur-de-lis* ring is a source for the ring in the present passage has been advanced by

Roger Brooks, Director of the Armstrong Browning Library, at Baylor University. Professor Brooks has examined the photograph for Fig. 258 and has identified an iris flower as the decoration located in the upper right-hand corner—at one o'clock high—on the outer edge of the ring. The iris, as explained below under IV.320-25, is, according to Christian symbolism, interchangeable with the lily. Professor Brooks also perceives that the decoration on the ring next to the one described above—at two o'clock high—could also be an iris, although it is less distinct than the one at one o'clock high. Thus, if either or both of these observations are accurate, Browning's use in the text of the plural form "lily-*flowers*" (italics mine) is precise.

The possibility that Browning saw and remembered the *fleur-de-lis* ring when he was in Castellani's shop is further strengthened by the significance of three interrelated facts: first, the *fleur-de-lis* or *giglio* is the sign for the city of Florence; second, a *fleur-de-lis* design is embossed on the Medici coat of arms on Baccio Bandinelli's statue of John of the Black Bands, in the Piazza San Lorenzo, in Florence (Figs. 140 and 257); and third, two tapestries with Medici coat of arms formed part of the Browning collection (KEL, 524, items H672 and H673). In June, 1860, five months after visiting Castellani's shop in Rome, Browning discovered the Old Yellow Book in the market place next to Bandinelli's statue (DEVA, 319). Under I.38-52, 91-95, and 110-116 above, Browning describes the discovery and then relates how he walked back to Casa Guidi while reading the Old Yellow Book. At the end of *The Ring and the Book*, Browning refers to the tablet of Tommaseo over the portal of Casa Guidi that was put up by the citizens of Florence. The tablet, described below under XII.870-74, commemorates the death of Elizabeth Barrett Browning and presents the ring metaphor, which conveys the idea of a marriage between Elizabeth's poetry, England, and Italy. Thus the Castellani ring with the *fleur-de-lis* design reinforces several associations in the poem: it ties the Medici family with the discovery of the Old Yellow Book near Bandinelli's statue, it connects the Medici family and the discovery of the Old Yellow Book with Casa Guidi and the Brownings, and it links Casa Guidi and Florence with England and Italy.

Dr. Bordenache Battaglia and I have not been able to locate the former site of the Castellani shop on the Via Poli, in Rome, where the Brownings visited and signed the guestbook in 1860, but it is compensating to note that the Via Poli is a short street running into the Piazza di Trevi, and that in the square, next to the famous Fountain of Trevi, the Castellani palace that served the family after 1869 is boldly marked with the name of Augustus Castellani over the portal (DIZ, 598; Fig. 251; Map R:7I). (Continued below under I.38,45-49.)

I.38, 45-49 (cont.)

I found this book,

. . .

Toward Baccio's marble, ay, the basement-ledge
O' the pedestal where sits and menaces
John of the Black Bands with his upright spear,
'Twixt palace and church, Riccardi where they lived,
His race, and San Lorenzo where they lie.

In the Cappella de' Principi of the Church of "San Lorenzo where they lie," that is, where there are tomb monuments of the Medici family, there is a *fleur-de-lis* design inlaid in one of the walls in *pietra dura*—in hard stone (Fig. 253). Marvin Eisenberg submits this fact as reinforcement for the connection between the statue of "John of the Black Bands," the discovery of the "book"—the Old Yellow Book, and the Castellani *fleur-de-lis* ring, discussed above under I.1-5, 15-17. In addition, as I have observed, there are four other *fleur-de-lis* designs inlaid on the hard stone pavement of the Cappella de' Principi as devices on Medici coat of arms, and there is a *fleur-de-lis* device embossed on the Medici coat of arms over the arcade in the courtyard of the "palace . . . where they lived," Palazzo Medici-Riccardi.

Also related to Medici landmarks in Florence surrounding Browning's discovery of the Old Yellow Book are the sculptured, painted, and inlaid diamond rings that decorate the landmarks. In this supplement, above under "James Lee's Wife," VIII.43-48, the diamond betrothal ring of the Brownings is presented as a source for the wedding ring of James Lee's wife. Eisenberg, upon being informed of the betrothal ring of the Brownings, called to my attention the fact that a diamond ring is associated with Lorenzo the Magnificent, of Medici fame. My subsequent investigations revealed that there are two bas-relief diamond rings of Lorenzo the Magnificent carved on the "pedestal" of "John of the Black Bands" (Figs. 140 and 257). And Professor Eisenberg has further brought to light a couple of other facts about Lorenzo the Magnificent's ring: First, in Benozzo Gozzoli's famous frescoe the *Procession of the Kings*, in Palazzo Medici-Riccardi, the stewart attending Piero de' Medici's horse has a diamond ring device on the front of his tunic (Fig. 156). And, second, in the 1550 edition of Vasari's *Lives*, an edition that was known to Browning (KEL, 200, item A2378), information about the diamond device is given in the Life of Pontormo. In the third volume of the 1927 edition of Vasari's *Lives* (J. D. Dent, London, ed. by Ernst Rhys and trans. by A. B. Hinds), the pertinent passage from the 1550 edition is translated as follows (EISE):

> The head of one of these [a company of lords and nobles in the city of Florence] called the Diamond, was Sig. Giuliano de' Medici, the Pope's brother, and it was so called because the diamond was the device of Lorenzo the elder, his father.

Finally, I have observed that large diamond-shaped rings hang from the ends of the tomb monuments of the Medici family in the Cappella de' Principi of the Church of San Lorenzo, that is, they hang from the real tomb monuments and from the tombs depicted in *pietra dura* on the walls of the Chapel.

That Browning was aware of all these diamond rings representing Lorenzo the Magnificent is highly probable. That he connected in his mind the diamond betrothal ring with the diamond ring of Lorenzo "the elder"—the Magnificent—seems possible in light of a notable correspondence: there is a crown on the betrothal ring (Fig. 252) and a crown on the *fleur-de-lis* design in *pietra dura* in the Medici Chapel (Fig. 253), where stands Lorenzo the Magnificent's diamond-designed tomb monument. Could it be that Browning was aware of this correspondence and identified himself with the princely Lorenzo, who, as a patron of art, encouraged writers and was an eminent poet in his own right?

I.1391-1401 (cont.)

> O lyric Love, half angel and half bird,
> And all a wonder and a wild desire,—
> Boldest of hearts that ever braved the sun,
> Took sanctuary within the holier blue,
> And sang a kindred soul out to his face,—
> Yet human at the red-ripe of the heart—
> When the first summons from the darkling earth
> Reached thee amid thy chambers, blanched their blue,
> And bared them of the glory—to drop down,
> To toil for man, to suffer or to die,—
> This is the same voice: can thy soul know change?

In 1861, three years before Browning began work on *The Ring and the Book*, Elizabeth died in the master bedroom of Casa Guidi while Robert held her in his arms (GRI, 222). In the center of the wedgewood blue ceiling of the master bedroom are two white stucco doves in bas-relief (Fig. 259). The reference to Robert's "lyric love, half angel, half bird," then, could be to these doves as the angelic, bird-like Elizabeth transported from Casa Guidi to her "sanctuary within the holier blue—amid [her] chambers . . . blue" in heaven. Philip Kelley informs me in conversation that the wedgewood blue ceiling of the master bedroom today is a reduction, after recent cleaning, to its former appearance, which probably means that the room was also blue in Browning's time.

IV.320-25

> . . . one child
> The strange tall pale beautiful creature grown
> Lily-like out o' the cleft i' the sun-smit rock
> To bow its white miraculous birth of buds
> I' the way of wandering Joseph and his spouse,—
> So painters fancy. . . .

Pompilia as a "beautiful creature grown / Lily-like out 'o the cleft i' the sun-smit rock" calls to mind the two versions of Leonardo da Vinci's *Madonna of the Rocks*. But the version in the Louvre, I think, is more likely a source here than the one in the National Gallery of London. During Browning's time the version in the National Gallery was in private hands before it was acquired by the gallery in 1880, and so Browning could only have seen copies of it before publishing *The Ring and the Book* in 1868. The Paris version was in the Louvre, however, by the early nineteenth century, and Browning undoubtedly saw it during his many visits to the city between 1846 and 1868 (KELL, 493-95; EISE). Another feature that distinguishes the version in the Louvre from the one in the National Gallery is the depiction of irises in the left-hand foreground of the former painting and none, apparently, in the latter. James Hall, in his *Dictionary of Subjects and Symbols in Art* (Harper and Row, New York and London, 1974), page 162, notes that in Christian symbolism connected with the Virgin, the iris is many times used instead of the lily, and Browning could easily have interchanged the two flowers in his mind. Moreover, the *giglio* (lily) of Florence, illustrated in Fig. 253 and discussed above under I.1-4, 15-17, 38, 45-49, is actually an iris (EISE). Finally, the irises in the "Lily-like" version in the Louvre are, as the text describes, clearly growing "out o' the cleft i' the sun-smit rock" (Fig. 260).

For a collateral source for the picture that "painters fancy," see the description of Gaudenzio Ferrari's *Flight into Egypt* below under IX.26-27, 120-30. For another reference to a lily, see the presentation of the *fleur-de-lis* ring above under I.1-4, 15-17.

VI.1249-55

> Once she asked, "What is it that made you smile,
> At the great gate with the eagles and the snakes,
> Where the company entered, 't is a long time since?"
> . . .
> That was a certain bishop's villa-gate,
> I knew it by the eagles. . . .

Cook places the Bishop's "villa-gate" near Spello but does not identify the structure that it is part of (COOK, 129). I propose that the villa does not exist but is rather the Old Bishop's Palace of Foligno, which is six miles south of Spello. The "great gate with the eagles and the snakes" is probably the Romanesque portal to the lateral façade of the Duomo of Foligno, which adjoins the Old Bishop's Palace facing left from the Piazza della Repubblica (Fig. 242). A fairly large natural looking eagle, representing St. John the Evangelist, is under the inner arch of the portal (Fig. 243). Also represented under the inner arch of the portal are the other Evangelists: St. Matthew (himself), St. Luke (an ox), and St. Mark (a lion). A small stylized eagle, possibly representing Frederick Barbarossa, is part of the decoration on the left inner portal pilaster. A fairly large dragon with a serpentine body is under the left end of the consoled stringcourse of the lateral façade (Fig. 242). A small serpentine figure, either a snake or an eel-like fish, is part of the decoration on the right inner pilaster of the portal. Eisenberg corroborates these identifications and adds that Browning might have seen the running fringe of each pilaster as eagles and snakes because the heavy, paired leaves resemble the spread of an eagle's wings, and the rinceau of the right pilaster suggests intertwined snakes (EISE; Fig. 243). Furthermore, it should be noted that Foligno is mentioned in line 1275 as part of the escape route taken by Pompilia and Caponsacchi on their way from Arezzo to Rome. Browning, too, we know, visited Foligno in 1860 (KELL, 494), four years before beginning *The Ring and the Book* while in London (DEVA, 322).

From Pompilia's untutored point of view, as quoted here by Caponsacchi, and/or Browning's dim recollection of his visit to Foligno, a confusion could have been made between an imaginary bishop's villa with a great gate decorated with eagles and snakes, and the Old Bishop's Palace and the Romanesque portal and lateral façade of the Duomo of Foligno.

VII.186-92 (cont.)

> And, since there hung a tapestry on the wall
> We two agreed to find each other out
> Among the figures. "Tisbe, that is you,
> With half-moon on your half-knot, spear in hand,
> Flying, but no wings, only the great scarf
> Blown to a bluish rainbow at your back:
> Call off your hound and leave the stag alone!"

Another painting in the Dulwich Picture Gallery that is unquestionably a source for Pompilia's imaginary "tapestry" is Tiepolo's *Diana* (DULW, 54, no. 186). As Fig. 245 shows, the painting corresponds in every way with the text. Diana has a "half-moon on . . . [her] hair knot, spear in hand, / Flying, but no wings, only the great scarf / Blown to a bluish rainbow at . . . [her] back" (partly visible on the left), and a "hound . . . and stag" are also in the picture. The bluish color of the scarf has been verified by G. A. Waterfield, Director of the Dulwich Gallery, who has observed the painting for me in its original state. The painting was received in the Bourgeois estate of 1811 (DULW, 54) and so was on hand for Browning to see during his many visits to the gallery (GRI, 12-14).

The third picture in Pompilia's imaginary tapestry is no doubt the *Perseus and Andromeda* that is identified above under VII.390-93, Figs. 121 and 122.

VIII.634-41

>   . . . why, trait for trait,
> Was ever portrait limned as like the life?
> (By Cavalier Maratta, shall I say?
> I hear he's first in reputation now.)
> Yes, that of Samson in the Sacred Text.
> That's not so much the portrait as the man!
> Samson in Gaza was the antetype
> Of Guido at Rome. . . .

Carlo "Maratta"—or Maratti—is not known to have done a "Samson," and so this presumed painting is imaginary. But Browning, we know, made regular visits to the Dulwich Picture Gallery in his youth (GRI, 12-14), and he could be recalling two paintings in the gallery that match the present text and the one above under III.58-62, which also refers to Maratta. One of the paintings, a *Holy Family with St. Anne, the Baptist and Zacharias*, is by Maratta (DULW, 28, cat. no. 274), and the other, a *Samson and Delilah*, is by Van Dyck (DULW, 40, cat. no. 40). That Browning could have confused the work of Maratta with Van Dyck is understandable, for, according to M. Murray's entry in the 1980 Dulwich catalogue, the *Samson and Delilah* is influenced by Rubens (p. 53) and dated to 1618/20. Prior to that, in the early 1600's, Rubens had familiarized himself with and had been influenced by the Italian style while living in northern Italy. Eisenberg, upon comparing the paintings (Figs. 247 and 248), agrees with me that there is enough similarity between the use of classical faces and columns to justify Browning's possible confusion in identifying the Van Dyck with the work of Maratta (EISE). The correspondence between the characters in the paintings and the literary texts is close, too. The reference to a Madonna by Maratta under III.58-62 above ties in with Half-Rome's sympathetic conception of Pompilia as the Virgin, and thus relates to Maratta's *Holy Family*; and the reference in the present passage to a presumed Samson by Maratta—by Van Dyck—connects with Archangelis's defense of Guido as analogous to Samson betrayed by Pompilia as represented by Delilah. Both the Maratta and Van Dyck paintings were acquired by the Dulwich Gallery in the Bourgeois bequest of 1811 (DULW, 49, 52, 55), which, of course, was many years earlier than Browning's first visit to the gallery.

IX.26-27, 120-30 (cont.)

> Suppose that Joseph, Mary, and her Babe
> A-journeying to Egypt, prove the piece....
> ...
> Thus then, just so and no whit otherwise,
> Have I,—engaged as I were Ciro's self,
> To paint a parallel, a Family,
> The patriarch Pietro with his wise old wife
> To boot (as if one introduced Saint Anne
> By bold conjecture to complete the group)
> And juvenile Pompilia with her babe,
> Who, seeking safety in the wilderness,

> Were all surprised by Herod, while outstretched
> In sleep beneath a palm-tree by a spring,
> And killed—the very circumstance I paint. . . .

Two paintings by Mazzolino could be conflated sources for
Bottinus's imaginary picture of the Holy Family being "killed"
by "Herod." One of the paintings is his *Madonna with St. Anne,*
and the other is his *Slaughter of the Innocents.* What brings
these particular paintings to mind is the fact that they are both
lodged in the Uffizi Gallery, that the painting of the Madonna
specifically includes a "Saint Anne," that both were rendered by
one artist, and that they were probably placed close together
when Browning no doubt saw them during his long stay in
Florence— his long stay before leaving the city for good in 1861
and starting *The Ring and the Book* in 1864. The paintings,
listed in the gallery's inventory as nos. 1347 and 1350, have been
in the Uffizi since 1773 and 1704, respectively.

A third possible source, I think, could have caused
Browning to have used the name of "Ciro" Ferri—his full name
is stated in line 117—instead of Mazzolino. In *Legends of the
Madonna,* in the section on the Flight into Egypt, Mrs. Jameson
describes a painting by Gaudenzio Ferrari, in the Church of the
Minorites, in Varallo, Italy (JAMESO, 275). By contracting the
name "Ferrari" into "Ferri," it is easily seen how Browning
could have confused the two painters. Furthermore, not only
are "Joseph, Mary, and her Babe / A-journeying to Egypt" in the
painting, as described here and by Mrs. Jameson, but the "palm-
tree" mentioned in the present passage is also included in Mrs.
Jameson's description, for she writes, "In the background the
palm-tree inclines its branches." The legendary tradition of a
palm-tree lowering its branches so that the Holy Family can
readily gather its dates is picked up in the passage above under
IV.320-25, where a lily plant, rather than a palm-tree, "bow[s] its
white miraculous birth of buds / I' the way of wandering Joseph
and his spouse. . . . " We have no evidence that Browning
visited Varallo, and so the specificity of Mrs. Jameson's description of the inclining palm tree is crucial to identifying this
source. Also, it should be pointed out that Mrs. Jameson, who
was a good friend of Browning, probably caught his attention by
judging Ferrari's painting "the most beautiful Flight into Egypt"
she had "ever seen." *Legends of the Madonna* was written in
1852, and Browning, who no doubt was familiar with all of Mrs.

Jameson's writings, probably read about Ferrari's painting long before publishing *The Ring and the Book* in 1868. For another reference to Ciro Ferri, see above under V.487-89.

IX.177-80

> What is this Tale of Tarquin, how the slave
> Was caught by him, preferred to Collatine?
> Thou, even from thy corpse-clothes virginal,
> Look'st the lie dead, Lucretia!

"Lucretia" was the virtuous wife of Lucius Tarquinius Collatinus, that is, "Collatine," who was the second cousin of Sextus Tarquinius, or simply, "Tarquin." According to tradition, Tarquin, influenced by Lucretia's beauty, visited her during her husband's absence and threatened to kill her and a slave unless she would give in to his lust. Tarquin's excuse was to be that, should she refuse, he had caught Lucretia and the slave in adultery and had killed them to avenge her husband's honor. Fear of her own dishonor and use of force by Sextus induced Lucretia to yield, but afterwards she told her relatives what had happened, swore them to vengence, and then stabbed herself to death.

Bottinus, in prosecution of Guido's murder of Pompilia, takes the position that Lucretia, like Pompilia, "look'st the lie dead"—the lie of Tarquin—that the "slave . . . she preferred to Collatine" was like Caponsacchi, whom Pompilia preferred to her husband, Guido, but to whom she was not unfaithful.

Browning, who depicts Bottinus arguing through word pictures—"just one portrait, but life-size" (IX.164)—could be referring to an actual painting he saw at the Dulwich Picture Gallery, the *Death of Lucretia*, a painting by Guido Reni, from the 1811 Bourgeois bequest (DULW, 54, no. 204; Fig. 249). What brings this particular version of the subject to mind is the fact that five other paintings in the Dulwich Picture Gallery are nominated in this study as sources in *The Ring and the Book*. These paintings are entered under I.1391-92 (Fig. 157), VII.186-96 (Figs. 237 and 245), III.58-62 (Fig. 247), and VIII.634-41 (Fig. 248). Also, Browning might have made the connection with the present source through his use of Guido Reni's paintings entered above under II.83-96 (Fig. 158) and "Cenciaja," 15-29 (Fig. 19). Finally, the first names of Guido Reni and Guido Franceschini could have been associated in Browning's mind.

XII.870-74 (cont.)

Render all duty which good ring should do;
And, failing grace, succeed in Guardianship,—
Might mine but lie outside thine, Lyric Love
Thy rare gold ring of verse (the poet praised)
Linking our England to his Italy!

A. N. Kincaid makes a strong case for two gold rings given to the Brownings by Isa Blagden as sources for the rings in the present passage.   One ring, inscribed "*Vis Mea*," which means "my strength," was given to Robert and is presently in the Balliol College Library; the other, a small signet inscribed "*A.E.I.*," which is Greek for "always," was given to Elizabeth and is currently stolen out of the British Museum.   Robert's larger ring surrounds the smaller one of Elizabeth and will, as Book XII concludes, "In guardianship . . . lie outside thine, Lyric Love" (KI, 151-58, with an illustration of the *Vis Mea* ring on p. 155). For the *Vis Mea* ring as a composite source in another context, see above under I.1-4, 15-17.

THE STATUE AND THE BUST

187-93

But long ere Robbia's cornice, fine,
With flowers and fruits which leaves enlace,
Was set where now in the empty shrine—

(And, leaning out of a bright blue space,
As a ghost might lean from a chink of sky.
The passionate pale lady's face. . . .

Although mainly confined to her Florentine palace by her jealous husband, the "lady" of Browning's poem might have been allowed to visit the churches in Florence in order to tend to her devotions.   In one of these, Santa Maria Novella, she could have seen a work by Giovanni Della Robbia that passes as a model for her portrait in the present passage.   In the sacristy is "Robbia's" *Lavabo*, which has a "cornice, fine, / With flowers and fruits which leaves enlace," while "leaning out of the bright blue space" is the image of the Virgin, which could serve for the "pale lady's face" (Fig. 246; Map F:G7).

TIME'S REVENGES

22

> ... Saint Paul's [bell] is striking two.

DeVane dates the poem to 1845, when Browning was in London courting Elizabeth (DEVA, 179-80). The reference is undoubtedly to the famous Cathedral of St. Paul, in London.

UP AT A VILLA—DOWN IN THE CITY

56-57

> They have clapped a new tax upon salt, and
> what oil pays passing the gate
> It's a horror to think of. And so, the villa for
> me and not the city.

Edward McAleer quotes the above passage in reference to the economic advantage Isa Blagden had in living in villas outside of Florence, but McAleer does not determine which of the Florentine residences that Isa Blagden lived in best fits his chosen text (MCA, xxii). On several counts Villa Brichieri, I think, is the logical choice for McAleer's unspecified nomination of a Blagden abode as the poem's out-of-town residence. DeVane dates "Up at a Villa—Down in the City" to 1853 (DEVA, 215). McAleer places the meeting of the Brownings and Isa Blagden to about 1850 (MCA, xxiii), five years before the poem was published. And Villa Brichieri is advanced above as the setting for the opening of "Old Pictures in Florence," which, along with "Up at a Villa—Down in the City," was published in 1855.

An alternate to the above proposal could be DeVane's choice of the Villa Poggio al Vento, in Marciano, where Browning stayed outside of Siena in 1850 (DEVA, 215; KELL, 493).

A third possibility is the residence where the Brownings sojourned in Bagni di Lucca in 1853. This idea follows from the dating of the present poem by Griffin and Minchin to 1853, while the Brownings were in Bagni di Lucca (GRI, 199). Kelley and Hudson identify the residence of the Brownings in Bagni di Lucca at this time as Casa Tolomei (KELL, 493).

SUMMARY OF COMPOSITE SOURCES

A significant theory of Browning's creative method emerges from this study. It is his apparent use of composite sources for references and allusions to unspecified and imaginary art, sculpture, and architecture. Whether or not this is a deliberate method, however, is not known. Perhaps in the cases of unspecified art objects it is intentional poetic license. Perhaps in the instances of imaginary art objects it is poetic license and carelessness. But carelessness, at least in the case of *The Ring and the Book*, is ruled out by Pen Browning in favor of absent-mindedness combined with a desire to be historically accurate. In a letter to Hodell, Pen writes (HOD, 334, item 536):

> . . . certainly it [an error in *The Ring and the Book*] was not caused by carelessness, for he [Browning] was painstaking to a degree and had a proper horror of blundering, which is the word he would have used. I can only account for such a mistake as this—which he would have been the first to pronounce unpardonable—by his absent-mindedness, his attention being at the moment absorbed by something else. Absent-mindedness was one of his characteristics, over instances of which he used to laugh most heartily. My father's intention, I know, was to be scrupulously accurate about the facts in this poem.

Apart from these insights into Browning's creative process, it is sufficient to say that there are enough conflated possibilities in this study to justify a composite theory. The entries below, then, are listed in order to support the theory and to provide source materials for future research. Entries that are marked "(I)" are imaginary, and those that are designated "(U)" are unspecified. The fact that 13 out of the 40 composite entries below, that is, that about one out of every three conflated entries is imaginary rather than unspecified, might indicate that factual confusion, in addition to poetic license and absent-mindedness, characterizes Browning's creative process; that inasmuch as even the imaginary conflated sources are, along with the unspecified ones, probably based on actual models, it would appear that Browning's use of composites is almost always concerned with history if not historical accuracy.

And,   **103-12 (U)**
Copy of a painting by Raphael: *Virgin of the Palazzo Tempi, Leo X with Two Cardinals*, by Raphael; copy of Raphael's *Leo X with Two Cardinals*, by Andrea del Sarto

148-51 (U)
Work of Andrea del Sarto in France: *Portrait of the Infant Dauphin; Charity*

259-63 (I)
Four walls painted together by Andrea del Sarto, Raphael, Michelangelo, and Leonardo da Vinci: Cloister of the Madonna, Church of the Santissima Annunziata; Sala Grande, Villa di Poggio a Caiano; Uffizi Gallery; Life of Michelozzo, from Vasari's *Vite*

Any,   **77-78 (U)**
Painting of Venus by Titian: *Venus of Urbino; Venus and Cupid; Venus with the Organ-player; Venus with the Lute-player; Venus, Pardo*

Bi,   **666-68 (U)**
Painting of St. Michael: *St. Michael*, by Mabuse; *St. Michael*, by Innocenza da Imola

Bis,   **56-61 (I)**
Tomb in the Church of Santa Prassede: *Pan and Syrinx*, by Gerard Hoet; *Pan Pursuing Syrinx*, by Hendrick van Balen; *Pan and Syrinx*, by Hendrick Goltzius; *Pan and Syrinx*, by Rubens-Brueghel; tombs of Cardinal Cetti and Cardinal Anchero in the Church of Santa Prassede

By,   **2:6-8 (U)**
Fireplaces: in the Dining Room and Drawing Room of Casa Guidi

18:86-90 (I)
Chapel in the Alps with a fresco of John in the Desert on the façade: *Life of John the Baptist, Birth of John the Baptist,* by Filippo Lippi; Oratorio di Rifubbri, near Bagni di Lucca; John Murray's *Handbook for Travellers in Switzerland, the Alps of Savoy and Piedmont*

Fra,   70-75 (U)
Painting of St. Jerome: *Four Fathers of the Church, Madonna with the Christ Child, Death of St. Jerome, Adoration of the Christ Child, Trinity and Saints, Suffering Christ among St. Francis and St. Jerome, Three Saints, St. Jerome,* by Filippo Lippi; *Penitent St. Jerome,* by Toscani; "Bishop Blougram's Apology," lines 704-07

145-63 (U)
Figures representing monks: *Innovation of the Rule of the Carmelites,* by Filippo Lippi; *Consecration,* by Masaccio

Paintings of the Crucifixion: *Trinity and Saints, Crucifixion and Saints* (2), by Filippo Lippi, Filippo Lippi and Pesellino, and the school of Lippi **(U)**

Painting representing a girl on tiptoe: *Madonna and Child and Life of St. Anne, Birth of St. Stephen,* by Filippo Lippi **(U)**

189-90 (U)
Paintings of a saint praising God: *St. Francis Glorified in Heaven,* by the school of Giotto; *Life of St. Francis,* a series attributed to Giotto

265-69 (U)
Paintings and sculpture representing Eve: *The Temptation,* by Masolino; *The Expulsion,* by Masaccio; *Creation of Eve,* by Ghiberti; *Creation,* by Jacopo della Quercia; *Creation of Eve,* by Uccello

286-90 (U)
Florentine landscapes: Numerous landscapes as backgrounds for pictures by Filippo Lippi; *Tribute Money*, by Masaccio; *Alton Locke* and *Yeast*, by Charles Kingsley

323-32 (I)
Fresco of St. Lawrence by Filippo Lippi in Prato: *Martyrdom of St. Lawrence*, by Mario Balassi and Carlo Dolci; *Martyrdom of St. Lawrence*, by Fra Angelico; *Christ of the Column*, by Andrea del Castagno

345-87 (I)
Details in Filippo Lippi's *Coronation of the Virgin*: *Madonna and Child with Four Saints*, by Filippo Lippi; Legend of St. Lucy, from *Sacred and Legendary Art*, by Mrs. Jameson

In, 190-93 (U)
Painting of Mary Magdalen: *Magdalen*, by Titian; *Magdalen*, attributed to Giorgione

Jam, VIII.27-32 (I)
Anonymous clay cast of a hand with a ringed finger: *Clasped Hands of the Brownings*, by Harriot Hosmer; *Loulie's Hand*, by Hiram Powers; Kenyon's marble hand of Hilda, in Hawthorne's *The Marble Faun*

My, 1-4 (U)
Portrait of Lucrezia de' Medici: *Lucrezia de' Medici*, by Agnolo Bronzino and Alessandro Allori (5); medals nos. 473-476 of Lucrezia de' Medici, by Pastorino da Siena; a bronze medal of Lucrezia, by Francesco Salviati; a medal of Lucrezia by Domenico Poggini; *A Young Lady*, from the Italian School in the Dulwich Picture Gallery; statue scene from *The Winter's Tale*, by Shakespeare

47-48 (U)
Site of Renaissance court in Ferrara: Castel Estense, Ferrara; Ducal Palace, Venice

54-56 (I)
Neptune statue by Claus of Innsbruck: *Wonders of the Little World,* by Wanley; *Neptune,* by The Master of the Dragon and Severo da Ravenna (5); *Neptune,* by Alessandro Vittoria; statue of Neptune owned by Isabella d'Este; bronze tomb-monument in the Court Church of Innsbruck; statue of Neptune in the Piazza della Borsa, Trieste; two statues of Neptune by Jacopo Sansovino; fountain group sculpture of Neptune by Giongo, in Trent; Neptune chalice and Neptune vase in the Residenz of Munich; *Venice Receives the Homage of Neptune,* by Tiepolo

Old,   13:97-104 (U)
Classical sculpture representing Alexander: *Dying Alexander,* in the Uffizi Gallery; *Alexander Sarcophagus,* in the Istanbul Museum

24:185-87 (U)
Damaged frescoes in Florence: *Innovation of the Rule of the Carmellites,* by Filippo Lippi; *Portrait of Dante,* attributed to Giotto; *Last Supper,* by Ghirlandaio; *Lives of the Virgin and St. John the Baptist,* by Orcagna; *Christ at the Column,* by Andrea del Castagno; frescoes in the refectory of the Church of Santa Croce

26:201-08, 31:241-43 (U)
Paintings in the Church of Ognissanti: *St. Jerome,* by Botticelli; *St. Jerome,* by Ghirlandaio; *Last Supper,* by Ghirlandaio

One,   2:5-17 (U)
Paintings by Raphael representing his loved one: *La Velata, La Fornarina, Sistine Madonna,* Mary Magdalen in the *St. Cecilia, Portrait of a Lady*

Sonnets written on sketches for the *Disputa* and *La Fornarina,* by Raphael (U)

16:164 (U)
Towers used for Galileo's experiments: Galileo's Villa Gioiello, Arcetri; Bell-tower (Leaning Tower) of Pisa; Torre del Gallo, Arcetri

Pic, **25-26, 31-33 (U)**
Painting of a Madonna carried in procession: *Rucellai Madonna* (Vasari's *Lives*), *Madonna Enthroned*, by Duccio

Pip, **III.162-63 (U)**
Painting by Titian in Treviso: *Annunciation*, *Portrait of Speroni*

Rin, **I.1-4, 15-17; XII.870-74 (I)**
Etruscan style gold ring by Castellani with lily design: Robert Browning *Vis Mea* ring; Castellani *fleur-de-lis* ring; Godfrey Wentworth ring in Isa Blagden's book *Agnes Tremorne*; Elizabeth Barratt Browning *A.E.I.* ring

I.1391-1401 (U)
Image of Elizabeth Barratt Browning as a "lyric Love, half angel and half bird": *Jacob's Dream*, a printing by Aert de Gelderin; bas-relief doves on ceiling of the master bedroom in Casa Guidi

IV.320-25 (I)
Painting of Flight into Egypt with bowing lily plant among rocks: *Madonna of the Rocks*, the version in the Louvre, by Leonardo da Vinci; *Flight into Egypt*, by Gaudenzio Ferrari

VI.400-06 (I)
Painting of a Madonna in Arezzo by Raphael: *Madonna and Child*, by Betto di Francesco and Giovanni di Francesco; *Small Cowper Madonna*, *Madonna del Granduca*, by Raphael

VI.1249-55 (I)
Bishop's Villa: Old Bishop's Palace of Foligno; lateral facade of the Cathedral of Foligno

VIII.186-92 (I)
Tapestry: *Daphne and Apollo,* by Aert de Gelder; *Diana,* by Tiepolo; *Perseus and Andromeda,* by Polidoro da Caravaggio, and the copy by Volpato

IX.26-27, 120-30 (I)
Painting of the Holy Family slaughtered during the Flight into Egypt: *Holy Family with St. Anne, Slaughter of the Innocents,* by Mazzolino; *Flight into Egypt,* by Gaudenzio Ferrari

Sor,   **I.567-83 (U)**
Sculpture representing Christ by Nicola Pisano: *Descent from the Cross,* pulpits in the Baptistry of Pisa and the Duomo of Siena

Up,   **26-30 (I)**
Fountain in Italy representing a naked woman and sea horses: *Fountain of Good Fortune,* Fano; *Birth of Venus,* by Botticelli; *Fountain of Neptune,* Trent, by Giongo; *Fountain of Neptune,* Florence, by Ammanati; *Fountain of Trevi,* Rome

56-57 (U)
Villa representing the title of the poem: Villa Brichieri, Florence; Villa Poggio al Vento, Marciano (environs of Siena); Casa Tolomei, Bagni di Lucca

INDEX OF ARTISTS

Only names of painters, sculptors, and architects that are specifically mentioned or clearly implied in Browning's poems are listed in this index. The poems and the line numbers in which the names are mentioned are listed under each of the names. The line numbers are taken from *A Concordance to the Poems of Robert Browning*, by Leslie N. Broughton and Benjamin F. Stelter (New York: Stechert, 1924-25).

CLASSICAL (6th and 5th centuries B.C.)
    Greek
        Phidias
            "Cleon," 141

MEDIEVAL (13th and 14th centuries)
    Italian
        Cimabue
            "Old Pictures in Florence," 180
        Dello Delli ("Dellos")
            "Old Pictures in Florence," 64
        Fra Angelico
            "Fra Lippo Lippi," 235
            "Old Pictures in Florence," 204
            The Ring and the Book, XI.2114
        Gaddi, Taddeo
            "Old Pictures in Florence," 205
        Giotto
            "Fra Lippo Lippi," 189
            "Old Pictures in Florence," 15, 17, 24, 133, 233, 287
            "Of Pacchiarotto, and How He Worked in Distemper," 44
        Guido da Siena ("Guidone")
            Sordello, I.576
        Guido da Bologna
            Sordello, IV.608

RENAISSANCE 15th and 16th centuries)
Italian (cont.)
        3, 27, 43, 64, 193, 226, 232, 282, 291
  Polidoro da Caravaggio
    "Waring," 152
  Pollaiuolo, Antonio ("Pollajolo")
    "Old Pictures in Florence," 210
  Primaticcio ("Primatice")
    "Cristina and Monaldeschi," 106
  Raphael ("Rafael")
    "Andrea del Sarto," 119, 131, 136, 152, 177-78, 185, 194, 197, 263
    Fifine at the Fair, 518, 523, 533, 536, 553, 700, 755
    "Old Pictures in Florence," 51
    "One Word More," 5, 14, 15, 17, 20, 58, 198
    "Parleyings with Christopher Smart," 40, 90
    "Parleyings with Francis Furini," 166
    The Ring and the Book, IV.376; VI.402, 661, 899; XI.2110
    A Soul's Tragedy (advertisement)
    Prince Hohenstiel-Schwangau, Saviour of Society, 853
  Robbia, della (which one not specified)
    "The Statue and the Bust," 169, 187
  Rosso Fiorentino ("Le Roux")
    "Cristina and Monaldeschi," 107
  Schedone ("Schidone")
    "In a Gondola," 186
  Titian ("Tizian")
    "Any Wife to Any Husband," XIII.5
    "Beatrice Signorini," 122
    "Cenciaja," 22
    "Filippo Baldinucci on the Privilege of Burial," 402, 419, 439
    "Founder of the Feast," 3
    "How It Strikes a Contemporary," 76
    "In a Gondola," 193
    Pippa Passes, III.163
    The Ring and the Book, XI.2114
  Vasari
    "Andrea del Sarto," 106
    "Old Pictures in Florence," 72
  Volpato
    "A Likeness," 61

BAROQUE (17th century)
   Flemish
      Lairesse, Gérard de
         "Parleyings with Gerard de Lairesse," 5, 23, 39, 115, 157,
            363
      Rubens
         In a Balcony, 130, 677
   French
      Du Pré, Abraham
         The Two Poets of Croisic, 377
      Daret, Pierre
         The Two Poets of Croisic, 378
   Italian
      Albano
         The Ring and the Book, XI.270
      Bernini, Gian Lorenzo
         The Ring and the Book, I.891
      Carracci, Annibale
         Pippa Passes (Porter and Clarke, I, 320, identify the
            reference in Act I, line 447, to "Hannibal Scratchy"
            as a play on Carracci's name)
      Dolci, Carlo ("Carlino")
         "Old Pictures in Florence," 232
         The Ring and the Book, III.58, IX.34
      Ferri
         The Ring and the Book, V.487, IX.117
      Furini
         "Parleying with Francis Furini," 1ff
      Gentileschi, Artemisia
         "Beatrice Signorini," 29, 67, 84, 106, 151, 241, 246
      Giordano, Luca ("Haste-thee-Luke")
         "In a Gondola," 188
      Guercino
         "The Guardian Angel," 36, 47
      Maratta
         The Ring and the Book, III.59, VIII.630
      Pietro da Cortona
         "Beatrice Signorini," 4, 5, 6
         The Ring and the Book, V.486, IX.116
      Reni, Guido
         "One Word More," 27, 29
         The Ring and the Book, II.83

BAROQUE (17th century)
   Italian (cont.)
      Romanelli, Francesco
         "Beatrice Signorelli," 12
      Romano, Guilio
         "Bishop Blougram's Apology," 516

CLASSICAL (18th century)
   English
      Blake
         Red Cotton Night-Cap Country, IV.772
      Gainsborough
         The Inn Album, I.353
      Reynolds
         Fifine at the Fair, 724
   Flemish
      Lairesse, Gérard de
         "Parleying with Gerard de Lairesse," 5, 39, 115, 157, 363
   French
      Ingres
         "Dis Aliter Visum," 38
   Italian
      Canova
         Pippa Passes, I.346, 377, 389, 393

ROMANTIC (19th century)
   French
      Corot
         The Inn Album, I.77
      Doré
         Fifine at the Fair, 35:551
      Gérôme
         Fifine at the Fair, 709
      Meissonier
         The Inn Album, IV.772
      Pradier, James
         Prince Hohenstiel-Schwangau, Saviour of Society, 186
   Italian
      Ademollo, Luigi
         The Ring and the Book, I.364

VICTORIAN (19th century)
  English
    Barry
      The Inn Album, III.7
    Gibson, John
      "Youth and Art," 8, 55
    Hunt, William Holman
      The Inn Album, I.37
    Landseer
      The Inn Album, I.35
    Leighton ("Kaunian painter")
      Balaustian's Adventure, 2674
      "Eurydice to Orpheus: a Painting by Leighton"
      "Parleyings with Christopher Smart," 90
      "Yellow and pale as ripened corn"
    Millais, John
      The Inn Album, I.37
    Pugin
      "Bishop Blougram's Apology," 6
    Watt, John
      "Parleyings with Christopher Smart," 91 (name identified by Porter and Clarke, XII, 340)
    Woolner, Thomas
      "Deaf and Dumb: A Group by Woolner," 1-8

INDEX OF SOURCES WITH LOCATIONS

This index gives a summary of possible sources for art and architecture in Browning's poetry that have definite locations. It also gives a detailed account of the author's contribution to the study of original sources, and together with the Index of Miscellaneous Sources provides the data summarized in the first paragraph of the Introduction to this study. An asterisk after an entry indicates an original source nominated by the author. Other symbols used in this index are the head letters indicating the titles of the poems covered in this study, and the numbers indicating the line numbers of the citations from the poems (*e.g.*, My, 1-4, means "My Last Duchess," lines 1-4).

ENGLAND
  Bedford
        Jail of Bedford, doors kept in the Moot Hall of Elstow and the Bunyan Meeting Church (Fig. 94)
           Ned, 328
        John Bunyan, a statue by Boehm (Fig. 93)
           Ned, 328
  Birmingham
    City Museum and Art Gallery
        First Anniversary of the Death of Beatrice, a pen-and-ink drawing by Dante Gabriel Rossetti (Fig. 250)
           One, 5:32-35
  Cambridge
    Fitzwilliam Museum
        Emily Augusta Patmore, a portrait by Millais (Fig. 38)
           Fac, 1-3, 11-13
  Chistlehurst
    Murial and Betty Edwards
        Carved wood gilt mirror of the Brownings (Fig. 149)
           Rin, I.472-83
  London
    British Museum, Archaic Rooms
        Omphalos Apollo, a marble statue (Fig. 97)
           Old, 13:97-104 (*)
        Racers' Frieze, a metope from the Parthenon (Fig. 99)
           Old, 13:97-104
        Theseus, a statue from the east pediment of the Parthenon (Fig. 95)
           Old, 13:97-104
    British Museum, Dept. of Medieval and Latin Antiquities
        Signet Ring of Mrs. Browning (presently stolen)
           Rin, I.1-4, 15-17; XII.866-70
    British Museum, Print Room
        Andromeda and Perseus, from an engraving by Volpato (Fig. 122)
           Lik, 60-61
           Pau, 656-67
           Rin, VII.186-96 (*), 390-93; IX.965-70 (*)
        Crucifixion and Saints, a sketch by Filippo Lippi
           Fra, 145-63 (*)
        Sketch for the *Disputa* with a sonnet by Raphael (Fig. 107)
           One, 2:5-17

ENGLAND (cont.)
  London (cont.)
    National Picture Gallery (cont.)
      Seven Saints, Sacred Conversation, a painting by Filippo Lippi (Fig. 45)
        Fra, 47-49, 245-46
      Trinity and Saints, a painting by Filippo Lippi
        Fra, 70-75 (*)
      Trinity and Saints, a painting by Filippo Lippi and Pesellino
        Fra, 145-63 (*)
    National Portrait Gallery
      Bronze cast of the clasped hands of the Brownings, by Harriet Hosmer (Fig. 81)
        Jam, VIII.27-32 (*), IX.18-20
        Lik, 49-50
        Pro, 27-28 (*)
    St. George's Cathedral, Southwark (Fig. 11)
        Bi, 3-9 (*)
    St. Margaret's Church
      Jub
    St. Paul's Cathedral
      Bell-tower
        Tim, 22
      The Light of the World, a painting by William Holman Hunt (Fig. 77)
        Inn, I.34-37
    T. Agnew and Son
      The Huguenot, a painting by John Everett Millais (Fig. 76)
        Inn, I.34-37
    Tate Gallery
      A Distinguished Member of the Humane Society, a painting by Landseer (Fig. 75)
        Inn, I.34-37
      The Hunted Stag, a painting by Landseer (Fig. 74)
        Inn, I.34-37
    Victoria and Albert Museum
      Life of Christ, cartoons for tapestries, by Raphael
        Pri, 850-55 (*)
    Westminster Abbey (Fig. 85)
        Bi, 3-9
        Las, 6:65-66

GERMANY (WEST) (cont.)
  Munich
    Alte Pinakothek
      Madonna of the Palazzo Tempi, a painting by Raphael (Fig. 4)
        And, 103-12
      St. Michael, a painting by Mabuse (Berneart van Orley)
        Bi, 666-68 (*)
    Glyptothek
      Paris, a statue from the Aeginetan Sculptures (Fig. 96)
        Old, 13:97-104
    Residenz
      Neptune, a 16th-century chalice (Fig. 240)
        My, 54-56 (*)
      Neptune Vase (see Index of Miscellaneous Sources)

GREECE
  Athens
    Stoa Poecile ("Poikilè")
      Bal, 2672-97
      Cle, 51-54

IRELAND
  Clandeboye
    Tower of Lady Helen Dufferin (Fig. 64)
      Hel, 12-13
ITALY
  Abano
    Archeological Zone
      Fountain of Tiberius, today a circular bed of gravel eight feet in diameter in the garden where the "fount" once stood (added at publication time)
        "Pietro of Abano," stanza 54 (*)
  Arezzo
    Bishop's Palace (Fig. 172)
      Rin, VII.757
    Cathedral
      Ferdinand I, a statue by Giovanni da Bologna (Fig. 172)
        Cle, 174-80 (*)
        Rin, VI.249-56
      Life of Christ, stained-glass windows by Guillaume de Marcillat
        Rin, VI.460-62

ITALY (cont.)
  Florence (cont.)
    Churches, Convents, and Monasteries (cont.)
      San Gaetano (Map F:7G)
        Crucifixion and Saints, a statue from the school of Lippi
          Fra, 145-63 (*)
      San Lorenzo (Map F:7H; Fig. 141)
        Cappella de' Principi, statues by Michelangelo in the Medici Chapel (Figs. 119, 253)
          Fra, 61-67
          Par, 3:176-81
          Rin, I.38-52 (*)
          Sta, 214-16
      San Marco (Map F:6I)
        Façade (Fig. 49)
          Fra, 138-44
        Portrait of Savonarola, a painting by Fra Bartolommeo (Fig. 225)
          Pic, 38-41 (*)
      San Miniato al Monte (Fig. 113)
          One, 15:144-52
      Santa Croce
        Frescoes in the Refectory
          Old, 24:185-87
        New Cloister, *Christ at the Column,* a fresco by Andrea del Castagno (destroyed)
          Fra, 323-32
      Santa Maria degli Angeli ("Camaldolese") (Map F:7I; Fig. 48)
        Façade
          Fra, 138-41
      Santa Maria del Carmine (Map F:8F)
        The Expulsion, a fresco by Masaccio (Fig. 223)
          Fra, 265-69 (*)
        Façade (Fig. 41)
          Fra, 138-41
        Innovation of the Rule of the Carmelites, a fresco by Filippo Lippi (Fig. 50)
          Fra, 145-63
        Portrait of Pollaiuolo, a fresco by Filippino Lippi
          Old, 27:209-16
        The Temptation, a fresco by Masolino (Fig. 55)
          Fra, 265-69 (*)

ITALY (cont.)
  Florence (cont.)
   Houses (cont.)
    Casa Guidi: balcony, fireplaces, master bedroom (ceiling), mirror, memorial tablet by Tommaseo, (Map F:9G; Figs. 149, 150, 197, 259)
      By, 2:6-8
      Rin, I.1-4, 15-17, 110-16, 472-83, 1391-1401 (*); XII.470-74
      Up, 51-52
  Museums
   Accademia delle Belle Arti (Map F:7I)
    Awakening Captive, a statue by Michelangelo (Fig. 238)
      Fif, 52:757-59, 777-79
   Archeological Museum (Map F:6I)
    Chimera of Arezzo, a marble statue (Fig. 188)
      Rin, XI.1115-25
   Bargello (National Museum) (Map F:8H,8I; Fig. 86)
    Portrait of Dante, a detail of a fresco attributed to Giotto; sketch of the same by Seymour Kirkup (Figs. 209, 210)
      Lur, I.297-300
      Old, 24:185-92
      Sou, verso of title page (*)
   Museo dell' Opera del Duomo (Map F:7I),
    A design of the Bell-tower of Florence, attributed to Giotto (Fig. 106)
      Old, 35:278-80; 36:281-88
   Palazzo Pitti (Map F:9G)
    La Velata, a painting by Raphael (Fig. 108)
      One, 2:5-17
    Lucrezia de' Medici, a painting by Bronzino (Fig. 222)
      My, 1-4
    Madonna and Child and the Life of St. Anne, a painting by Filippo Lippi (Fig. 51)
      Fra, 145-63
    Madonna del Granduca, a painting by Raphael (Fig. 111)
      One, 3:18-25
      Rin, VI.400-06, 460-62, 668-73 (*)
    Portrait of a Man and Woman, a painting once attributed to Andrea del Sarto (Fig. 1)
      And, 1-3
    St. Mary Magdalen in Penitence, a painting by Titian (Fig. 73)
      In, 83-99 (*)

ITALY (cont.)
  Florence (cont.)
    Street
      Borgo Allegri (Map F:8I)
            Pic, 25-26; 31-38
    Tower
      Torre del Gallo
            One, 16:164 (*)
  Foligno
    Duomo
        Portal with eagles and serpentine figures on lateral
        façade (Figs. 242 and 243)
            Rin, VI.1249-55 (*)
      Old Bishop's Palace (Fig. 242)
            Rin, VI.1249-55 (*)
  Galli Islands, Amalfian Coast
    Tower of Robert of Naples (Fig. 32)
            Eng, 207-38
  Goito
    Castle (ruins)
            Sor, I.381-82
  Loreto
    Santuario della Santa Casa
        Life of the Virgin, marble panels by Andrea Sansovino
            Bi, 377 (*)
    Museo della Santa Casa
        Life of Christ, copies of tapestries by Raphael
            Pri, 850-57 (*)
  Lucca
    Church of San Martino
        Descent from the Cross, a lunette on the façade by
        Nicola Pisano (Fig. 208)
            Sor, I.567-83 (*)
  Mantua
    Palazzo Ducale
        Life of Christ, copies of tapestries by Raphael
            Pri, 850-55 (*)
  Massa
    Malaspina Castle (Fig. 255)
        Tower below the castle (Fig. 256)
            Chi, title, 31:181-84 (*)
  Merluzza ("Baccano")
    Inn (Fig. 163)
            Rin, III.1633-36; IV.1397-98; X.846-49

ITALY (cont.)
Milan
  Brera Gallery
    St. Michael, a painting by Innocenza da Imola
      Bi, 666-68 (*)
  Church of Santa Maria delle Grazie
    Judas, from the *Last Supper,* a fresco by Leonardo da Vinci (Fig. 43)
      Fra, 25-26
  Private collection
    Magdalen, a painting attributed to Giorgione
      In, 83-89
Naples
  Duomo
    Chapel of the Treasury of St. Janarius, reliquary for the blood and silver box for the bones of the head of St. Janarius (Fig. 232)
      Bi, 728-29
  Palazzo Capodimonte
    Leo X with Two Cardinals, a painting by Andrea del Sarto, after a painting by Raphael
      And, 103-12
Padua
  Duomo (Fig. 79)
      Ita, 73-75
  Governor's Palace ("Podesta")
      Sor, I.150
Palermo
  Palazzina Cinese (Fig. 202)
      Sor, III.119-21
  Palazzo della Zisa
      Sor, III.119-21 (*)
Parma
  National Art Gallery
    Virgin with St. Jerome and Mary Magdalen, a painting by Correggio (Fig. 12)
      Bi, 113-17, 704-07 (*)
Piano di Sorrento
  Church of the Santissima Trinità (Fig. 34) (*); Mount Vicoalvano (Fig. 35)
    Effigy of the Madonna del Rosario (Fig. 33)
      Eng, 260-91 (*)

ITALY (cont.)
  Pisa
    Baptistery
      Crucifixion, a panel from the pulpit, by Nicola Pisano
        Sor, I.567-83
    Bell-tower (Leaning Tower)
      One, 16:164
    Camposanto
      Triumph of Death, a fresco by the Master of the Triumph of Death (Fig. 244)
        Fra, 183-93
  Possagno
    Gipsoteca
      Muse or *Psyche*, a plaster head by Canova
        Pip, I.375-94
      Pietà, a group sculpture by Canova (Fig. 130)
        Pip, I.375-94
    Temple of Canova (Fig. 125); copy of Canova's *Pietá*, by Bartolommeo Ferrari
        Pip, Intro., 130-31; I.375-94
  Prato
    Duomo
      Birth of St. John, a fresco by Filippo Lippi
        By, 18:86-90 (*)
      Birth of St. Stephen, a fresco by Filippo Lippi
        Fra, 145-63
      Decapitation of John the Baptist, a fresco by Filippo Lippi (Fig. 44)
        Fra, 31-36, 194-98
      Feast of Herod, a fresco by Filippo Lippi (Figs. 52, 53)
        Fra, 31-36, 194-98
      Martyrdom of St. Lawrence, a painting by Mario Balassi and Carlo Dolci (Fig. 57)
        Fra, 323-32 (*)
      St. John in the Desert, a detail from the *Life of John the Baptist*, a fresco by Filippo Lippi (Fig. 18)
        By, 18:86-90 (*)
    Museo dell' Opera del Duomo
      Death of St. Jerome, a painting by Filippo Lippi
        Fra, 70-75

ITALY (cont.)
  Rome (cont.)
  Prison
    Carceri Nuove (Map R:8F; Fig. 168)
        Rin, I.1284-85; V.324-25; XII.138-46
  Squares
    Barberini (Map R:7I)
        Rin, I. 896-903
    Colonna (Map R:7H; Fig. 193)
        Rin, IV. 439-42; XI.138-46
    Montecitorio (Map R:7H; Fig. 164)
        Rin, IV. 168-70
    Navona (Map R:7G; Fig. 194)
        Rin, IV.1282-83; XII. 138-46, 159-65
    Pantheon (Map R:7H; Fig. 169)
        Rin, V.703-05; XII.138-46
    Pasquino (Map R:8G; Figs. 175, 192)
        Rin, VI.1658-59; XII.138-46
    Pietra (Map R:7H)
      The Exchange (Fig. 190)
        Rin, XII.51-52
    Popolo (Map R:5H,6H; Fig. 196)
        Rin, I.350-60; X.2106-11; XII.138-46
    Silvestro (Map R:7H)
        Pau, 656-67
    Spagna (Map R:6H,6I)
      Boat Fountain, by P. Bernini (Fig. 161)
        Rin, III.388-93
      Palazzo di Spagna
        Rin, VII.608
    Verità (Map R:9H; Fig. 185)
        Rin, XI.187-88
  Streets
    Babuino (Map R:6H)
        Rin, II.200-07; III.388-93
    Bocca di Leone, Browning's residence (Map R:6H)
        Rin, VII.425-30
    Corso (Map R:6H,8H; Fig. 196)
        Hol, 9:52
        Rin, VII.425-30; XII.138-46
    Convertite (Map R:7H)
        Rin, II.1229-31; VIII.1064

ITALY (cont.)
   Siena (cont.)
      Via Stalloreggi
         Pac, 5:64-75
   Solagna
      Parish Church
         Tomb and effigy of Ecelin II (Fig. 207)
            Sor, I.138-39; VI.687-90
   Trent
      Square of the Duomo; Palazzo Communale (Fig. 92)
         Neptune Fountain, by Giongo
            My, 54-56 (*)
            Up, 26-30 (*)
   Treviso
      Bailo Museum
         Sperone Speroni, a portrait by Titian
            Pip, III.162-63
      Duomo
         Annunciation, a painting by Titian (Fig. 131)
            Pip, III.162-63
   Trieste
      Piazza della Borsa
         Neptune, a statue by Mazzolan da Bergamo (Fig. 221)
            My, 54-56 (*)
   Turin
      Accademia Albertini
         Four Fathers of the Church, a painting by Filippo Lippi
            Fra, 70-75 (*)
      Palazzo Rivoli (environs; Fig. 83)
            Kin, stage directions
      Piazza Carlina (Carlo Emmanuelle II)
            Kin, II.77-79
   Urbino
      Palazzo Ducale
         Life of Christ, copies of tapestries by Raphael
            Pri, 850-55 (*)
   Vallombrosa
      Monastery of Vallombrosa
         Rin, XI.902-09
   Varallo
      Church of the Minorites
         Flight into Egypt, a painting by Gaudenzio Ferrari
            Rin, IV.420-25 (*); IX.26-27, 120-30 (*)

ITALY (cont.)
  Venice (cont.)
    Church and Square of St. Mark (Fig. 216); columns surmounted by a statue of the Lion of St. Mark and a statue of St. Theodore (Fig. 201)
        Fif, stanzas 94, 95, 104, 107, 117
        Pip, I.28-29
        Sor, I.820-21; III.136-37, 876-77
        Toc, 5-8
    Ducal Palace (Fig. 204)
      Neptune, a statue by Jacopo Sansovino (Fig. 201) (*); *Venice Receives the Homage of Neptune*, a painting by Tiepolo (Fig. 241) (*)
        My, 54-56
    Navel Museum
      Small model of *Bucentaur* (state barge)
        Toc, 5-8 (*)
    Piazza San Bartolommeo
      Statue of Goldoni (Fig. 61)
        Gold, 1-2
    Piombi (prisons) (Fig. 204)
        Sor, III.876-77
    Ponte dell' Angelo, Palazzo Soranzo, marble bas-relief on façade (Fig. 132)
        Pon, 7-12
    Rialto Bridge (Fig. 217)
        Toc, 508
    Teatro la Fenice
        Pip, I.417
  Verona
    Church of Sant Eufemia, sacristy
        Sor, I.567-83
    Piazza delle Erbe
      Madonna of Verona, a fountain statue (Fig. 203)
        Sor, III.586-87
  Vicenza
    Governor's Palace ("Podestà")
        Sor, I.535
  Viterbo
    Romanelli House (Fig. 9)
        Bea, 306-15 (*)

UNITED STATES (cont.)
Waco, TX (cont.)
Armstrong Browning Library (cont.)
The Delivery to the Secular Arm, a painting by Robert
Wiedemann Browning (Fig. 197.5)
Sc, 1-5
The Serenade, a painting by D. Maclise (Fig. 71)
In, 1-7
Wonders of the Little World, by Nathaniel Wanley,
the copy owned by Browning
My, 54-56
Washington, D. C.
National Gallery
Small Cowper Madonna, a painting by Raphael (Fig.
228)
Rin, VI.400-06, 668-73
Wellesley, MA
Wellesley College Library
Bronze cast of the clasped hands of the Brownings, by
Harriet Hosmer
Jam, VIII.27-32 (*), IX.18-20
Pro, 27-28 (*)

INDEX OF MISCELLANEOUS SOURCES

This index complements the Index of Sources with Locations. It comprises sources that cannot be located or which, for one reason or another, have been omitted from the Index of Sources with Locations. Imaginary and unspecified art objects for which no sources are nominated are listed for the sake of future research. This index also provides a detailed account of the author's contribution to original source work, and together with the Index of Sources with Locations constitutes the data summarized in the first paragraph of the Introduction. An asterisk after an entry indicates an original source nominated by the author. Other symbols used in this index are the head letters indicating the titles of the poems, and the numbers indicating the line numbers of the citations from the poem (*e.g.*, My, 1-4, means "My Last Duchess," lines 1-4).

Admollo, Luigi, unspecified prints by, Rin, I.66-75, 369-72.

Andrea del Sarto, lost painting of *A Portrait of the Dauphin*, And, 149-152.

Aphrodite, unspecified statue of, Chr, II.678-82.

Bacon, Brazen Head, Rin, VIII.985-87; also see below under Byron.

Baldinucci, *Notizie*:
 Life of Andrea del Sarto, 103-12.
 Life of Artemisia Gentileschi, Bea, 17-24, 306-15.
 Life of Filippo Lippi, Fra, 194-98.
 Life of Francesco Furini, Par, I:3-7.
 Life of Francesco Romanelli, Bea, 17-24, 306-15.
 Life of Lodovico Buti, Fil, 241-44ff.
 Life of Pacchiarotto, Pac, 5:64-75.

Baldovinetti, *Virgin and Child*, Old, 27:209-16.

Balen, Hendrick van, Bis, 56-61 (*); see below under Brueghel I, Goltzius, and Rubens.

Bartoli, Daniel, *De'simboli trasportati al morale*, Bis, 68-69.

Bellori, Giovanni Pietro, *Descrizione della imagini dipinte da Rafaello d'Urbino delle camere del Palazzo Apostolico Vaticano*, Sou.

Blagden, Isabella, *Agnes Tremorne*, Rin, I.1-4, 15-17.

Browning, Elizabeth Barrett, *Casa Guidi Windows*, Old, 33:257-58, 35:278-80, 36:281-88; Par, 3:176-81; Pic, 25-26, 31-33.

Browning, Robert, source for "Fra Lippo Lippi," 70-75, see Bi, 704-07 (*).

Browning, Robert Wiedemann, *Joan of Arc and the Kingfisher*, Par, 11:601-07; *A Scene in the Building of the Inquisitors at Antwerp*, Sce, 1-5.

Brueghel, I, *Pan Pursuing Syrinx*, Bis, 56-61 (see below under Rubens).

Byron, *Don Juan*, I, stanza 217, Rin, VIII.985-87 (see above under Bacon). Special thanks for encouragement goes to Dr. Clement T. Goode, Professor of English at Baylor University.

Buti, Ludovico, *Madonna* and *Crucifixion*, Fil, 31:241-44ff.

Caponsacchi, Florentine house of, Rin, VI.231-34.

Casa Tolomei, Bagni di Lucca, Up, 56-57.

Colossus of Rhodes, Chr, 12:749-52.

Comparini, Roman house (now destroyed), Rin, II.200-07, VII.77-81.

Domenico Gazzadi da Sassuolo, "Andrea del Sarto: i due ritratti ambidue di sua mano," And, 1-3 (*).

Margheritone, *Crucifixion*, Old, 28:217-24.

Master of the Dragon, statuette of Neptune, My, 54-56.

Masaccio, *Consecration*, Fra, 145-63.

Milton, *Paradise Lost*, Abt, 13-24 (*).

Moscheles, *The Isle's Enchantress*, Isl, 1-5.

Mote House, Bedford (now destroyed), Ned, 278 (*).

Murray, John, ed., *Handbook for Travellers in Central Italy*, Bis, 56-61 (*); *Handbook for Travellers in Switzerland, and the Alps of Piedmont*, By, 14:66-68.

Neptune Vase, Treasury Room, Residenz, Munich, My, 54-56 (Treasury Catalogue No. 328, Neptune surmounting ornate vase holding trident; added at publication time) (*).

New Place, house of Shakespeare in Stratford-on-Avon (now destroyed), Bi, 513-16.

Pacchiarotto, house in Siena (now destroyed), Pac, 5:64-75.

Palazzo della Zisa, Palermo, Sor, III, 119-21 (*).

Persian Sword, "A Forgiveness," 281-87; sold by Sotheby to Maggs Brothers, London; presently untraced (late entry at publication time).

Pietro da Cortona, unspecified painting by, Rin, V.487-89.

Portico of Livia, Rome (now destroyed), Imp, 56-58.

Powers, Hiram, sculptured hand of Loulie, Jam, VIII.27-32 (Fig. 239) (*).

Primaticcio, imaginary painting of Juno striking Ixion, Cri, 105-12.

Pugin, A. W., *Contrasts*, Bis, 106-12.

KEY TO BIBLIOGRAPHY

The purpose of this key is to provide, through head letters, easy access to the bibliographical references in the notes. Also, this key coordinates with the Preface in that it lists the various reference librarians, art curators, museum directors, and church historians to whom the author is indebted for many of his findings.

AL   Alberti, Judith Fay. "Robert Browning and Italian Renaissance Painting." Unpublished Ph.D. dissertation. University of California, Berkeley, 1979.

ALB   Albrecht, Mary Louise. "The Palaces and Art Objects in 'The Statue and the Bust.'" *Studies in Browning and His Circle*, 11 (Spring 1983), 47-60.

ALL   Allot, Kenneth, ed. *Selected Poems of Robert Browning*. London: Oxford University Press, 1967.

BAE   *Rome and Central Italy*. Leipzig: Karl Baedeker, 1930.

BAI   Letter to the author dated October 14, 1985, from D. M. Bailey, representing the Greek and Roman Antiquities Department of the British Museum.

BAL   Baldinucci, Filippo. *Delle notizie de' professori del disegno da Cimabue....* 20 vols. Florence, 1767-74.

BAN   Letter to the author from D. G. Banwell, of the Dulwich Picture Gallery, in London, dated November 11, 1976.

BAR   Barfucci, Enrico. *Giornate fiorentine*. Florence: Vallecchi Editore, 1958.

BART   Bartolini, Roberto. *Florence.* Florence: Bartolini
              Publications, n.d.

BEC   Becci, F. *Delle Stinche di Firenze.* Florence: Le
              Monnier, 1839. This book may be found in the Bib-
              lioteca Marucelliana, in Florence.

BED   Letter to the author dated May 18, 1978, from the
              Bedfordshire County Librarian.

BEL   Bellori, Giovanni Pietro. *Descrizione delle imagini
              dipinte da Rafaelle d'Urbino delle camere del Palaz-
              zo Apostolico Vaticano.* Roma, 1695; facsimile rpt.
              Farnborough, Hants: Gregg International, 1968.

BEN   Bénézit, E. *Dictionnaire critique et documentaire
              des Peintres, Sculpteurs, Dessinateurs et Graveurs.*
              10 vols. Paris: Librairie Gründ, 1911-23.

BER   Berdoe, Edward. *The Browning Cyclopaedia.* New
              York: Barnes & Noble, 1891.

BERE   Berenson, Bernard. *Italian Pictures of the Renais-
              sance: Florentine School.* 2 vols. London: Pheidon,
              1963.

BERM   Berman, R. J. *Browning's Duke.* New York:
              Richards Rosen Press, 1972.

BERT   Berti, Luciano. *Masaccio.* University Park: Penn-
              sylvania State University Press, 1967.

BIO   *Biographie Universelle.* 52 vols. Paris: Michard
              Bros., 1811-62.

BOA   Boas, Louis Schultz. "The Glove." *Explicator,* 11
              (November 1943), item 13.

BOC   Bocchi, Francesco. *Le bellezze della città di Firenze.*
              Florence: n.p. (but Medici emblem is given), n.d.

BOL   Bolton, Frances.   "Robert Browning's *Dramatic Idyls.*"   Unpublished Ph.D. dissertation.   Yale University, 1934.

BON   Letter to the author dated January 29, 1986, from Dr. Carla Guiducci Bonanni, director of the Biblioteca Marucelliana, Florence.

BRI   Bright, Michael H.   "Browning's Celebrated Pictor Ignotus."   *English Language Notes,* 13 (1976), 192-94, 209-15 (including reply to BULL).

BOR   Borenius, Tancred.   *Catalogue of the Pictures and Drawings at Harewood House.*   Oxford: The University Press, 1936.

BRO   *The Complete Poetical Works of Browning.*   Cambridge Edition.   Boston: Houghton Mifflin, 1895.

BROW   *Browning Society Papers.*   Comp. by F. J. Furnivall.   3 vols.   London: Trubner, 1881-1891.

BUL   Bullen, J. B.   "Browning's 'Pictor Ignotus' and Vasari's 'Life of Fra Bartolommeo di San Marco.'"   *Review of English Studies,* NS 23 (1972), 313-19.

BULL   —.   "Fra Bartolommeo's Quest for Obscurity."   *English Language Notes,* 13 (1976), 206-09.

CAL   Calcraft, M. B. M.   "'A Place to Stand and Love In': By the Refubbri Chapel with the Brownings."   *Browning Society Notes,* 16 (Spring 1986), 12-22.

CAP   In conversation on August 15, 1978, with Luciano Capra, director of the Biblioteca Comunale, Ferrara.

CAR   Carrington, C. E. "My Last Duchess," *Times Literary Supplement,* November 6, 1969, p. 1288.

CARR   Carr, Cornelia, ed.   *Harriet Hosmer: Letters and Memories.*   New York: Moffat, Yard, 1913.

CHA   Champneys, Basil. *Memoirs and Correspondence of Coventry Patmore.* London: George Bell, 1900.

CHI   Letter to the author dated December 6, 1979, from Dr. Marco Chiarini, Director of the Galleria Palatina di Palazzo Pitti.

CHIA   Chiavacci, Egisto. *Guida della Galleria del Palazzo Pitti.* 2nd ed. Florence: M. Cellini, 1862. The annotation reads as it does below under DOM.

CON   Conroy, Marilyn Ann. "Browning's Use of Art Objects." Unpublished Ph.D. dissertation. Indiana University, 1971.

COO   Cook, Eleanor. "Browning's 'Bellori.'" *Notes and Queries* (September 1970), 334-35.

COOK   Cook, A. K. *A Commentary upon Browning's "The Ring and the Book."* Hamden, Connecticut: Archon Books, 1966.

COOKE   Cooke, George Willis. *A Guide-Book to the Poetic and Dramatic Works of Robert Browning.* Boston: Houghton-Mifflin, 1891.

COR   Corson, Hiram. An Introduction to the *Study of Robert Browning.* Boston: Heath, 1885.

CRI   Letter to the author dated July 2, 1981, from Miss C. Crichton-Stuart, Secretary to the Surveyor of the Queen's Pictures, Lord Chamberlain's Office, St. James's Palace, London.

CRO   Crowder, Ashby Bland, Jr. "Browning's *The Inn Album.*" Unpublished Ph.D. dissertation. University of London, 1972.

CROW   —. "The Inn Album: A Record of 1875." In *Browning Institute Studies,* 2. Ed. by William S. Peterson. New York: Browning Institute, 1974, pp. 43-64.

CROWE   Crowe, Sir Joseph Archer and Giovanni Battista
             Cavalcaselle. *A New History of Painting in Italy:
             from the II to the XVI Century in Italy.* Ed. by
             Edward Hutton. 10 vols. London: Dent, 1908-09.

DAH   Dahl, Curtis. "Browning, Architecture, and John
             Ruskin." *Studies in Browning and His Circle*, 6
             (Spring 1978), 32-45.

DAR   Letters to the author dated March 25 and August 1,
             1983, from Dr. Alan P. Darr, Curator in Charge of
             European Sculpture and Decorative Arts, The De-
             troit Institute of Arts.

DAV   Davies, F. "Browning's 'The Guardian Angel.'"
             Times Literary Supplement, 32, 1933, p. 692.

DE   DeVane, William Clyde. "The Landscape of Brown-
             ing's 'Childe Roland.'" *PMLA*, 11 (1925), 426-32.

DEL   DeLaura, David J. "The Context of Browning's
             Painter Poems: Aesthetics, Polemics, Historics."
             PMLA, 95 (May 1980), 367-88.

DELA   —. "Some Notes on Browning's Pictures and Paint-
             ers." *Studies in Browning and His Circle*, 8 (Fall
             1980), 7-16.

DEV   DeVane, William Clyde. *A Browning Handbook.*
             1st ed. New York: F. S. Crofts, 1935.

DEVA   DeVane, William Clyde. *A Browning Handbook.*
             2nd ed. Appleton-Century-Crofts, 1955.

DEVAN   —. *Browning's Parleyings.* New Haven: Yale Uni-
             versity Press, 1927.

DIZ   Bordenache Battaglia, Gabriella. "Castellani." In the
             Dizionario biografico degli italiani. Vol. 21, July
             1972, pp. 590-605.

DO   Dooley, Allan C. "Another Detail from Vasari in 'Fra Lippo Lippi.'" *Studies in Browning and His Circle*, 5 (Spring 1977), 51.

DOO   —. "Browning's Prince Hohenstiel-Schwangau: An Annotated Edition with an Introductory Study of Napoleon III in Victorian Literature." Unpublished Ph.D. dissertation. Northwestern University, 1970.

DOOL   —. "Andrea, Raphael, and the Moment of 'Andrea del Sarto.'" *Modern Philology* (August 1983), 38-46.

DOM   Domenico Gazzadi da Sassuolo. "Andrea del Sarto: i due ritratti ambidue di sua mano." In *L'imperiale e reale galleria Pitti*." Ed. Luigi Bardi. Florence: coi tipi della Galileliana, 1837, 1: no page number. The annotation reads in the original as follows:

> Sembra questo quadro alludere al passo doloroso della vita d'Andrea. Quando invitato per lettere da Francesco I a ritornare in Francia, gli fu della moglie impedito.

DOU   Douglas, Norman. *Siren Land and Fountains in the Sand*. London: Secker and Warburg, 1957.

DUF   Duffin, Henry Charles. *Amphibian: A Reconsideration of Browning*. London: Bowes & Bowes, 1956.

DUL   *Catalogue of the Pictures in the Gallery of Alleyn's College of God's Gifts at Dulwich*. Revised in 1914 by Sir Edward Cook. By order of the Governors, 1926 (n.p.).

DULW   *Catalogue of the Pictures in the Dulwich College Picture Gallery*. By order of the Governors, 1953 (n.p.).

DUP   Dupres, Joseph A. "'An Epistle . . . of Karshish' and Froment's *Lazarus Triptych*: The Uffizi Connection." *Studies in Browning and His Circle*, 9 (Fall 1981), 50-56.

DUS   Dussler, Luitpold. *Raphael: A Critical Catalogue of His Pictures, Wall-paintings, and Tapestries.* London: Phaidon, 1971.

EIS   Eisenberg, Marvin. "'The Penitent St. Jerome' by Giovanni Toscani." *The Burlington Magazine,* 118 (May 1976), 274-83.

EISE   Correspondence to the author between 1983-89 from Professor Marvin Eisenberg, of the Department of History of Art, University of Michigan.

               Special appreciation is expressed to Professor Eisenberg, who, as one of the readers listed in the Preface of this study, has gone far beyond the task of proofreading copy for correctness, precision, and clarity, as important as these matters are. He has also systematized the form of the captions for the illustrations, standardized the foreign terms and names, resolved research problems with pertinent documentation, and, most important, contributed numerous original source possibilities. The bulk of Professor Eisenberg's contributions, both original and auxiliary, are listed in this work under And, 259-63; Bi, 666-68; Bis, 56-61; Fra, 70-75, 265-69, 323-32, 344-81; My, 54-56; Old, 26:201-08; and Rin, I.1-4, 15-17, 38-52; IV.420-25; VI.400-06, 1249-55; and IX.26-27, 120-30.

EISS   Eissenstat, Martha Turnquist. "Robert Browning's Use of Italian Renaissance Sources." Unpublished Ph.D. dissertation. University of Kansas, 1968.

ELI   *Elizabeth Barrett Browning: Letters to Her Sister, 1847-1859.* Ed. by Leonard Huxley. New York: Dutton, 1930.

ESP   This information was obtained through interviews in early June, 1982, with Antonio D'Esposito, Parroco of the Santissima Trinità, in Piano di Sorrento, and former Parroco Don Antonino Alberino, of the same church. For further documentation concerning the connection between the Dominican order and the Feast of the Madonna of the Rosary, inquire into letters from Dominican priests in the archives of the Church of the Santissima Trinità and consult Pasquale Ferraivolo's *Chiese e monasteri di Sorrento: cenni storici ed artistici,* ed. by the Congregation of the Servi di Maria, Sorrento, 1974, pp. 110-13.

FAL   Faldi, Italo. *Pittori viterbesi di cinque secoli.* Rome: Ugo Bozzi Roma, 1970.

FRE   Freedberg, S. J. *Andrea del Sarto: Catalogue Raisonné.* Cambridge, Mass.: Harvard University Press, 1963.

FRI   Friedland, Louis. "Ferrara and 'My Last Duchess.'" *Studies in Philology,* 33 (1936), 656-84.

GERK   Letter to the author dated June 7, 1982, from Dr. Gerhard Gerkins, director of the Kunsthalle, Bremen.

GIP   *La Gipsoteca di Possagno.* Elena Bassi, ed. Venice: Neri Pozza Editore, 1957.

GRE   Greenberg, Robert A. "Ruskin, Pugin, and the Contemporary Context of 'The Bishop Orders His Tomb.'" *PMLA,* 84 (1969), 1588-94.

GRI   Griffin, W. H. and H. C. Minchin. *The Life of Robert Browning.* Hamden, Conn.: Archon, 1966.

GRIF   Griffo, Mary. "Robert Browning and the Sister Arts." Unpublished Ph.D. dissertation. University of California, Riverside, 1983.

GUI   *Les Guides Bleus, Paris.* Paris: Librairie Hachette, 1952.

HA   Hardy, Florence Emily. *The Early Life of Thomas Hardy, 1840-91.* New York: Macmillan, 1928.

HAR   Hare, Augustus J. C. *Florence.* London: George
           Routledge, n.d.

HARE   —. *Walks in Rome.* 2 vols. London: George Allen,
           1903.

HARP   Harper, J. W., ed. *Men and Women, and Other
           Poems.* London: J. M. Dent, 1975.

HARR   Harrington, Vernon C. *Browning Studies.* Boston:
           Richard G. Badger, 1915.

HAZ   Hazlitt, William. *Sketches of the Principal Picture-
           galleries in England.* London: Taylor and Hessey,
           1824.

HER   Herford, C. H. *Robert Browning.* New York: Dodd,
           Mead, 1905.

HOD   Hodell, Charles W., ed. and tr. *The Old Yellow
           Book: Source of Robert Browning's "The Ring and
           the Book."* Baltimore: The Lord Baltimore Press,
           1908.

HUM   Letter to the author dated July 15, 1985, from Dr. N.
           Humburg, Director of the Museum Hameln.

IRV   Irvine, William and Park Honan. *The Book, the
           Ring, and the Poet.* New York: McGraw-Hill, 1974.

IST   The archives are at the Instituto Tedesco di Storia
           dell' Arte, in Florence. The books dealing with the
           façade of the Duomo are as follows: Luigi del Moro,
           Facciata di S. Maria del Fiore (Florence: Giuseppe
           Ferroni, 1888); Walter and Elisabeth Paatz, *Die Kir-
           chen von Florenz* (Frankfurt: Vol. III, Vittorio Klos-
           termann, 1952), pp. 320ff; and Voti and Pareri, et al,
           Sulla facciata del Duomo (Florence: M. Cellini,
           1865). The Paatz volume contains an extensive bib-
           liography and specifically locates the designs today.

JAC   Jack, Ian. *Browning's Major Poetry.* Oxford: At the
           Clarendon Press, 1983.

JAM   James, Henry. *William Wetmore Story and His Friends*. 2 vols. Boston: Houghton-Mifflin, 1903.

JAME   Jameson, Anna. *Sacred and Legendary Art*. 2 vols. London: Longman, Green, 1870. First published in London in 1848.

JAMES   —. *Sketches of Art, Literature, and Character*. Boston: Ticknor and Fields, 1847. First published in London as *Art, Literature, and Social Morals*.

JAMESO   Jameson, Mrs. Anna. *Legends of the Madonna*. In *The Writings of Anna Jameson*. Vol. 4. Boston: Houghton Mifflin, 1897. First printed in 1852.

JER   Jerrold, Blanchard. *Life of Gustave Doré*. London: W. Allen, 1891.

KEL   Kelley, Philip and Betty A. Coley. *The Browning Collections: A Reconstruction with Other Memorabilia*. Winfield: Wedgestone Press, 1984.

KELL   Kelley, Philip and Ronald Hudson. *The Brownings' Correspondence: A Checklist*. New York/Winfield, Kansas: The Browning Institute and Wedgestone Press, 1978.

KEN   *The Letters of Elizabeth Barrett Browning*. Ed. by Frederic G. Kenyon. 2 vols. London: Smith, Elder, 1897.

KI   Kincaid, A. N. "The Ring and the Scholars." In *Browning Institute Studies*, 8. Ed. by William S. Peterson. New York: Browning Institute, 1980, pp. 151-59.

KIN   *The Letters of Robert Browning and Elizabeth Barrett Barrett, 1845-46*. Ed. by Elvin Kintner. 2 vols. Cambridge, Mass.: Belknap Press, 1969.

KING   King, Roma A., Jr., et al., eds. *The Complete Works of Robert Browning*. Vols. 1-5, 7, 8. Athens, Ohio: Ohio University Press, Baylor University Press, 1969-86.

KNI   Knickerbocker, Kenneth Leslie. "A Critical Analy-
        sis of Robert Browning's *Pacchiarotto* Volume with
        a Study of the Background (1867-1876)." Unpub-
        lished Ph.D. dissertation. Yale University, 1933.

KNIG   Knight, Charles, ed. *London*. 6 vols. London: H.G.
        Bohn, 1861.

KO   Korg, Jacob. *Browning and Italy*.   Athens, Ohio:
        Ohio University Press, 1983.

KOR   —. "Browning's Art and 'By the Fireside.'" *Vic-
        torian Poetry*, 15 (1977), 147-58.

KRY   Krynicky, Harry Thomas.   "*Christmas-Eve and
        Easter-Day* by Robert Browning: A Variorum Text."
        Unpublished Ph.D. dissertation.   University of
        Pennsylvania, 1974.

LAI   Lairesse, Gerard de. *The Art of Painting in All Its
        Branches*. Tr. by J. F. Fritsch. London: S. Vanden-
        bergh, 1778.

LEI   Leisgang, Waltraud. "'Fra Lippo Lippi': A Picture
        Poem." *Browning Society Notes*, 3 (December 1973),
        20-32.

LEV   Levi, Karen, ed. *The Power of Love: Six Centuries
        of Diamond Betrothel Rings*. London: Diamond In-
        formation Center, 1988.

LIN   Lindsay, J. D. "The Central Episode in Browning's
        By the Fireside." *Studies in Philology*, 39 (1942), 571-
        79.

LUC   Letter to the author dated March 15, 1979, from the
        Soprintendenza per i beni ambientali, architet-
        tonici, artistici e storici per le province di Pisa,
        Livorno, Lucca, e Massa Carrara.

MA   Marabottini, Alessandro. *Polidoro da Caravaggio*. 2
        vols. Rome: Edizioni dell' Elefante, 1969.

MAC   Mackendrick, Paul. *The Greek Stones Speak.* New York: St. Martin's Press, 1962.

MAJ   Major, Mabel. "Robert Browning and the Florentine Renaissance." *TCU Quarterly,* 1, nos. 2 and 3 (1924), 5-74.

MAR   Marchini, Giuseppe. *Filippo Lippi.* Milan: Electa Editrice, 1975.

MARK   Markus, Julia. "Browning's 'Andrea' Letter at Wellesley College: A Correction of DeVane's *Handbook.*" *Studies in Browning and His Circle,* 1 (Fall 1973), 52-55.

MARKUS Markus, Julia. "'Old Pictures in Florence' Through *Casa Guidi Windows.*" In *Browning Institute Studies,* 6. Ed. by William S. Peterson. New York: The Browning Institute, 1979, pp. 43-61.

MART   Martin, Gregory. *Catalogue of the Flemish School, 1600-1900.* London: National Gallery, n.d.

MARTI Martindale, Andrew and Edi Baccheschi, eds. *The Complete Works of Giotto.* New York: Abrams, 1966.

MCA   McAleer, Edward C., ed. *Dearest Isa: Robert Browning's Letters to Isabella Blagden.* Austin: University of Texas Press, 1951.

MEL   Melchiori, Barbara. "Where the Bishop Orders His Tomb." *Review of English Literature,* 5 (1964), 7-26. Also published in Melchiori's *Browning's Poetry of Reticence* (New York: Barnes & Noble, 1968), pp. 20-39.

MES   Letter to the author dated June 22, 1982, from Professor Fede Messedaglia, of the Comune di Goito, Province of Mantova, Italy.

MIC   *Michelin Benelux.* Paris: Services de Tourisme, 1972.

MICH   *Michelin Italy.* 6th ed. London: The Dickens Press, 1966.

MIL   *John   Milton: Complete   Poems   and   Major   Prose.* Ed. by Merrit Y. Hughes.   Indianapolis: Dobbs-Merrill, 1957.

MILL   Letter to the author dated November 25, 1982, from Dr. Albrecht Miller, director of the Bayerische Verwaltung der Staatlichen Schlösser, Gärten und Seen, Munich.

MUR   *Handbook for Travellers in Central Italy.*   London: John Murray, 1843.

MURR   *Russia.* London: John Murray, 1893.

MURRA   *Handbook for Travellers in Switzerland and the Alps of Savoy and Piedmont.* London: John Murray, 1828.

MURRAY   *Handbook for Travellers in Northern Italy.*   London: John Murray, 1846.

NA   Letter to the author dated November 9, 1979, from the Archives du Département et du Comte Nantais, in Nantes, Loire-Atlantique, France.

NE   *New   Poems   of   Robert   Browning   and   Elizabeth Barrett Browning.*   Ed. by Sir. Frederic G. Kenyon. New York: Macmillan, 1915.

NEW   *New Letters of Robert Browning.*   Ed. by William C. DeVane and Kenneth L. Knickerbocker.   New Haven: Yale University Press, 1950.

NEY   Ney, Marie.   "Was it a Procession of the Service Order in 'Down in the City'? a Query." *Browning Society Newsletter,* 5 (March 1975), 27.

OFF   Letter to the author dated August 10, 1979, from the librarian of the Offentliche Bibliothek, in Aachen, West Germany.

OG   *Elizabeth Barrett Browning's Letters to Mrs. David Ogilvy, 1849-1861.* Ed. by Peter N. Heydon and Philip Kelley. New York: Quadrangle/The Browning Institute, 1973.

ON   D'Onofrio, Cesare. *Le Fontane di Roma.* Rome: Staderin Editore, 1957.

OR   Orr, Mrs. Sutherland. *A Handbook to the Works of Robert Browning.* London: G. Bell, 1927. First published in 1885.

ORM   Ormond, Leonée. "Browning and Painting." In *Robert Browning.* Ed. by Isobel Armstrong. Athens, Ohio: Ohio University Press, 1974, pp. 184-210.

ORMO   — and Richard. *Lord Leighton.* New Haven, Conn.: Yale University Press, 1975.

ORMON   Letter to the author dated September 10, 1983, from Leonée Ormond, of King's College, London.

ORMOND   Ormond, Richard. *Early Victorian Portraits.* 2 vols. London: HMSO, 1973.

ORR   Orr, Mrs. Sutherland. *Life and Letters of Robert Browning.* London: Smith, Elder, 1908.

PAR   Parr, Johnstone. "Browning's 'Fra Lippo Lippi,' Baldinucci, and the Milanesi Edition of Vasari." *English Language Notes,* 3 (March 1966), 197-201.

PARR   —. "Browning's 'Fra Lippo Lippi,' Vasari's Masaccio, and Mrs. Jameson." *English Language Notes,* 5 (June 1968), 277-83.

PAS   Pasqui, V. *Guida d'Arezzo.* Arezzo: Società Tipografica Aretina, 1925.

PET   Pettigrew, John and Thomas J. Collins, eds. *Robert Browning: The Poems.* 2 vols. New Haven: Yale University Press, 1981.

POR   Porter, Charlotte and Helen A. Clarke. *The Complete Works of Robert Browning*. 12 vols. New York: Thomas Crowell, 1898.

POU   Pouncey, Philip and J. A. Gere. *Italian Drawings in the Department of Prints and Drawings in the British Museum: Raphael and His Circle*. London: British Museum, 1962.

PRA   Praeger, Robert Lloyd. *Official Guide to Co. Down*. Belfast: Belfast and Co. Down Railway, 1900.

PRO   Procacci, Ugo. *La Casa Buonarroti di Firenze*. Florence: Electa Milano, 1965.

QUA   Quarles, Francis. *Emblems, Divine and Moral*. London: Milton Press, 1839.

RAD   Radford, Ernest. "The Moorish Front to the Duomo in 'Luria.'" *Browning Society Papers*, 2 (1881-1884), 251-52. In a footnote on p. 251 the description of the design for the façade reads,

> Progetto per la facciata della Metropolitana di Firenze composto e disegnato nel 1822 dall'Architetto Giovanni Silvestri ed inviato all I. R. Accademia delle belle Arti. —Giovanni Silvestri e Felice Francolini Architetti dedicano al loro concittadini. 1833.

RIC   Richter, Gisela. *The Sculpture and Sculptors of the Greeks*. New Haven: Yale University Press, 1970.

RIG   Letters to the author dated October 31, 1978, and April 4, 1981, from Dr. Fernando Rigon, Director of the Museo, Biblioteca, e Archivio di Bassano del Grappa.

RIO   Rio, Alexis François. *The Poetry of Christian Art*. Trans. by Miss Wells. London: Bosworth, 1854.

RIZ   *Rizzoli classici dell' arte: Canova #85*. N.p., n.d.

ROL   Rolfe, William S. and Heloise E. Hersey, eds. *Select Poems of Robert Browning*. New York: American Book Co., 1886.

ROM   Letters to the author dated January 1 and September
        5, 1983, from Giandomenico Romanelli, Director
        of the Civic Museums of Art and History in Venice.

RUS   *The Works of John Ruskin.* Ed. by E. T. Cook and
        Alexander Wedderburn. 39 vols. London: George
        Allen, 1903-12.

SAM   Letters to the author dated August 9, 1976, and Sep-
        tember 15, 1977, from Jean-Pierre Samoyault, Con-
        servateur du Musée National du Château de
        Fontainebleau.

SAN   Letter to the author dated January 9, 1980, from
        Bettini Santo, parish priest of Santa Maria a Olmi
        and Sant' Ansano, Mugello, Italy.

SC   Schweik, Robert C.   "Bishop Blougram's Miracles."
        Modern Language Notes, 71 (June 1956), 416-18.

SH   Shearman, John. *Andrea del Sarto.* 2 vols. Oxford:
        Clarendon Press, 1965.

SIR   Sirugo, Marilyn S. "The Site of 'Love Among the
        Ruins' Revisited."   *Studies in Browning and His
        Circle*, 4 (Spring 1976), 41-48.

SMI   Smith, Arthur Hamilton.   *A Guide to the Collec-
        tion of Casts of Sculpture in the Department of
        Greek and Roman Antiquities in the British
        Museum.*   London: By Order of the Trustees,
        1913.

SOS   Letter to the author dated August 14, 1978, from Dr.
        Piero Sospecchi, attaché for the Pinacoteca, Siena.

SOT   Sotheby, Wilkinson, and Hodge.   *The Browning
        Collections.* London: The Dryden Press, 1913.

SOTH   *Sotheran's Price Current of Literature: Illustrated
        Catalogue.*   Vol. 757.   London: Henry Sotheran,
        1913, p. 122, item 413.

SPO   In consultation on August 17, 1972, with Father Pierdamiano Sportono, Curator of the Vallombrosan Monastery.

STE   Stevens, L. Robert. "'My Last Duchess': A Possible Source." *Victorian Newsletter*, 28 (Fall 1965), 25-26.

STEV   Stevenson, Lionel. "The Pertinacious Victorian Poets." In *Victorian Literature: Modern Essays in Criticism*. Ed. by Austin Wright. New York: Oxford University Press, 1961, pp. 16-31.

STU   Stubblebine, James H. *Duccio di Buoninsegna and His School*. 2 vols. Princeton, New Jersey: Princeton University Press, 1979.

TAP   Taplin, Gardner B. *The Life of Elizabeth Barrett Browning*. New Haven: Yale University Press, 1957.

TAY   Taylor, Gerald, ed. *Finger Rings: From Ancient Egypt to the Present*. London: Lund Humphries, 1978.

TER   Terreni, Jacopo and Antonio. *Viaggio pittorico della Toscana*. Vol. I. Florence: Giuseppe Tofani, 1801.

THI   Thieme, Ulrich and Felix Becker. *Allgemeines Lexikon der bildenden Künstler*. 37 vols. Leipzig: Verlag von E. A. Seemann, 1908-50.

THO   Thomas, Charles Flint (formerly Charles Lynde-Flint Waterman). "The Painting of St. Laurence in 'Fra Lippo Lippi': Its Source at Prato." *Studies in Browning and His Circle*, 6 (Fall 1978), 45-51.

THOM   —. "The Setting for 'Bishop Blougram's Apology': St. George's Cathedral, Southwark." *Studies in Browning and His Circle*, 5 (Spring 1977), 27-33.

THOMA   —. "The Browning Busts at the South London Art Gallery." *Studies in Browning and His Circle*, 3 (Spring 1975), 96-101. This article provides background for the bust of Browning by Henry Charles Fehr that is used as the Frontispiece for this work.

THOMAS   —. "Robert Browning's Poetic Art Objects: An Illustrated Compendium." Unpublished Ph.D. dissertation. Baylor University, 1979.

TIM   Timbs, John. *Curiosities of London*. London: John Camden Hotten, 1855.

TON   Letter to the author dated August 13, 1974, from Dr. Giorgio Tononi, director of the Azienda Autonoma Turismo, Trent.

TRE   Treves, Frederick. *The Country of "The Ring and the Book."* London: Cassell, 1913.

TUR   Turner, Paul, ed. *Browning: "Men and Women."* Oxford: Oxford University Press, 1972.

UFF   *Nuovo catalogo dell' Imperiale e Reale Galleria di Firenze, 1851.* Florence: Tipografia Soliani, 1851.

VA   *Le Vite de' piu eccellenti pittori, scultori e architettori.* Compilatori: Gaetano Milanesi, Carlo Milanesi, Carlo Pini, Padre Vincenzo Marchese. 13 vols. Florence: Felice Le Monnier, 1846-57. (Vol. XIV added in 1870.)

VAS   Vasari, Giorgio. *Lives of Seventy Painters, Sculptors, and Architects.* 4 vols. Ed. by E. H. and E. W. Blashfield and A. A. Hopkins. Trans. by Mrs. Jonathan Foster. New York: Charles Scribner, 1897.

VASA   Vasari, Giorgio. *Lives of Seventy of the Most Eminent Painters, and Architects.* Trans. by Mrs. Jonathan Foster. 5 vols. London: Henry G. Bohn, 1850-1864. (Vol. VI, a commentary by J. P. Richter, added in 1865.)

VASAR   Vasari, Giorgio. *Lives of the Most Eminent Painters, Sculptors and Architects.* Trans. by Gaston du C. De Vere. 10 vols. London: Macmillan and the Medici Society, 1912-15.

VAU   Vaughan, Herbert. *Florence and Her Treasures.* New York: Macmillan, 1911.

WET   Wethey, Harold Edwin. *The Paintings of Titian.* 3 vols. London: Phaidon, 1969-75.

WH   White, John. *Duccio: Tuscan Art and the Medieval Workshop.* Great Britain: Thames and Hudson, 1979.

WHI   Whiting, Lilian. *The Brownings: Their Life and Art.* Boston: Little, Brown, 1911.

WIT   Withers, Sara and Samuel. "The Palazzo in 'The Statue and the Bust.'" *Browning Newsletter,* 8 (Spring 1972), 45-46.

WOR   Worsfold, Basil, ed. *Browning's "Men and Women."* 2 vols. London: Chatto and Windus, 1907.

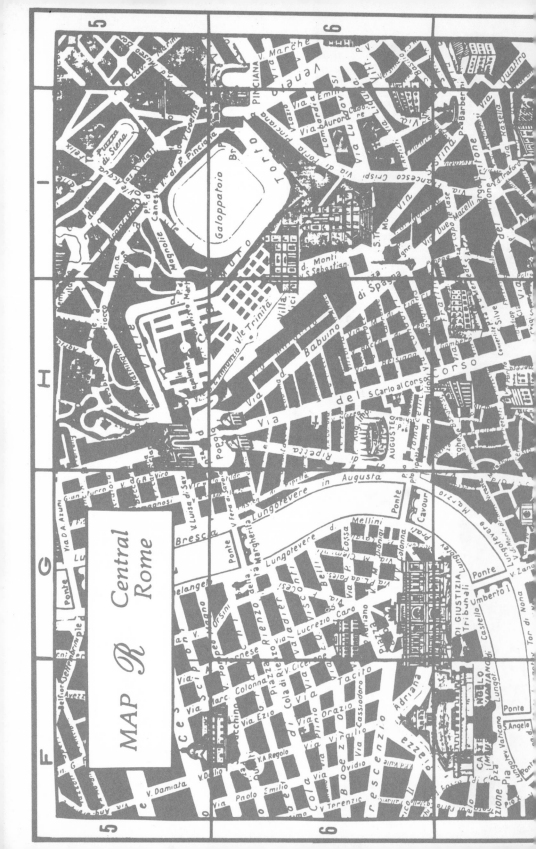

MAP R Central Rome